The Garland Library of Medieval Literature

General Editors
James J. Wilhelm, Rutgers University
Lowry Nelson, Jr., Yale University

Literary Advisors
Ingeborg Glier, Yale University
William W. Kibler, University of Texas
Norris J. Lacy, Washington University
Giuseppe Mazzotta, Yale University
Fred C. Robinson, Yale University
Aldo Scaglione, University of North Carolina

Art Advisor
Elizabeth Parker McLachlan, Rutgers University

Music Advisor
Hendrik van der Werf, Eastman School of Music

The Song of Aspremont
(La Chanson d'Aspremont)

translated by
MICHAEL A. NEWTH

Volume 61
Series B
GARLAND LIBRARY OF MEDIEVAL LITERATURE

Garland Publishing, Inc.
New York & London
1989

© 1989 Michael A. Newth
All rights reserved

Library of Congress Cataloging-in-Publication Data

Chanson, d'Aspremont. English
　　The song of Aspremont.

　　　(Garland reference library of the humanities ; v. 61.
Series B)
　　　Translation of: La chanson d'Aspremont.
　　　Bibliography: p.
　　　1. Charlemagne, Emperor, 742–814—Romances.
2. Chansons de geste.　I. Newth, Michael A.　II. Title.
III. Series: Garland library of medieval literature ;
v. 61.
PQ1425.A57E5　1989　　841'.1　　88-31024
ISBN 0–8240–5618–3　(alk. paper)

Printed on acid-free, 250-year-life paper
Manufactured in the United States of America

FOR SUE

'Sa prode feme doit on forment cierir
 Et chier tenir et amer et joïr;'

Chanson d'Aspremont LL.1452-3

Preface of the General Editors

The Garland Library of Medieval Literature was established to make available to the general reader modern translations of texts in editions that conform to the highest academic standards. All of the translations are originals, and were created especially for this series. The translations attempt to render the foreign works in a natural idiom that remains faithful to the originals.

The Library is divided into two sections: Series A, texts and translations; and Series B, translations alone. Those volumes containing texts have been prepared after consultation of the major previous editions and manuscripts. The aim in the editing has been to offer a reliable text with a minimum of editorial intervention. Significant variants accompany the original, and important problems are discussed in the Textual Notes. Volumes without texts contain translations based on the most scholarly texts available, which have been updated in terms of recent scholarship.

Most volumes contain Introductions with the following features: (1) a biography of the author or a discussion of the problem of authorship, with any pertinent historical or legendary information; (2) an objective discussion of the literary style of the original, emphasizing any individual features; (3) a consideration of sources for the work and its influence; and (4) a statement of the editorial policy for each edition and translation. There is also a Select Bibliography, which emphasizes recent criticism on the works. Critical writings are often accompanied by brief descriptions of their importance. Selective glossaries, indices, and footnotes are included where appropriate.

The Library covers a broad range of linguistic areas, including all of the major European languages. All of the important literary forms and genres are considered, sometimes in anthologies or selections.

The General Editors hope that these volumes will bring the general reader a closer awareness of a richly diversified area that has for too long been closed to everyone except those with precise academic training, an area that is well worth study and reflection.

James J. Wilhelm
Rutgers University

Lowry Nelson, Jr.
Yale University

Contents

Introduction	xi
Select Bibliography	xxvii
The Song of Aspremont	1
Glossary	269

INTRODUCTION

AUTHORSHIP

The ninety or so surviving Old French epic poems called *chansons de geste* or "songs of deeds", written mainly in the twelfth and thirteenth centuries, form a vital and varied but comparatively neglected body of medieval French verse. The earliest and best of these poems, the *Chanson de Roland*, has represented the literary achievements of the genre almost exclusively for generations of scholars and consequently to general readers. It is in an effort to convey some of the richness and excitement contained in all these poems, and because indeed the *Roland* is in several ways an atypical example of its kind, that the present verse translation of the *Chanson d'Aspremont* has been prepared.

The *chansons de geste*, as they have come down to us, are the literary culmination of a long and largely unknown oral tradition of epic chant inspired originally by the legendary history of Emperor Charlemagne and by his role as Defender of Christianity. As such the early oral versions of these songs were enthusiastically received by both the aristocracy and the Church. They were enjoyed by the barons, whose delight in combat they reflected, and their development was fostered in the monasteries along pilgrimage routes to important shrines. The composition of the *Chanson de Roland*, generally accepted to be the first of the written epics, dates from the early years of the twelfth century at a time when the interests of both these ruling forces were united by the First Crusade.

The original *chansons de geste* were composed by the *trouvères* and intended for public performance by the *jongleurs*, who chanted them to the accompaniment of a *vielle*. During the centuries of their popularity they were performed across the country before audiences of differing and changing tastes, and the content and tone of their narratives were altered accordingly. The deeds of local heroes like William of Orange and Girart of Roussillon were exploited in addition to those of Charlemagne, and episodes of romance were included in response to the growing popularity of the *roman courtois* with the more literate and literary aristocracy. The tastes of the popular audience were accommodated by the introduction of comic and satiric elements and scenes of parody involving a *vilain* - hero character type. Successful songs were continued either backwards or forwards in time and new tales containing the *enfances* or last days of particular heroes, or the doings of their ancestors or descendants were added to the *jongleurs'* repertoires. At the height of their popularity in the thirteenth century the *chansons de geste* were grouped by the *trouvères* into three main cycles, each named after the figure which united them in some way-- Charlemagne, Garin de Monglane (or William of Orange) and Doon de Mayence (the rebel barons cycle).

Unlike the *Chanson de Roland*, which owes much of its aesthetic appeal and dramatic success to the unity of its plot and the sustained severity of its tone, the vast majority of the extant *chansons de geste* bear much more clearly the imprint of this oral tradition. Their tone varies, often jarringly to modern taste, from the elevated to the humorous and even crude, while their narratives are made up of numerous uneven episodes of adventure, violence, romance and tragedy, feudal crisis and religious fervor, during which details of the original plot are often distorted and sometimes lost. The live performer is still and always present in the written text as the omniscient narrator. He controls the attention and emotions of his "audience" by commenting constantly on the action with humor, horror or homespun philosophy.

With this in mind, the *Chanson d'Aspremont* affords us an excellent and artistically successful example of a *chanson de geste*. Using the stereotyped descriptions and structural features characteristic of much oral poetry, the unknown author of this poem presents a complete gallery of the themes, episodes and character types which are the life-blood of the Old French epic genre. Against a background of religious zeal and feudal loyalty, scenes of combat and perilous adventure are mixed skillfully and originally with episodes of humorous and openly comic intent. We are told of perfect knights and rebel barons, of loyal and libidinous ladies, of grumbling gray-beards and high-spirited youngsters, of the craven and the noble-hearted. Above all we are given an expansive and entertaining rendition of that religious sentiment which pervades the noblest of the epics and which is most succinctly phrased in the *Roland* (1015):

Pagans are wrong and Christians are right.

This sentiment undoubtedly held a direct appeal at the

Introduction   xiii

time and place of our poem's composition.

　　The *Chanson d'Aspremont* belongs to that cycle of epic poems having the Emperor Charlemagne himself as their central figure and which are known collectively therefore as the "*geste de roi*." According to Roelof van Waard (p.263)* the present poem was written in Sicily or Calabria at some time during the preparations for the Third Crusade, which set out from Messina in the spring of 1191. Its author was certainly familiar with the area of southern Italy and also well acquainted with the local legend concerning Charlemagne.

　　Before the mighty Emperor's successful but ill-fated campaign in Spain, of which the *Chanson de Roland* so movingly tells, his legend has it that he fought several times in Italy against the Saracen invaders. Although there is no authentic historical evidence to suggest that Charlemagne ever set foot in southern Italy, it is apparent from the chronicles of certain Latin authors of the ninth and tenth centuries that the enduring fame of his exploits was readily identified and indeed confused with the contemporary aspirations of the Ottonian dynasty and their achievements in that region. Thus, for example, the monk Benoît de Saint-André distorts a passage from Eginhard's *Vita Caroli* to tell of Charlemagne's military progress through Calabria and his departure for the Holy Land from a port on the Strait of Messina, while a second monk, the so-called Annalist of Saint-Gall, attributes to Otto II the very exploits accredited by Benoît to Charlemagne himself (Van Waard, pp.49-52). By the middle of the tenth century the belief in a great victory won by Charlemagne in the vicinity of Reggio was current at the Saxon court. However, the establishment of this legend in northern France and in southern Italy itself can be attributed to the success of the Norman expedition to Calabria in the second half of the twelfth century (Van Waard, p.262).

　　Our poem is the most significant of a small group of epics which exploit the theme of a Saracen invasion of the Italian peninsula. Historically this theme is thought to echo the Arab incursions of 813, 846 and 870, the latter two of which did indeed succeed in menacing Rome (Riquer p.208).

　　　　　　　　　　　***************

* All names and page references relate to authors and works in the Select Bibliography which follows.

ARTISTIC ACHIEVEMENT

The themes of religious and feudal loyalty dominate the "story" of the *Chanson d'Aspremont*. The entire narrative is constructed upon the understanding of the mutual obligation between lord and liege, both sacred and secular, and the action turns upon the superiority, alike understood by poet and audience, of the followers of the One True Faith. The poem, although at times anticlerical, is a profoundly religious one. The tenets of the Christian faith--the sin of Man and his redemption through the Passion of Christ and through baptism--are constantly recalled and its superiority confirmed through frequent allusion to the miracles of both the Old and New Testaments and to the resurrection of Christ. Charlemagne as feudal lord calls upon the knights of his Empire to avenge the unwarranted attacks on his territories, but more importantly as God's representative on Earth to repel the incursions of the Infidels and to pay back the debt of their Faith. His call is echoed by all the Christian leaders in the poem and accepted wholeheartedly by the rank and file (3969-73):

> "While I've good arms and a good horse beneath me
> Why would I not strike mighty blows for Jesus
> And pay to God the debt of all believers?
> Body and soul I'll give him here quite freely,
> Prepared to die for Him as He for me did."

The faith of Charlemagne's fighters is as strong as it is simple. Battle against God's foes is at once a penance and a privilege, and death brings only honor and reward (5102-105):

> "Welcome the wounds, brave men!" old Girart cries;
> "You will be martyrs if you should lose your lives,
> Served with the Saints who dwell in Paradise,
> All garlanded with the blest crowns of Christ,
> There to enjoy whatever you desire."

In return, the miracles performed upon the battlefield--the blazing Cross, the unbreakable helm, the appearance of Saints--make manifest the presence of God and the supremacy of His cause. The Saracen religion, on the other hand, is depicted as a parody of faith and faithfulness. The Paynims (i.e. Pagans) worship a curious infernal trio of idols--Mahom (Mohammed), Tervagant and Apollo--which are stolen and smashed to bits by Charlemagne's troops in the early stages of the battle and vilified constantly by the Infidels themselves thereafter.

Introduction

Similarly, although the empire of the Emir Agolant is credited with much the same feudal structure as that of the Emperor Charlemagne, his dues of fealty are decidedly less well paid. His realm, we learn, has been racked by civil strife, and there is still much rivalry between his own house and that of the evil Almanzor. His son, Aumon, driven himself by the desire for personal glory, is let down by his vassals and loses both the Paynim idols and his father's best soldiers in two disastrous engagements. He refuses obstinately to call upon his father's aid and is ultimately defeated when two of his vassal kings, Amargon and Esperrant, nephews of the Almanzor, desert their post as flag-bearers. One whole section of the poem (Part Seven in this translation) is devoted to the trial and punishment of these two kings, the extent of whose guilt is the cause of much debate between the two rival houses (6527-540):

"By Mahomet, you speak with words unreasoned,
Such high-born men as these to treat so cheaply,
Condemning them to pain and death for treason!
We still know not where lies the fault of fealty;
That these two held the flag, this is indeed so,
Till in low wise they were both forced to flee it;
But even if they'd stopped there, though defeated,
Aumon their liege was not there to relieve them;
And all their friends would now be fiercely grieving--
For had they stayed they would have died quite clearly;
We must judge here as fits the misdemeanor;
If we rush off to the Emir with these two,
I know for certain he will kill them unheeding;
The gold of all the world would not redeem them."

It is the subsequent execution of these two kings which brings about the final and fatal act of disloyalty by the Almanzor himself, who with his clan deserts the Emir at the height of the battle and sails back home to lay claim to Africa.

In sharp contrast to this are the eagerness and unquestioning loyalty shown to Charlemagne, Girart d'Eufrate and young Roland at all stages of the action. There is an internal conflict here too between the Emperor and the rebel baron Girart, but it is the overriding allegiance of both to Lord God which turns this conflict to good and decisive account. It is Girart's feats which lead directly to the defeat of both Aumon and Agolant.

The most original and appealing literary aspect of the

Chanson d'Aspremont is the unusual degree of individual characterization which the poet has achieved in presenting the traditional epic types. In the course of his long narrative (the average *chanson de geste* is 8,000 lines, the *Roland* 4,000) our poet introduces nearly two hundred different characters, many of them indeed of peripheral importance and passing interest. However, in his protagonists he has created and sustained a range of psychologically valid and interesting personalities. They are presented as easily recognizable opposing pairs which may be categorized thus:

CHRISTIAN	SARACEN	CHARACTER TYPE
Charlemagne	Agolant	Supreme ruler
Roland	Aumon	Proud young hero
Naimes	Balan	Bravest and wisest knight
Girart	Almanzor	Rebel baron
Lady Emmeline	the Queen	Leader's wife

It is the distinctive personality of each one, the comparison each invites with his or her opposite number and their conflicts with each other, which provide much of the excellent drama and humor in the poem. The portrayal of Charlemagne aptly illustrates this point. His character in *Aspremont* is three-dimensional. On one level he is the idealized figure familiar to the audience from the *Chanson de Roland*. He is the champion of his faith and the perfect liege lord--a virile patriarch, "fierce-faced" but generous, careful but confident. On another level he displays a more human side to his character--his deep affection for his nephew and Duke Naimes and his grief for his soldiers are two signs of this. But in *Aspremont*, quite originally, we are given glimpses of an equally human but weaker side of his nature which, if detracting somewhat from his imperial stature, add a satisfying dimension to his credibility as a man. When, at the start of the poem, Charlemagne is jolted out of his buoyant mood by the sudden insults thrown at him by the Pagan envoy Balan, he loses his temper and moves to strike the intruder. It is only after Duke Naimes intervenes that the Emperor regains his normal composure and addresses the envoy as "brother" thereafter. On several subsequent occasions the Emperor vents his spleen at the frustrations of his office and at the lack of appreciation he receives from those he serves (10614-630):

> "My lords," says Charles, "I seek not to gainsay;
> When we for war came here to Calabray,
> Of men eight thousand score our force was made;
> Two thirds of these shall never breathe again,

Introduction

> Who three days back were healthy men and hale;
> Yet I came not to capture lands or take,
> But rode here rather the Lord our God to aid
> And to uphold and glorify His faith;
> Now when I hear some of our own men say
> That I began this war and am to blame
> For all the hurt and hardship we've sustained,
> And that the fault is mine for all their pain,
> I'm sorely tempted to give up all my claims,
> And devil take the thought of further gain--
> Save that I'm loath to change all for their sakes!
> Let God give France to him whom more she craves!
> I pay too dearly, who dear enough have paid!"

His counterpart, the Emir Agolant, is shown quite bluntly to be well past his prime both as a leader and as a man. His control over events in Africa and in the war in Italy has been usurped by his son Aumon and he is left to fret over a succession of disasters and to blame a succession of defeated generals. Arrogant, cruel and quick-tempered he develops into a helpless, comic and almost pathetic figure ruined by his son's pride, betrayed by the Almanzor, deceived by his wife and derided by both Charlemagne and Duke Naimes in their exchanges with him or with his equally arrogant representatives.

It is, however, the personality and doings of the Emir's son Aumon which dominate the first half of the poem. The portrayal of this character is one of the many borrowings made by the poet from the *Chanson de Roland*, for it is clear that this proud prince is a Saracen duplicate of the older Roland himself. He is a tragic anti-hero whose fatal flaw is his *démesure*, his pride. In his quest for personal glory he leads his own troops away from the rest of the Pagan forces and embarks upon a local "crusade" of pillage and cruelty. He is his father's champion, yet humiliated when his raiding gang is defeated by Charlemagne's vanguard. Like Roland at Roncevaux he refuses to blow his horn to summon help, and as a result eventually loses all of his men and his own life. He is slain by the young Roland, who gains possession this way of his horn, the famous Olifant of the older poem, and of the equally famous sword Durendal. Aumon indeed "bequeathes" them to his literary *alter ego* (6040-44):

> "I pray Mahom, my great god, and request it
> That this lad have my sword Durendal henceforth;
> For it would be too wrong and too offensive
> If a weak, wavering man wielded Durendal,
> Who lusted not for battle and its perils..."

True to his promise of the first stanza the poet provides us with a lively and entertaining account of the *enfances* of the hero Roland. Given the frequency of their appearance throughout the pages of the *chansons de geste* there can be little doubt that the exuberant exploits of noble-hearted youngsters provided the medieval audience with a welcome comic relief from the dramas of the battlefield. The vivid picture of youth painted in *Aspremont*, in scenes contrasting uncaring violence with innocent clumsiness, aggressive impatience with affectionate zeal, is one of the finest and funniest of its kind.

Within the boundaries of their traditional type the individual personalities of the three remaining role pairs are defined and developed in terms of their awareness of God. Duke Naimes and Balan are the best and wisest knights of either side, and as such the defiant speeches made by each in their role of envoy are an early highlight of the poem. But Balan's conversion to Christianity, initiated and nurtured by Naimes, adds a more personal dimension to the character of each. Balan develops as an honorable man plunged into a dilemma of divided loyalties, while the Duke's ministrations effectively illustrate the wisdom traditionally associated with his name. Girart d'Eufrate and the Almanzor are both arrogant, cruel and rebellious warlords. But Girart's disdainful attitude towards organized religion and its representatives is clearly and at times humorously opposed to the religious zeal inspired in him by his wife Emmeline. His uneasy cooperation with Charlemagne, a psychological mainspring of the drama, is a reflection of this contradiction--one of the many in his character. The Christian constancy of Lady Emmeline herself lends sharper focus to the conversion of the Emir's wife. The latter's amorous dalliances, both before and after her baptism, betray her true role as the stock comic figure of the Saracen Princess.

Paynim (i.e. Pagan) soldiers, women and the clergy constitute three major groups whose appearance in the *chansons de geste* frequently cause laughter. The Pagans in *Aspremont*, known variously as Saracens, Africans, Turks, Persians and Slavs, all bear the physical and moral brand of their anti-Christianity. They are endowed by the poet with names, physical features and a general deportment both on and off the battlefield which parody the Christian and the chivalric ideal. Their leaders lack little in terms of bravery, but it is their arrogance which makes them laughable opponents. Their constant, exaggerated taunts are turned aside or back upon them with pithy comment or

Introduction xix

elaborate cruelty throughout the poem by Duke Naimes and Charlemagne in particular. Their rank and file are lampooned for their cowardice, their collective light-headedness and brittle obedience.

The range of roles gradually accorded to females in the development of the Old French epic genre is well illustrated in our poem. Firstly there is the part of womanhood in general, both as the helpless victim of warfare and wanton cruelty and as the sex of Eve which always makes men suffer. Then in particular there is the role of the strong-minded wife, such as Lady Emmeline, who is in every way a match and worthy mate for her intemperate and stubborn husband Girart d'Eufrate. Her type goes back to the energetic Guibourc of the early *Chançun de Willame*. Although essentially not a comic figure at all it is her strength, her ability to dictate to him who dictates to everyone else, which makes us smile. The most prominent female role in the genre is however that of the amorous Saracen Princess, represented in our poem by the Emir's unnamed wife. Injected into the epic poems in direct response to the popularity of the female-dominated courtly romance, her role is certainly intended to be comic. As an erotic figure "the loveliest Queen and bride/Who ever had breasts upon her chest inclined," the young wife of King Agolant amuses us with the number, speed and intensity of her affairs. She is the lover of Gorhan and probably Balan too, she desires Duke Naimes as soon as she sees him, and even after her baptism alongside her equally attractive attendants she flirts with a suddenly rejuvenated Girart d'Eufrate. She increases our humorous contempt for her husband the Emir, whom she herself describes as a "ravaged relic", and adversely affects the fighting prowess of her "courtly" lover Gorhan, who in combat with Naimes "feels sore regret that he was ever inspired."

There are several examples of clerical and anti-clerical humor in the poem. The sympathetic figure of Turpin the fighting Archbishop, familiar to the medieval audience from the *Chanson de Roland*, evokes nothing but admiration for his ready zeal and selfless common sense. But his dual role as pastor and fighter is totally bemusing to his superior, Milon the Pope (9312-320):

"Milon, my lord, pray do not be annoyed!
I would give back this holy Cross of yours;
For I've a hauberk and a good horse of war,
A bright steel helm and at my side a sword;
I am an Archbishop and knight withal;
I would now show the worth of my employ."

The Pope replies: "I thank the Lord God for it;
For as I see I have but little choice!"

Turpin himself is scathing in his criticism of those miserable prelates such as Abbot Fromer, for whom the accumulation of personal wealth is more important than the selfless performance of their Christian duty. The undignified verbal battle between both churchmen on this point at the start of the poem amuses even an affronted and fuming Charlemagne.

The anti-clerical element in *Aspremont* is most apparent in the speeches of Girart d'Eufrate. He insults Archbishop Turpin and treats his threats of excommunication with contempt. He fulminates against the "ignobility" of the bishops and tells his nephew Claron to never trust a priest "save at confession time." The wry humor of these comments made at the Church's expense is carefully controlled however, as befits a work of art which draws its impetus and intensity from the strength of the One True Faith.

Despite its "literary" length the *Chanson d'Aspremont* remains in essence poetry for public recitation not private reading. As such it bears many of the stylistic features of verse composed and presented orally for the enjoyment of an audience. It is indeed drama in song and the realities of any live performance are present in the text. The narrator-performer introduces successive episodes and repeats salient details. He establishes a lasting rapport with his listeners by communicating his own enthusiasm for his tale. His interjections are frequent but timely. He compliments or criticizes, urges or warns, jokes or worries along with the audience and thus succeeds in gaining and guiding their attention.

Conflict is presented through dialogue with little other explanation, while soliloquy is limited to lament and prayer. There is little of the verbal wit to be found in earlier epics such as *Gormont et Isembart* and the *Chançun de Willame*, but there is a more original and developed use of the simile. It is however the frequent employment of stereotyped "formulaic" expressions, used to classify a character, sketch a scene, repeat, sustain, vary or embellish a particular statement, description, emotion or action, which characterizes the oral style of *Aspremont* and all its genre. Easy to learn and to perform originally no doubt, these epic formulas serve not only as an aid to audience understanding, but their repetition mesmerizes and their skilful management arouses the emotions (see

Aspland, p. 36). The use of this formulaic technique is most obvious in the descriptions of men and weapons and in the lengthy accounts of conventionalized battle-scenes. To any follower of modern sporting broadcasts this style will not be unfamiliar.

The action of the poem is presented and propelled in verses of varying length called *laisses*. The final syllables of all the lines in one laisse are traditionally assonanced together, but in *Aspremont* they are also rhymed. The assonance or rhyme changes with each laisse and is either, but not alternatively, masculine or feminine--the addition of an unstressed syllable not counting in the scansion. The self-contained laisse provides an excellent structure for episodic unity and dramatic emphasis. It is indeed the lengthening of the laisses, already evident in this poem, which gives one indication of the breakdown of the oral tradition in the epics of the thirteenth century.

As with most *chansons de geste* the line itself in *Aspremont* is strictly decasyllabic with strong internal accent and heavy end-stopping, although there are rare examples of enjambement. The break in the line usually falls after the fourth but occasionally after the sixth syllable, which again may be either masculine or feminine and may vary from line to line within one laisse. It is these half-lines which are the real building blocks of the Old French epic, for it is they which contain the four-syllable or six-syllable formulas. The considerable syntactic flexibility of these formulas when used in combination with the changing laisse assonance allows the skilful poet to sustain or embellish any description to create a heightened effect. It is this technique, known as that of the similar or parallel laisse, which produces the finest moments of the Old French epic genre.

SOURCES AND INFLUENCES

The *Chanson d'Aspremont* owes much, both in construction and content, to its more famous elder brother, the *Chanson de Roland*. Both epics consist of two distinct halves which deal with the death of a proud young hero and the revenge sought subsequently on his behalf. Key episodes of our poem, the embassies of King Balan and Duke Naimes, the destruction of the Pagan gods, the trial of the Almanzor's nephews and the conversion of the Emir's wife, contain passages which are identical in motif and expression to those found in the *Roland*. The imitation is even plainer on the level of characterization--the Pagans of Agolant and Aumon all threaten, fight and die using the very words and weapons of those of Baligant and Marsilion, whilst the similarity between the character of Aumon himself and his behavior on the slopes of Aspremont and that of Roland on the plain of Roncevaux is particularly obvious. As the level-headed but unheeded "hero's friend" there is also much of Roland's companion Olivier in the figure of King Balan.

Two other epics are cited by Van Waard as providing the inspiration for important elements of *Aspremont*. He sees the character of Guibourc in the *Chançun de Willame* as the model for the strong-minded Dame Emmeline in our poem, and the antics of young Gui, Count William's nephew, as the source for the *enfances* Roland section (p. 144 *et seq.*). *Aspremont* also contains material from an eleventh-century epic *Giroud dou Frates*, which supplies the background for the feud between Girart and Charles and the characterization of the rebel baron himself (Van Waard, pp.82 *et seq.*). The other major literary influences upon our poem appear to have been the enormously popular *Roman de Thèbes**, where the adventures of Polynices foreshadow those of Duke Naimes upon Mount Bitter, and the so-called Pseudo-Turpin chronicle, which provides much of the religious debate to be found in *Aspremont* as well as the name of the Pagan emperor Agolant.

The stock themes and stylistic features of the *fabliaux*, composed and presented alike by the *jongleurs*, are more evident in our poem than in many other epics. The following tirade against women, for example, made by the Emir Agolant, is in tone and content the very stuff of the shorter genre (8971-982):

> "King Uliens, I'll not conceal this thought:
> Whoever seeks the counsel or support
> Of womenfolk or weak and wavering sorts
> Should never rule a mighty realm at all;
> A woman marries and weds within the law,
> Then undertakes to try to lure some lord;
> She tries her best to flirt with him and flaunt
> And soften him up for what she has in store;
> But if she sees him hesitate or baulk
> From doing that about which I'll not talk,
> Or should he even abandon her perforce,
> She'll find her pleasure with someone else in short..."
> **********************

*in GLML trans. by J.S. Coley, Vol.44 (Garland, 1986).

Introduction xxiii

Ironically enough it is the Emir's wife herself who fits this description exactly. She exposes her older husband to ridicule by her own deceit and unflattering remarks--a common motif in the *fabliaux* (Herman, p. 222). The slapstick violence of the *fabliaux* is present also in the boisterous behavior of young Roland and his band. Their bashing of the uncooperative porter and Breton squires provides a timely scene of comic relief. Most strikingly, the tendency of the fabliau-teller to moralize upon behavior, a procedure not common in the epics, is evident in the first half particularly of our poem (for examples of this see lines 80-81, 756-57, 797-98, 452-54 and 4162-163).

The popularity of the *Chanson d'Aspremont* in the late twelfth and thirteenth centuries is attested firstly by the number of surviving manuscripts containing all or parts of this long poem. Roepke (pp. 1-5) lists seventeen. Secondly, the number of specific allusions made in later epics to *Aspremont* by name or to the characters therein is considerable (see Szogs, p. 88 *et seq.*). In particular, many of the *enfances* episodes in later *chansons de geste* appear to have been heavily influenced by the motif's treatment in our poem. Sections of *Aspremont* are to be found in the *Chronique rimée* of Philippe Mousket, a "historical novel" in verse, composed around 1260, and in the fourth part of the Old Norse prose epic *Karlamagnus saga* written around 1300. At least two later prose compilations dealing with the life and deeds of Charlemagne contain extensive amounts of material culled from our poem--the *Myreur des Histors* of Jean d'Outremeuse (d. 1400) and *Les Cronicques et Conquestes de Charlemaine*, attributed to David Aubert and completed in 1458. In addition, a *chanson de geste* called *Aspramonte*, written in Franco-Italian dialect in 1508 or 1509 and in the possession of the library of St. Mark in Venice, bears witness not only to the popularity of certain Old French epics and their legends but to the survival of the genre itself in Italy during the fourteenth and fifteenth centuries.

By contrast the decidedly cool reception accorded to the poem by the consensus of late nineteenth and early twentieth-century scholarship (see Van Waard, p. 1) is disconcerting if not entirely surprising. Even Alfred Jeanroy, one of the few critics to concern himself with *Aspremont* at all, concludes that the work is "an almost inextricable tangle of repetition, digression and exhausting, drawn-out episodes" (1934, p. 121, my translation). Such a lack of literary appreciation, I would suggest, stems more from the defective critical approaches to oral-based poetry of that era, than from the intrinsic qualities of the verse itself.

EDITORIAL POLICY FOR THIS TRANSLATION

The only edition of the *Chanson d'Aspremont* is that of Louis Brandin, published by the *Classiques Français du Moyen Age* in two volumes in 1923 and 1924 and reprinted in 1970. In consultation with the nine other major manuscripts, which all appear to stem from a lost original, Brandin presents the version contained in "the manuscript of Lord Middleton preserved at Wollaton Hall in Nottinghamshire." He dates this text from the end of the thirteenth century and shows it to be written by two different scribes in variant forms of the Picard dialect. In 1925 Brandin also published an illustrated, much condensed version of the same text in modern French prose. It is Brandin's Wollaton Hall manuscript which is translated here.

In this translation I have tried to preserve all the formal properties of the original text. Given the nature and purpose of the *chansons de geste* such an approach seems to me to be essential if the modern reader is to appreciate something of the energy and effectiveness of this art form. Within the laisses I have used the traditional assonance pattern rather than the full rhyme which is predominant in the original, but which it would have been impossible to copy. In the interests of fluency I have also allowed myself the luxury of many more run-on lines and feminine laisses than occur in the original and some of my lines themselves are hypermetric for the same reason. The occasional archaisms and misplaced accents remain, however, and bear witness to the, at times, grim battle with the decasyllabic meter, as do the liberties taken with some proper names (thus, for example, Charlemagne is called variously Charlemayn, Carlon and Charles, while Agolant is both the Émir and the Emír). These contrivances apart, however, this translation of the *Chanson d'Aspremont* is as strict yet natural as I could make it.

I have maintained Brandin's division of the poem into two books and have further divided the whole translation into twelve parts, each one except the last of approximately one thousand lines. Ideally these should be *declaimed* by the "reader," so that something of the tempo and flavor of the original may be recaptured.

Introduction

My first debt of gratitude is to Associate Professor C.W. Aspland of Macquarie University, from whom I have received constant encouragement over the several years of this translation and to whom I owe such Old French scholarship as I possess. My warm thanks go also to Dr. John Ward of Sydney University. His unfailing enthusiasm for this and previous translations I have made as well as his practical help and advice have meant much to me. I am grateful alike to my friends in general for their patient interest in this project and to Mrs. Lucy Croci and Mr. Gary Heap in particular, the former for her knowledge of details relating to the Italian setting and the latter for his collaboration on the map. I am indebted to the School of Modern Languages at Macquarie University for the use of their word-processing facilities and to my two typists, Heather Hyndes and Barbara Albertini for their painstaking labors on my behalf. In the preparation of this edition the assistance of James J. Wilhelm has been invaluable. Last but not least I owe thanks to the members of my family for their understanding and practical support.

SELECT BIBLIOGRAPHY

1. CRITICAL STUDIES OF THE *CHANSON D'ASPREMONT*

Bédier, Joseph. *Les Légendes Epiques*. 4 vols. Paris: Champion, 1908-13; rpt. 1914-21. Vol.2 pp. 200,207 *et seq.*; Vol.3, p.97; Vol.4, pp. 183,301,329 *et seq.* The *travail de base* of Old French Epic studies.

Benary, Walter. "Mitteilungen aus Handschriften der Chanson d'Aspremont." *Zeitschrift für romanische Philologie*, (1920), 1-25.

Haase, C. *Weitere Studien zur "Chanson d'Aspremont."* Greifs--wald, 1917.

Jeanroy, Alfred. "Compte-rendu de S. Szogs, Aspremont." *Romania*, LX (1934) 119-121.

─────────── "La Chanson d'Aspremont." *Studi Medievali*, XI (1938) I-III.

Mayer, Josef. *Weitere Beiträge zur "Chanson d'Aspremont."* Greifswald, 1910.

Roepke, Fritz. *Studien zur "Chanson d'Aspremont."* Inaugural Dissertation, Greifswald, 1909.

Szogs, S. "Aspremont," *Romanistische Arbeiten*, Halle, 1931.

Van Waard, Roelof. *Etudes sur l'origine et la formation de "La Chanson d'Aspremont."* Groningen, 1937. A detailed analysis of the legendary and literary sources for the poem, as well as a discussion of all criticism up to that point.

2. GENERAL STUDIES OF THE *CHANSONS DE GESTE*

Altman, Charles F. "Interpreting Romanesque Narrative: Conques and the *Roland*." *Olifant*, 5 (1977), 4-28.

Aspland, Clifford W. *A Syntactical Study of Epic Formulas and Formulaic Expressions Containing the -ant Forms in 12th Century French Verse*. Queensland: University Press, 1970. An analysis of the formation and function of epic diction in the *chansons de geste*. The introduction examines various theories concerning the oral transmission of the poems.

Benton, John F. "Nostre Franceis n'unt talent de fuïr": *The Song of Roland* and the Enculturation of a Warrior Class." *Olifant*, 6 (1978-9), 237-258.

Brault, Gerard J. *The Song of Roland: An Analytical Edition*. Pennsylvania: State University Press, 1978.

Calin, William C. *The Epic Quest: Studies in Four Old French chansons de geste*. Baltimore: John Hopkins Press, 1966.

Colby, Alice M. *The Portrait in Twelfth-Century French Literature*. Genève: Droz, 1965.

Comfort, William W. "The Character Types in the Old French *Chansons de Geste*." *PMLA*, XXI (1906), 279-434.

_____. "The Literary Role of the Saracens in the French Epic." *PMLA*, LV (1940), 628-59.

Cook, Robert F. "Unity and Esthetics in the Late *Chansons de Geste*." *Olifant*, 11 (1986), 103-114.

Crosland, Jessie. *The Old French Epic*. New York: Haskell Howe, 1970.

Daniel, Norman. *Heroes and Saracens: An Interpretation of the Chansons de Geste*. Edinburgh: University Press, 1984.

Doutrepont, G. *Les Mises en Prose des Epopées et des Romans Chevalresques du XIV au XVI siècle*. Bruxelles, 1939; Slatkine reprints Genève, 1969. Traces the adaptations of many *chansons de geste* and their legends by later French chroniclers and Italian poets of the Renaissance. The quality of the original often bears little relation to the number and success of its adaptations.

Duggan, J.J. *The Song of Roland: Formulaic Style and Poetic Craft*. Los Angeles, 1973.

_____ "Oral performance, writing and the textual tradition of the medieval epic in the romance languages: the example of the *Song of Roland*."*Parergon*, 2 (1984), 79-95. The variant texts of many epics are not corruptions of a primary written source but new "performances" of the original oral material, designed to suit new audiences and evolving tastes.

Faral, Edmond. *Les Jongleurs en France au moyen âge*. Bibliothèque de l'Ecole des Hautes Etudes, 187. Paris: Champion, 1910; rpt. 1964. A detailed study of the activities of the jongleurs.

Farnsworth, William Oliver. *Uncle and Nephew in the Old French Chansons de Geste: A Study in the Survival of Matriarchy*. New York: AMS Press Inc., 1966.

Gildea, Sister Marianna. *Expressions of Religious Thought and Feeling in the Chansons de Geste*. Washington: Catholic University of America Press, 1943.

Harden, A. Robert. "The Element of Love in the *Chansons de Geste*." *Annuale Medievale*, V (1964).

Herman, Gerald. *Aspects of the Comic in the Old French Epic*. Dissertation, Stanford University 1967. Comic elements are present in the genre from its very inception as an integral feature of all epic poetry. The amount of humor in any chanson depends upon the individual talent of the *trouvère*, not on its chronological place in the genre.

Hindley, Alan and Levy, Brian J. *The Old French Epic. An Introduction*... Louvain, 1983.

Holmes, Urban T. *A History of Old French Literature*. New York, 1948.

Jones, C. Meredith. "The Conventional Saracen of the Songs of Geste." *Speculum*, 17 (1942), 201-235.

Kibler, William W. "Bibliography of Fourteenth and Fifteenth Century French Epics." *Olifant*, 11 (1986), 58-100.

Koch, Sister Marie Pierre. *An Analysis of the Long Prayers in Old French Literature with Special Reference to the "Biblical-Creed-Narrative" Prayers*. Washington:Catholic University of America Press, 1940.

Moroldo, Arnaldo. "Le Portrait dans la *Chanson de Geste*." *Le Moyen Age*, LXXXVI (1980), 387-419 and LXXXVII (1981) 5-44.

Nichols Jr., Stephen G. *Formulaic Diction and Thematic*

Composition in the "Chanson de Roland." Chapel Hill: University of North Carolina Press, 1961.

―――――――――――― "The Generative Function of *Chant* and *Récit* in the Old French Epic." *Olifant*, 6 (1979) 305-352.

―――――――――――― *Romanesque Signs: Early Medieval Narrative and Iconography*. See esp.: Chapter 5: Roncevaux and the Poetics of Place/Person in the *Song of Roland*.

Picherit, Jean-Louis G. "L'"Apostoile" dans l'épopée." *Olifant*, 9 (1981) 113-128.

―――――――――――― "L'évolution de quelques thèmes épiques: La dépossession, l'exhérédation, et la reconquête du fief." *Olifant*, 11 (1986) 115-128.

Riquer, Martin de. *Les Chansons de Geste Françaises* trans. I.-M. Cluzel. 2nd ed. Paris: Nizet, 1957.

Rychner, Jean. *La Chanson de Geste: Essai sur l'art épique des jongleurs*. Société de publications romanes et françaises, LIII. Genève: Droz, Lille: Giard, 1955. The classic study of the jongleur's art.

Sayers, Dorothy. *The Song of Roland*. Harmondsworth: Penguin Classics, 1957. Both the preface and verse of this translation of the *Roland* are written with a true artist's intuition of the genre.

Shen, Lucia Simpson. *The Old French "Enfances" Epic and their Audience*. University of Pennsylvania, 1982.

Taylor, S.E. *The Saracen Princess in the Medieval "Chansons de Geste"*. University of Sheffield Press, 1982.

The Song of Aspremont
(La Chanson d'Aspremont)

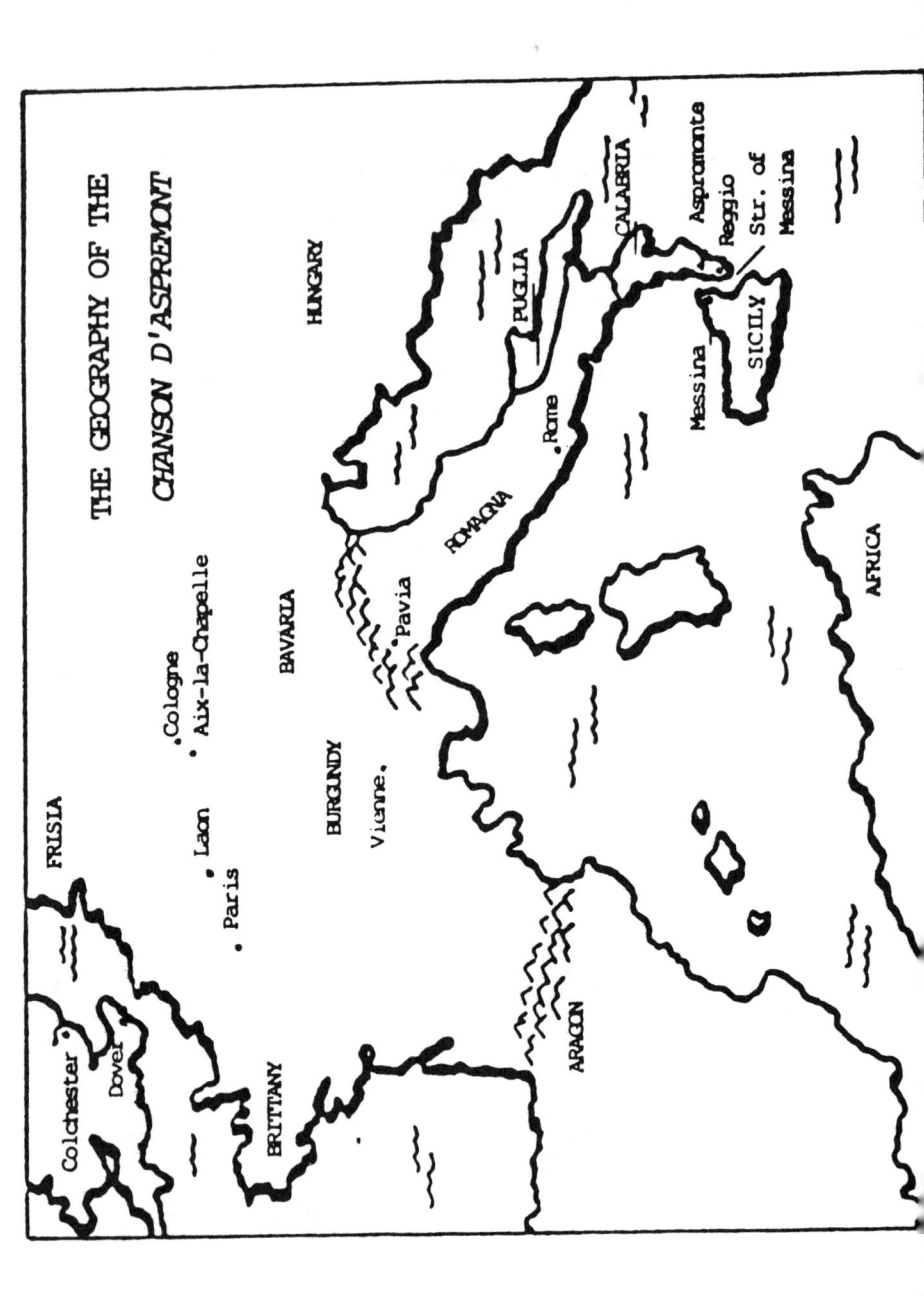

BOOK 1

PART I

THE SONG OF ASPREMONT TELLS OF AUMON AND AGOLANT

1

Will you hear a good song, a worthy one
Of Charlemayn the powerful Emperor
And Naimes the Duke, whom the King loved so much?
The French ne'er had so wise a counsellor;
No word of his would harm the barons' luck;   5
In matter great or small he never once
Advised a knight that he do such and such
That by that man was not directly done;
And Charles knew well that his words brought results
And all his life he honored him and loved;   10
Now of Aumon I'll tell and Agolant,
Of Aspremont and its great battle-fronts,
Of how the King first dubbed Roland the young,
How at his side the burnished blade he hung,
Sharp Durendal; the geste reveals it thus   15
And tells the first how he shed Paynim blood:
He killed Aumon, who was Agolant's son;
So listen well for what is now to come!
If it please you, a good song will be sung.

2

Let it be known, the good that Duke Naimes wrought!   20
He did not try to harm an honest cause
Nor seek to blacken a good man's name at court;
He praised good families when he and Carlon talked
And thus would bring a man's name to the fore,
Serve him so well with so little reward   25
No man could say his services were bought;
But as for villains or those he knew were false,
He kept them from the King and sent them forth;
And if he then could strike within the law
He had them tamed and tutored with such force   30
As one breaks in the forest sparrow-hawk;
Why should I make this matter any more?
His good advice brought Charles so to the fore

That following God, who judges each and all,
He started with just France to rule by law,   35
And ere old age robbed him of bed and board
Lands fifteen more in league with France he joined;
And now I shall begin the song, my lords;
Fierce-faced Carlon at Aix* is holding court
At Pentecost, and brave knights fill the hall;   40
King Didier, he is there and King Brunol,
King Salemon and Gaifier mighty lord,
Droon the King and Garnier strong and tall;
These wait on Charles, who wisely rules them all,
While at his feet sits Naimes Bavarian-born;   45
For pleasure's sake the Duke with Carlon talks:
"True Emperor, well may your heart rejoice!
Well may you praise and pray to God our Lord;
No man on earth dare anger you with taunts,
For if you cared to challenge him in war   50
You'd force him down and at your feet he'd fall;
So do not be so proud or fierce henceforth;
Your duty now is to befriend the poor;
Do not compel poor sons to leave your shores;
From seven lands knights come here to your court,   55
Whose seven kings keep danger from your door;
You should be happy--this is my honest thought;
Befriend them now and their pledge is assured;
Advise them well how they may seek rewards
And in two ways you'll benefit the more;   60
You'll have God on your side, now and henceforth,
And if they see you threatened, here or abroad,
They'll fight until they drop for you and yours;
Do not be mean with what lies in your vaults;
Those who come here to glorify your court,   65
To be with you and learn to love you more,
Deserve your thanks, which now must not fall short;
We who are here share every meal of yours,
Dress when you dress, put boots on when you walk;
You would be wrong to not give us a horse;   70
You would be wrong to hold on to one coin;
My wealth itself, dispense that first of all;
Dispense enough to knights who may be poor
So their poor wives feel happier than before;
Then if they see you're off to fight a war   75
They'll follow you without a second thought;
And if you send an envoy to their door
They'll bring their lands behind you in support;
Give them wealth now when they are all still poor,
For it is said and generally thought: 80

* Aix-la-Chapelle (Aachen).

He who gives first is no fool to be sure."

                    3

The Emperor, when he has heard this speech,
Replies: "Duke Naimes, may you be blessed indeed!
So many times your counsel has helped me;
When blows are struck with blades of naked steel   85
I've seen you out in front leading the field
And all our soldiers rallying around your shield;
Before your wealth is brought to share out here
I'll give you mine, come morning, willingly;
And when you've seen it, I certainly believe   90
That you will say no richer has been seen;
As for the giving, I would not have you grieve;
You won it all, so give whatever you please,
That glad of heart all here may take their leave."

                    4

Now when Duke Naimes has heard his liege-lord talk   95
He feels such joy as never felt before:
"Heed these words well," he says, "barons my lords,
And serve this man unswervingly henceforth,
Who after God is greatest of them all!
To high and low I'll stand as guarantor: 100
Sons can come here of lowly vavasors
And leave as dukes or counts of Carlon's court."

                    5

The Archbishop is next to speak his mind;
A well-bred man in his young manhood's prime,
He's loved by all at court and much admired;   105
No duke in France, as hard as he might try,
Could bring to court so great a host to fight;
He much prefers good destriers to buy
And noble armor to dub and dress young squires
Than save his wealth and store it up in piles;   110
He will maintain until the day he dies
That any man who'd challenge Carlon's right
Should ride instead to battle at his side
And bear his arms, a good war-horse astride,
To fight for Charles, not plot for his demise;   115
Thus to the Pope he speaks now in this wise:
"Father, don't take amiss these words of mine;
It is our duty to cherish all brave knights;
For when we clerics sit down to eat at night,
Or in God's service sing matins at first light,   120
These men are fighting for our lands with their lives;

                    5

So Abbot Fromer here and you and I
Should empty all our coffers for their supplies;
Each one of us should give so much alike
They'll honor us and serve us all the time."

6

Before the King sits in the pine tree's shade,
Before he leaves his marble throne this day
Gold and silk cloth of Alexandrian make,
Fine goblets too and cups of gold ornate
And handsome hawks and falcons of the chase
Carlon, the son of Pepin, gives away
To men of noble rank and high estate.

7

He hands out coins, fine steeds and worthy palfreys;
Poor knights receive all these at Carlon's orders;
White furs and gray and fleet-footed war-horses,
Small hunting-falcons and caged sparrow-hawks also
Charles gives away to young men lithe and sporty;
While to brave soldiers and sons of noble forebears,
To high-born men, he offers mountain falcons.

8

The King bestows on all with great largesse;
Four sesterces he gives of all his wealth;
Three hundred horses that evening he gives them;
Naimes speaks for all, whose wisdom is his strength;
He says: "My lords, the truth must needs be said;
The royal crown should sit on this man's head,
Who after God has power above all men.

9

"Hear me, my lords! Whoever defies Charlemayn
Defies at once all of the German race,
Defies the Lombards and French and Bretons brave,
All of Apulia and all the Roman state;
Defies alike all those of Aquitaine;
No man, be he so bold, would tempt that fate;
Let just one squire of his put on his blade
And Charles find out, he'd rue it all his days;
He'd be hard-pressed to stop in his domain.

10

"Let no man now return to his own territory

And dub new knights for his own power and pleasure!
Bring them to Carlon's court when it's assembled
And he will give a sword or shield to everyone!

11

"He'll give each man both weapons and a charger,   160
Both coins to spend and a fine suit of armor;
Swords and war-horses will be theirs for the asking
If they agree to serve him ever after."

12

Now is the King well pleased and in high spirits;
None leaves his court who is not fully with him;   165
Seven thousand men have pledged and promise given
To serve Carlon with ready heart and willing,
Who ere this day would not have raised a finger;
Now two kings stand and Duke Naimes rises with them;
Before great Charles they kneel down in submission: 170
"True Emperor, we urge you now to listen
To what these knights at ease today are whispering,
All of these barons at rest on your silk pillows!
There's no land under heaven which, if you wished it,
By force of arms they could not capture quickly!   175
Yet Saracens are camped in neighboring Italy!
It hurts their hearts that you delay one instant."
The King hears this and thanks them for their
     diligence
And then replies as a true king befitting:
"I'll conquer them, then help them to be Christians,   180
If you will rule them within my jurisdiction."
The feast is ready and brought out from the kitchens,
Tablecloths laid and wines tasted for vintage,
Salt-cellars brought and knives placed in position;
Some hundred men the banquet-hall are filling,   185
Clothed all in vair and ermine cloaks close-fitting,
Sons all of counts and princes of the kingdom;
Yet ere the King shall get up from this sitting,
A plateful of such woe he'll have for dinner
That never before will he have felt so sickened,   190
Nor any there have felt so ill in spirit.

13

Before the King sits down this day to eat
Or even leaves his throne of stone and steel,
Behold a knight within their midst appear
Who has dismounted a big fawn-colored steed!   195
Lean now it looks and worn out with fatigue;

One month and two days more that horse has been
Without a rest of one whole day between;
But had you seen it as it set out for here!
No horse on earth were worthier than this beast   200
And none there were you'd covet more to keep.

14

Within their midst dismounts the warrior vassal;
His hair is fair, he wears it finely plaited;
Long on his shoulders it flows behind the back of him;
Down to his hips it falls in Paynim manner;   205
His eyes are bright, his face laughing and happy;
No girl has skin so fair nor maid so matchless,
Save that the heat of sunlight strong has tanned it;
His features are well-formed, his shoulders handsome;
His arms are long and strong, his bosom ample;   210
His waist and hips are slim and straight his stature;
His thighs are sturdy, his stance upright and agile;
How well he wears those spurs about his ankles!
You'd find few men as perfect as this Saracen;
He takes off now his silk gold-colored mantle;   215
Behold him, lords, in his plain tunic standing,
Slit to the waist his armor overhanging!
His sword he loosens, its hilt of gold enamelled,
And to a Turk behind him there he hands it;
Between both hands his right hand glove is balanced   220
As he steps forward approaching Charlemagne;
With full-lunged voice, so all may hear, he challenges:
"May Mahomet, whom Paynims worship gladly,
Who guards us all and makes us great in battle,
Save Agolant and Aumon our great Champion,   225
Gorhan the Glad and noble King Triamodes
And all the men with them in their encampments!
May he confound King Charlemayn the Arrogant
And all of those who influence your actions!
For much too long you've left us from your planning, 230
And now my lord has turned on you his anger;
For one month now he's ridden in the saddle,
Kingdoms and keeps all set to siege and captured;
Well might you say that you have acted rashly;
For your great pride, Carlon, you will be banished!   235
As for myself, sent here by royal Agolant,
When I was given this ring before I travelled,
Placed on my finger by one not unattractive,
I made a vow, for love of her enacted,
I'd not remove it nor would it be extracted   240
Until my lance lay low a Frankish baron."
"My friend," says Charles, "God pity what may happen!"

"Sir Emperor, now listen well to me!
Earth has three Empires and I shall name them each:
Asia is one and Europe is its peer 245
And Africa, no more are found save these;
Now these three realms are parted by the sea,
Which all mainlands and islands flows between;
The best of these my master rules and keeps;
His Paynims read the fates there recently; 250
Two realms should serve the third, these fates
    revealed;
Thus I am here, your land to claim and seize,
And to tell you to go to the Emir;
Do not resist! His army's coming here;
I am called Balan--my name I'll not conceal; 255
I serve my King and carry his decrees;
Nor do I waste my time with idle speech;
I stand prepared to prove this if needs be
To any knight who seeks proof in the field;
I'll go myself to buy the arms I'll need, 260
With Afric gold that I've brought with me here;
And if your man can bring me to my knees
I'll register a mark upon my seal,
Have it inscribed so that it can be seen,
And you can take it to the Emir my liege; 265
He would not cross the Strait* were this to be;
If you refuse, your fate itself is sealed;
You haven't got the men our men to beat;
We'll hunt you down, no matter where you flee;
No wood will hide you, no land nor any sea; 270
Unless you can sprout wings you'll not go free;
Accept my gage if you dare to agree!
Find your best man and let him challenge me!
Take now this brief, the text thereof to see!
If what it says and I've said disagree 275
Then punish me as harsh and horribly
As you would do a thief caught as he thieved!"
Down on his mantle he throws Carlon the brief;
Carlon requests that Abbot Fromer read;
He breaks the seal and ponders long and deep 280
And looks at it for a long time indeed;
From his soul's depths a heavy sigh he heaves;
Tears form and fall as Abbot Fromer weeps;
His hands go limp, the letter is released;
Turpin of Rheims moves quickly to retrieve: 285
"Sir Emperor, you act wrongly, I fear,
To give your letter to such a man as he;

* Of Messina.

When he was young, I say now what I've seen,
He spent his days in drinking wine and mead;
Generous in talk, in action he was mean;   290
Do you know why his eyes now fill with tears?
He's frightened now his wealth might disappear;
Wealth we should give to all of those in need;
Begone, sir Abbot! Go sing your matins, please!
You will read better the life of Saint Omer;   295
I'll read this letter and work out what it means."

                16

Fromer the abbot is nothing if not angry;
In self-defence he is both sharp and agile:
"My lord Archbishop, be not so angry at me!
If both of us were to be judged so frankly   300
Nor you nor I would save ourselves from hanging;
We are both here to counsel Charlemagne,
And any king with state affairs to handle
Can do without his clerk to be his advocate,
Except in matters that he is fit to handle--   305
Hearing his sins and helping him recant them;
For other counsel a king looks to a character
Who is some use to him in times of action,
Who'd give his life for his king's, if he had to."
The Emperor on hearing both clerics clashing   310
Is most amused and loses part his anger:
"Enough," he says, "let us hear now from Agolant!"

                17

The Archbishop in front of all stands up
And reads the letter at the top of his lungs:
"Your Majesty, King Agolant says thus: 315
Of Earth's three Empires he rules the largest one;
Now he has sailed the sea of Africa
And is arrived within Calabria,
Sparing no one, women or children none."
Balan exclaims: "Mahom and Tervagant!   320
I know full well what angers him so much:
Your faith in God and in Jesus His Son;
If you don't yield beneath his blade, Carlun,
And recognize his rule and faith at once,
Your life's not worth a bezant--your days are done."   325
The French all say: "Balan speaks well enough
And taunts with words as well as with his glove."

                18

Turpin continues: "There is more I can translate;

                10

King Agolant feels naught for Charles but anger;
With hate in heart he'll conquer Christianity;   330
He says he'll kill you, and with his own two hands, Sire,
And crown his son in Rome--Aumon his champion.

19

"Give ear, my lords, to what the Paynim boasts!
All Christendom he'll conquer and lay low;
He wants to crown Aumon his son in Rome;   335
He'll win the crown so it's his to bestow."

20

Turpin reads on--he's in no mood for laughter:
"King Agolant has come with all his armies;
Six hundred thousand, whatever's said hereafter,
Crossed overseas on this journey departing;   340
His oldest son, King Troiens, is their commander;
He brings so many no one can tell their vastness;
Before you reach the province of Romagna
And ere you see Vercelli or Ivrea,
All will be ravaged up to the Breton marches;   345
The Christian faith will be harassed so harshly
All Christian men shall lose their lives thereafter;
And as for you, who are their lord and master,
Who have allowed this folly and enhanced it,
Your neck shall lie beneath his blade well-sharpened;   350
Should he decide to grant your life a pardon,
He'll make quite sure your fighting days are past you;
In foreign parts fresh powers he will grant you;
His seneschal you'll serve as, Charlemagne;
The letter ends with this selfsame remark, Sire."   355

21

Then Balan calls on Charlemayn once more:
"What shall I say to Agolant my lord?
The day you could fight him will never dawn--
Can a wild duck hope to combat a hawk?
One hundred thousand men our front ranks form   360
And I myself strike the first blow of all;
It is my right and was my ancestors';
White as a flower is my fleet-footed horse
And indigo my flag is flying tall
With lions three, the largest of them small;   365
When you behold our men afield with yours
You'll be a fool if your heart doesn't fall;
If I don't turn your joy into remorse
Pluck out my eyes that witnessed such default."

Charles nearly dies with rage to hear such talk 370
And moves to strike him; Naimes runs over the floor:
"Please no, fine sir, by God who made us all!
To strike him here would be held a great fault."
"The villain lies!" the Emperor retorts:
"Tell your lord this, make no mistake withal, 375
That four months from this day Charles will have
   brought
The Oriflamme* to Aspremont for war!
While God protects my strength and guides my
   thoughts
I'll not bow down to any earthly lord."

22

The feast is high, the day is warm and clear; 380
They ask for water and Carlon washes clean;
The messenger does not waste time; indeed
He's off to Charles to ask him for his leave;
Duke Naimes, however, first takes his wrist and
   speaks:
"Balan, my lord, why do you make such speed? 385
No one who talks to Charles and journeys here
Can leave on that same day--what courtesy!
I beg you rather, come and behold our feast
While I bring forth three hundred of our steeds;
Put saddles on the best two you can see 390
And they'll be yours tonight before you leave!"
Balan looks hard at Naimes when this he hears:
"Christian, you're mad to try your tricks on me!
I've not come here to purchase property;
I came to bring a letter for Charles to read 395
And to take back an answer to the Emir;
And if we two on Aspremont should meet
These words of yours their guerdon will receive!"
"My lord," says Naimes, "let this bravura be!
Not every wish can always be achieved." 400
An ermine mantle is brought at his decree
And a silk top of Oriental weave;
When Balan's dressed, good Naimes attends his needs,
Gets him a faldstool so he may sit at ease;
The stool is placed where Carlon has his seat 405
So Charles can ask him questions during the meal.

23

Charles, son of Pepin, sits down now to his banquet;
Bruno, himself a king, serves his wine gladly,

*Sacred red banner of the Abbey of Saint Denis.

While on his plate waits brave Droon the Poitevin;
His finger-bowl is carried by King Salemon;   410
Balan, his gaze held low, surveys the gathering:
Sees in the hall so many mighty paladins
All clothed in vair and gray and ermine mantles,
In silken tunics, in gold and purple jackets;
Seven hundred goblets, silver and gold, Balan sees--   415
Constantine's treasure, Emperor of Byzantium,
Which Charles, crossing the Rhine, had won in battle
When he defeated King Witikin the Saxon;
He sees at table so many high-born barons,
So many furs, so many steel-blade daggers,   420
And sees them talking, companion to companion;
Balan swears by his gods--Apollo, Mahom,
That all kings else are beggars in comparison
To Charlemayn, his great sway and his standards:
"Alas," he thinks, "the day Sorbrin met Agolant!"--   425
Sorbrin the spy, who set them on this action.

24

While Balan eats he cannot help but notice
How Charlemayn stands out, his mark imposing;
His beard is long, its texture thick and flowing;
Compared to Carlon's he thinks how young his own is;   430
He sees the hall filled with so many nobles
Dressed in great mantles and such expensive clothing
That to himself he thinks over and over:
"If Charles had no one else except these soldiers
All drinking here his wine and mead so boldly,   435
King Agolant's intentions here are hopeless;
Charles does not rate our Paynim faith one groat's
     worth;
All other faiths he frowns on but his own one;
His One Lord God he loves and sets his hopes on;
He'd rather die than turn from Him one moment."   440

25

The Emperor calls on Balan and bids him:
"Envoy, good brother, conceal not, nor keep hidden:
King Agolant, what is it that he's thinking?
Does he seek to destroy all Holy Christendom?"
"Yes, Sire, indeed; the hatred of it fills him!   445
He plans, this summer, to take Puglia and Sicily,
Then to be crowned in Rome itself this winter;
He'll hunt you down, then capture you or kill you."
"Ah God", says Charles, "by that good Grace which is
     You,

Let me avenge this wrong as I would wish to! 450
Envoy, good brother, conceal not nor keep hidden;
Tell your lord well that this is my opinion:
I think he's being too hasty with his victories;
If he's in Puglia he'll meet with my resistance!"

26

"My lord, give ear to me!" Balan replies; 455
"King Agolant is here with all his knights;
In search of you he has crossed o'er the tide;
All Alexander himself conquered in life
My lord would have--he feels it's his by right;
For he indeed is of that sovereign's line." 460

27

"Envoy, good brother," King Charlemayn pursues,
"Is Agolant a noble lord or cruel?"
Balan retorts: "Why should I hide the truth?
His beard is full and white with years all through,
But in this world no nobler monarch rules: 465
He joys in life--he hates nothing, but you!
He loves you not because you have refused,
You and your realm, to pay him honor due;
But let us here and now end this dispute!
I'll buy my weapons, a shield and staff will do 470
To fight on foot, befitting such a duel;
In Carlon's court let honor be on view;
Let men not say I dealt in its abuse;
If I can beat the champion you choose
Then Aspremont is where I'll take you to 475
With your hands joined, to be his liege-man true;
Receive this land from his hand--as a boon!"
Says Charles: "Good brother, do you know what we'll do?
You will return, but I'll not leave this room!
He can have France when we decide to move!" 480

28

The King has eaten, the tables all are cleared;
The envoy now from Carlon takes his leave
Led by Duke Naimes, in whose room he's to sleep;
For his delight fresh fruit and tasty treats
Are brought from town, should he desire to eat; 485
In this one room both men now lie at ease;
They talk all night and all night disagree;
They ask each other: "What faith do you believe?"
Balan thinks Naimes a simpleton indeed

14

To love a God who on a Cross was pierced,   490
To hold a faith that's not changed one degree
Since Adam's time--and he likewise unreal!"
Says Naimes: "Good brother, you are greatly deceived!
God made the world and having this achieved
Created Adam and his companion Eve,   495
Prepared for them in Paradise a seat;
In Paradise all was theirs as they pleased,
Except one fruit which God forbade them eat;
But Eve told Adam to heed not His decree,
And Adam, ignorant, ate of that tree;   500
A naked wretch, cast out from Grace to grief,
His Paradise he lost and had to leave
And work to live, both he and all his seed;
And his seed prospered and humankind increased;
But in foul lust and sin they lived and breathed;   505
So in the Flood God drowned them all and each,
Except for one he spared--Noah was he,
From whom we all descend and born have been;
Woe for those others--Satan alone was pleased,
For they all went to fuel Hell's fiery heat;   510
All of the living were chased to Hell's dark deep,
As peasants drive to market their herds of beast;
When God pitied his children, as are all we,
He wrought Himself in Holy Trinity
And came to Earth to save souls and redeem.   515

                              29

"When our Lord God came down out of the skies
For our salvation Himself He so despised
That in the Virgin's womb He did reside
And took on flesh and blood of humankind
Until the time that He was born a child;   520
Three years and thirty He lived His earthly life;
By John in Jordan Lord Jesus was baptized,
That by baptism a man may have new life
And live as blessed eternally with Christ;
The Jews took Jesus, I'll not tell you a lie;   525
Upon the Cross He suffered pain and spite;
They pierced His heart with a great cutting pike;
And His last breath that left Him as He died
Drew down to Hell straightway, and once inside
Restored the Faithful whom the Flood had denied: 530
Abraham, Noah, Jacob, Joseph--alive!
On the third day He rose as God on High;
These things are as they are, and thus transpired;
The Truth of them consider now a while,
For by His death was Hell sealed for all time,   535
The Devil, ever since, losing his might."

"You have spoken enough," Balan replies;
"Now I must leave--I've overstayed my time;
When I've performed this task to me assigned,
Without delay I'll do what's in my mind." 540
Now breaks the dawn and day starts to grow light;
His horses saddled, Balan begins to ride
The metalled road and leave the town behind;
Yet several times he looks back and he sighs,
Loath now to leave King Charles and all his knights 545
And all the French so courtly and so kind;
He'd be baptized straightway, his heart confides,
If he'd not lose all honor in Paynim eyes;
Balan rides on each day and by and by
He crosses Puglia, Calabria in sight; 550
He finds the Emir beneath a well-branched pine:
"Did you find Charles and did you speak our mind?"
"Indeed I did; I left out nothing, Sire."

30

Balan dismounts where King Agolant's tent is,
His stirrups held by King Lanpal's son Hector; 555
He makes his way through crowds of Paynim felons
On foot and horse, soldiers and knights together;
He finds the Emir beneath a pine majestic
And greets the King with words of Paynim blessing:
"My lord, I come from royal France's territory; 560
Full many a pain and hardship have I met with,
High hills have climbed and valleys steep descended."
"Did you see Charles?"--"By our Mahomet, yes, Sire!
At Aix his seat during an annual festival
He wore his crown, enthroned amidst great splendor; 565
King Charles is brave and strong and fierce of mettle;
No man alive there is beneath the heavens
Who'd live for long incurring his displeasure;
The French compared to others seem so much better,
Like gold compared to copper or to metal; 570
He and his barons through me give you this message:
He will be here before four months have ended;
If race with race meets equally in melee,
You can be sure your sorrow will be heavy."

31

Triamodes replies to this with anger: 575
"Curse messengers whose only news is bad news!
If Charlemayn (may Mahom curse his arrogance)
Has given you gold and silver at his palace,
Try not to show so openly your gratitude!
Tell us your message and stop this other babbling!" 580

"A curse on him who'd stop me!" answers Balan;
"I found Carlon at court with all his barons;
They crowned him King at Aix, his seat and palace;
No stinging taunt that I thought to throw at him
Could make him angry or any way embarrassed;   585
He bade me choose the best from all his stallions,
More than one hundred, the slowest one a champion;
What can I say? To lie is not my habit;
By Lord Mahom I never saw such barons;
Whoever could live like them in mode and manners   590
Or witness them in their airs and their actions
And live among them and practise what they practise,
That man, I'd say, would live longer and happier;
But I've come back for this reason exactly,
So that this knowledge may help us with our tactics;   595
Don't ridicule my words as of no value;
I always strike first blow when we make battle,
It is my right and always was my family's;
When shields are raised and ranks made for attacking,
That man's a coward who'd leave his comrades stranded;   600
Judge either way of me when all this happens."

32

King Moysant up to his feet then jumps;
This is the man who bears the Olifant;*
He speaks his mind: "Give ear to me, Balan!
Tell us the truth, the whole truth, nothing but!   605
King Charlemayn--will he renege and run?
Will he take flight or will he wait for us?"
Balan laughs then and looks at Moysant:
"A curse on him who'd lie about Carlun!
To all his lands he has sent messengers;   610
Know this for certain--King Charlemayn will come;
His men are few, but they are brave each one;
If he finds you, he'll fight you sure enough
And you will be the worse off when he does;
Sirs, three days I've not eaten, and now I must."   615
He turns back to his lodgings and leaves them thus.

33

Balan moves off and leaves behind King Agolant
And Moysant and the Paynim King Danebus
And King Hector and white-haired old King Lanpal,
Triamodes and Gorhan his companion;   620
They talk together: "The way Balan's come back here
It's obvious they've paid him to abandon us;

* The famous ivory horn owned later by Roland.

If we can charge him and somehow prove what's happened
He should be drowned or hung for such an action."
Balan meanwhile arrives back at his campsite; 625
With joy he's met by comrades and companions.

34

Balan sits down and eats and drinks his fill
Then changes clothes to those his rank befits:
Close-fitting breeches embroidered in pure silk,
A silken tunic with golden thread sewn in, 630
And a silk mantle topped with an ermine trim;
He mounts a palfrey, well-groomed and closely-clipped,
And rides on back to where the Paynims sit;
From every side they look askance at him;
In such a rage is Agolant the King 635
He very nearly jumps up out of his skin;
Balan is tall and strong, broad-shouldered, big,
A better man than most and known as this;
Just like a falcon, which from its cage is slipped,
From smaller birds is quickly known and picked; 640
When Balan enters no words leave Paynim lips;
There is not one but bears him now ill will.

35

King Agolant is first to speak his mind: 645
"Balan, my lord, this thought I cannot hide;
I've cared for you and taught you from a child;
I hung that sword that hangs now at your side,
Gave you a crown for your prowess in fights;
You've suffered long and hard for me and mine, 650
And went to France to see Carlon this time,
Who holds by force a part of my birth-right;
He's promised you so much, I do surmise,
That you have told him all that his heart desires;
Your peers have judged you and they say you should
    die." 655

36

When Balan hears the words of the Emir,
Fast as he can he leaps up to his feet
And speaks out loud so that they all can hear:
"King Agolant, you are correct indeed;
Since I was young you have looked after me 660
And at my side you hung this sword of steel,
Then made me king and crowned me for my feats;
And now I ask--since I my arms received
Who is there here has served you more, my liege?

Not long ago I came back from the East;   665
I fought four jousts for you and won them each;
You have those lands, yet pain is all my fee;
Is it this pain that those about me seek,
Who sentence me to death as I stand here?
For if they do just let them leave their seats!   670
With this my glove I challenge the best man here!
I gained no gold from Charles nor bezant piece,
No war-horse, Moor horse, palfrey, hack nor steed,
Nor anything he offered did I keep;
No more did I agreement make or reach   675
With Charles whereby I would a traitor be
Or heed their law or in their God believe;
I say this now, whatever happens from here."

37

When Balan thus replies in his defence,
The King of Valorie, one Salatiel,   680
A wealthy lord of great omnipotence,
Of high degree and higher wickedness,
Before the King advances through the press:
"Lord Agolant, there's something must be said;
You've led us here upon this mighty quest;   685
It is our duty to guard you and protect;
You are our liege-lord and we are all your men;
But in my heart one nagging doubt I've held,
A doubt which now has blossomed to a dread;
All Balan's ever done for your success   690
He's now reversed, exposing you to death;
He's filled your army with fear of what's ahead;
If we weren't by the sea they'd all have fled."
Balan hears this and anger fills his breast.

38

What Balan hears in no way makes him happy: 695
"All this I hear is news to me, Lord Agolant;
Can you believe the words of King Salatiel,
Who massacred your men fighting in Africa
And in the battle of the Timorel valley?
In just one day ten thousand men he massacred;   700
I cut short his revolt and brought him back to you
And thirty towers and towns alike recaptured;
Within your court it's his head should be hanging;
He is the last whose good-will you should value;
He took Durant and Ospinel--think back, Sire,   705
Took both your nephews, sons of the good King Cadiel,
And placed strong chains about their wrists and ankles,
Then killed them both in cold blood with his dagger;

A man who'd plot so villainous an action
Should not be called your counsellor, your Majesty." 710

39

Triamodes now leaps up from his seat
And in full view he loudly starts to speak:
"Great Agolant, my lord, give ear to me!
Your King Balan I've heard and it is clear
How scared he is of all the French he's seen; 715
Sire, give me France! I urge you and entreat,
Make me commander of all your armies here
While you return to Africa in peace!
Take your ease there, don't risk it in the field,
And, by Mahom, I swear to you, Emir, 720
Calabria, then Puglia I'll defeat;
Then Lombardy, then France itself will yield;
I'll cut off Carlon's head for you to keep,
Then I'll return to Rome with my best speed
To be crowned King straightway if you agree; 725
Saint Peter's there, so have I heard indeed,
Whom Christians love and look to in their need;
I will destroy him while they look on in fear!
In Paradise no warrant more there'll be;
We shall erect the gods of our own creed; 730
By Eastertime or as the summer nears
I'll wear the crown of gleaming gold, Emir;
The whole of France I'll hold from you in fief;
And as for Balan, with him will I then deal
Like any man who in Lord God believes." 735
Balan hears this and his heart fills with grief.

40

Now is Balan both angry and dismayed;
He tells the King: "I've served you countless days
And aided you when most you needed aid;
I say once more, and let none hence gainsay: 740
I saw Carlon and all his court at Aix;
I heard his words and where he laid the blame;
When we raise shields and set out from this place,
And when you see the French dressed for the fray,
Armed and equipped astride their destriers, 745
Their bucklers braced, their burnished helmets laced,
If they seem not as I have said the same,
Which words of mine you treat now as betrayal,
Then banish me from all your lands and states!
My lord, trust not in cowards or in knaves; 750
See Triamodes! He sounds now very brave;

But wait and see--he'll turn from you, afraid;
I know full well why I'm the one he hates;
I threw him down before you once in chains;
He loves me not and he will never change;   755
Have you not heard or read this commonplace?
'A leopard does not change its spots' they say."

                    41

When Aumon now hears Balan's frank reply,
With hate in heart Triamodes he eyes;
He starts to speak and will not be denied: 760
"By Mahomet, do I hear this aright?
Triamodes, the King of Valorie,
In front of me the crown of France desires
While I stand here in my young manhood's prime?
And you'll have France, should my father comply?   765
Seven years before this force was raised to fight
The honors and the spoils of France were mine!
I'll be its King, whoever laughs or cries!
And you say too that Balan here should die,
As one who's done some death-deserving crime;   770
I tell you this--he'll not die in this wise;
I'll speak the truth, whoever laughs or cries,
Whoever hates me for it or calls me liar;
Balan, by force of character and mind,
By bravery and virtue as a knight,   775
Seven lands have added to our empire and might;
No king on earth would spurn such service, Sire;
I'll not stand by while Balan loses his life."

                    42

Aumon speaks thus and what he says persuades them;
And Balan adds, whose anger is still blazing: 780
"Lord Agolant, I've learnt from this occasion;
They used to say I was the Emir's favorite:
I see today how badly you've repaid me;
One moment hence you thought I could betray you;
There's no man here, no matter what his age is,   785
High-born or low, however strong he may be,
If he would lift his shield to fight against me,
I would not kill or conquer straightaway, Sire!"

                    43

Up on his feet stands Hector, Lanpal's son:
"Lord Agolant, curse him who would stand dumb   790
And let men here believe, as Balan does,
That Charles would dare to come and combat us!

Before he comes our ranks shall swell to such
That Carlon's force shall never dare confront;
Their ranks, in fear, will leave here in a rush;   795
All shame on him who sees it end but thus!
It's an old commonplace yet true enough:
'You'll be pursued once you decide to run.'"

44

Now Gorhan stands, a lion in his rage;
He casts his cloak and clasps his rod of state,   800
Dressed all in ermine close-fitting on his frame;
He's seneschal to Agolant the brave
And lover of the Queen, their vows exchanged;
He kneels down now before the King and says:
"Lord Agolant, now listen to me, pray!   805
I've served you well, yet now I'll seem a knave
To all my peers, whose censure I shall take;
On his behalf this solemn pledge I make
To the best man in your household today:
Balan, my father, has not betrayed our faith!"   810
These words strike home; the dispute falls and fades;
Now would I leave this quarrelsome debate,
Leave Agolant and Aumon for a space
And Balan too, the messenger I've named,
And tell you more of mighty Charlemayn;   815
Charles and his barons are holding court at Aix
At Pentecost after Ascension Day.

45

As soon as Balan has left great Carlon's court
Charles tell his knights their feasting now must halt;
Before each leaves strong pledges will be sworn: 820
"The time for jousts and jests is past, my lords;
It would be folly to spur our steeds in sport."
There's not one knight, be he long, short or tall,
Who does not sigh or shed a tear withal
When Carlon says that they must stay no more;   825
Each one must leave and to their lands report;
Prepare themselves as best they can for war,
To meet the menace that threatens each and all.

46

Our Emperor a mighty joy had felt
That the envoy had come to court just when   830
The French could hear the message for themselves;
Even the Pope, Milon, was there himself;
Above an arch his seat, set o'er the rest;

Now in clear tones he speaks to all of them:
"Brave Christian knights, God keep you in His
    strength! 835
Well might you say that you are lucky men,
That in your lifetime you can your faith defend;
You who are born in sin and wickedness,
For which you all are damned and your souls dead,
By striking blows with blades of steel unchecked 840
Your sins will be absolved and your souls blessed;
There is no doubt of this--you have my pledge;
Rise up at once sweet Jesus to avenge!
You will be saved--or may I go to Hell!"

47

Carlon, the King of Saint Denis, continues; 845
His voice is stern, there is no laughter in it:
"My noble knights, may God bless you as Christians!
Now you must leave and tarry not one instant!
And you young knights, whose knighthood's just
    beginning,
Who strive to live by doing deeds of chivalry, 850
But are still poor and have no wealth or riches,
Come now to me, for I say this and will it:
You'll all have arms, and none shall contradict it!
Let none for lack of money be uncommitted;
For I say this, sweet Mary be my witness: 855
No coin shall stop in abbey or in minster,
No cross, no chalice, nor any wealth within them;
For our own use I'll take it all and give it;
Whoever is loath to come upon this mission
Against the Emir, who's seized my lands and cities, 860
By my long beard I swear and tell you this much:
I brand him traitor, both he and all his kinsmen;
And none of them shall stay within my kingdom!

48

"My noble knights," says Carlon to his barons,
"Consider well the great shame and the damage 865
Which they have caused, this stinking race and savage,
Whose hordes have left Arabia and Africa
And taken over the land my father handed me!
As pilgrims all come with me and do battle!
He who comes not nor pays his debt of vassalage, 870
I brand him traitor, both he and all his family."

49

Carlon is fierce and full of wrath this day:

"My noble knights, don't fail me now," he says;
Let me not be disgraced or put to shame!
Help me instead my honor to maintain, 875
Which Saracens seek now to take away!
This pledge I give and willingly obey,
As monarch should who crown and court would claim:
At your disposal all of my wealth I place!
Let all the Lombards arm themselves and make 880
For Great Saint Bernard's Pass between the states,
So they can come and join me in the fray!"

50

The feast is high, the day is bright and clear;
The Emperor is in great haste indeed
To banish from his lands the Paynim breed; 885
With rapid hand the King his letters seals
And messengers straightway take charge of each;
He sends to England and asks its King Cahoer
To aid him now that he is in great need:
He should remember how Charles helped him defeat 890
The Danish hordes and caused them to retreat;
By force of arms Charles brought them all to heel;
Now Charles seeks help! Paynims from overseas,
Stealing his lands, Calabria have reached;
Come to him now so he can drive out these! 895
The envoy goes and sails across the sea;
At Colchester the English King he greets,
Hands him the letter, whose contents he reveals:
How Charlemayn requires him and entreats;
The king hears this: "Thanks be to God!" says he. 990

51

When King Cahoer hears the envoy's description,
And to his talk of Carlon's need has listened,
He says: "By God, I'll go to Charles right willing!
For he helped me when the Danes would have killed me!"
His will's proclaimed the length and breadth of
        England, 905
That all poor knights should come to him this instant;
Pure gold they'll get, and silver too he'll give them;
Ten thousand knights he gathers from his kingdom;
In Dover harbor they board a ship and fill it
With iron and steel, with finest gold and silver; 910
When all's aboard the next tide takes them thither;
They come to Paris and camp outside the city;
From there they'll go direct to fight the Infidel.

24

52

Carlon makes haste, the King of Saint Denis;
To Gondelbuef of Frisia word he seals   915
That Saracens, that race of vilest breed,
By Calabray the land have struck and seized;
With orders clear the envoy turns and leaves;
Through wind and storms he rides league upon league
Until he gives King Gondelbuef the brief;   920
The King beholds and asks his clerk to read;
Then when he hears the havoc Aumon's wreaked
And Agolant, who hates the Christian creed,
And hears that Charles requires his help in need:
"I'll go," he says, "for he's my lord and liege."   925

53

When Gondelbuef hears of Carlon's request
He tells the envoy: "It gives me great distress
That Charlemayn my liege is so hard-pressed;
With my whole realm, my people and myself
He can do as he wishes, as he thinks best;   930
I'll go to him, my duty is no less,
And take to him so stout a force of men
We'll give those Turks plenty that they'll regret!"
Ten thousand men King Gondelbuef takes thence;
They come to Paris in marvellous shape and strength; 935
For Christendom they'll fight till their last breath.

54

The King of Saint Denis, Carlon, makes haste,
Before the Paynims, that vile accursèd race,
Too much his land have taken and laid waste;
To the good Magyar king this plea he makes: 940
Bruno, the king who rules the Magyar state,
Come now to Charles and bring him help and aid;
For Saracens have entered his domain
Along the Eastern coast by Calabray."
King Bruno hears and heeds this message made;   945
He swears to God and in sweet Jesu's name,
Ten thousand men he'll take to Charles straightway:
"I will help Charles for I have pledged the same."
Throughout his realm he calls his barons brave,
Ten thousand fighters of the first rank and rate,   950
And comes to France with this fine cavalcade;
The ranks of Charles grow stronger now each day;
And may Lord God send His help too, I pray!

55

Carlon sends off a message very quickly
To Salemon, the worthy King of Brittany: 955
"Bring straightaway all aid and all assistance!
King Agolant has come and Aumon with him;
By Calabray they have laid waste my kingdom."
The King takes in this dread news as he listens;
He calls his Bretons--ten thousand come as bidden; 960
They come to Paris and join Carlon's contingent.

56

Our Emperor is hard-oppressed and angry;
With rapid hand four briefs he seals and waxes,
One to Droon, the overlord of Manseau:
"Help me," it says, "for mighty is the damage 965
Happening in Puglia and soon too in Calabria;
Paynims are here, the stinking race of savages."
"I'll go, says Droon, "I should and I am glad to."
Ten thousand men equipped and armed for action
Speed with the tide in one mighty battalion; 970
They come direct to Charles the King in Paris;
They will uphold his right against the Saracens.

57

Our mighty King Carlon is full of wrath;
To King Anseis in Cologne he writes off:
"Come help me now against the Arab throng! 975
They burn my land beyond high Aspremont."
When the King hears this message from Carlon
The pleasantries freeze on his lips with shock;
Ten thousand Germans, all knights of highest stock,
Mount Arab steeds, their shining armor donned; 980
They come to Paris to help him right the wrong.

58

Great Charlemayn our King is in high dudgeon
To think the Paynims have gained a hold in Puglia,
Burning the land and causing great destruction;
He sends to Cornwall, which good King David governs: 985
"Come to me now and help me with your courage!"
The king's jaw drops with rage to hear this summons;
Ten thousand men David of Cornwall musters;
They come to Paris and join ranks with the others.

59

Carlon makes haste to think of every detail; 990
To King Didier in his town of Pavia
He writes a letter, for he is very fearful
Lest in his land the food-stocks be too meagre;
For he must lead his lords this way and liege-men;
Does Didier know how many men he leads there? 995
Didier assures his messenger immediately
That in this matter the King's mind may rest easy;
For he'll give Charles all help and any needed;
Until the well-stocked walls of Rome he reaches
Didier himself will feed all Carlon's legion; 1000
They'll not pay for one apple all through his region;
Charles thanks Lord God, this welcome news receiving.

PART 2

60

King Charlemayn has finished with preliminaries;
His letters sent to all his lands and kingdoms
Bring back to him kings, dukes and worthy princes 1005
Armed and equipped for war against the Infidels;
Now Charles confers with Turpin the Archbishop:
"My lord," he says, "we've made a good beginning;
Our army swells each day as I envisaged;
Yet there is one whose presence here is missing, 1010
A powerful man and arrogant and wicked:
Girart d'Eufrate, I've not forgotten this man;
He's a rich man--I know of no one richer--
Yet he pays me no feudal rent or income;
He proudly heeds not me or my position; 1015
For far too long I have let him exist thus,
Demanding nothing nor punishing his impudence;
It is my wish a letter now be written
And you, Turpin, for love of me deliver it;
Ask for his aid against these Paynim brigands; 1020
By threatening me they threaten all of Christendom."
Turpin replies: "My lord, I will go willing;
Brazen Girart is after all my kinsman;
But I know him to be so wild and willful
He'd rather hurl his knife at me than listen." 1025

61

"My lord Archbishop" says fierce-faced Charlemayn,
"You must ride off to old Girart d'Eufrate,
Who holds Auvergne and the Burgundian state;
For love of God tell him to come with aid,
For never was our need of help so great;   1030
Fell Agolant would crush the Christian faith!"
"I will go willing," the good Archbishop says,
"But old Girart is fierce and quick to rage;
If I annoy him with one word that I say,
With his steel knife he'll strike me straightaway; 1035
He never loved you or cared about your fate."
"My lord," says Charles, "speak to him in this vein:
Tell him that if he helps me out this day,
Should he require it, I'll help him out the same;
Should he seek vengeance, tell him there is no knave 1040
I would not go and fight with for his sake;
Turpin, this message to Girart must not fail;
If Agolant defeats me in the fray
Then Christendom itself shall not be saved."

62

Says the Archbishop: "Fear not, I'll go directly;   1045
But old Girart is proud indeed and headstrong;
He is my kinsman, yet terrible and treacherous;
He has four sons, all fighters of great mettle;
Within his veins flows the blood of two Emperors;
He owns much land, whole cities, towns and centers; 1050
I know I'll find him in the vilest of tempers
When he receives your summons and your letter."

63

"My lord Archbishop," Carlon the King continues,
"We've gathered here men from so many kingdoms;
Now for your part do not delay one instant;   1055
I do not want their ranks to suffer injury
Ere we arrive in land held by the Infidel;
I charge you also to look after these children:
Roland the lad, Haton, Estous and Guion;
For I have raised all four of them from infants;   1060
Guard them for me until this fight is finished;
I cannot take young boys upon this business,
Nor sparrow-hawks for sport shall I take with me;
I'll have no pleasure save what my sword can give me."
"With the blessing of God!" says the Archbishop;   1065
"In Laon tower I'll see they're guarded strictly
Until you know the outcome of this mission,

If Girart's men will or will not assist you;
They can stay there while I go and see Girart."
Carlon replies: "God bless you and go with you!" 1070

64

Archbishop Turpin is nothing if not eager;
Without delay he rides and Laon reaching
Confines the boys in Berenger's strong keep there;
With cook and butler and seneschal to feed them
They are well-stocked with things to drink and
    eat there; 1075
As for the porter, he makes him swear to Jesus
That those four boys, at neither night nor evening,
Shall go out riding or be allowed to leave there.

65

Our good Archbishop is not one to delay;
To find Girart he rides as fast as he may, 1080
Reaching Vienne without a stop or stay;
For Christian folk this was a fasting day,
But old Girart was cleaning up his plate;
Turpin rides up and slacking not the reins
Comes to the porter and hails him at his gate: 1085
"My friend," he calls, "let me inside straightway!"

66

Says the Archbishop: "Gate-keeper, let me enter!"
And he replies: "Go seek your board and bedding!
Girart is eating, I dare not let in any;
He goes to church tomorrow, come back then, sir!" 1090
When Turpin hears how his call is rejected
He shouts out: "Porter, I am a royal envoy;
I've urgent news, I'm not afraid to tell you;
I'll give to you these four pure golden bezants
If you will lower the bridge as I've requested 1095
And then unlock the gate like a good fellow!"
This time the porter says: "In God's name, yes sir!"
The drawbridge drops--gold opened it directly;
Across the bridge Girart's knights have their
    dwellings,
And all his servants, his chamberlains and clerics; 1100
Turpin rides on, to Girart's hall ascending.

67

When to the hall the Archbishop has climbed
He finds my lord Girart about to dine,

With knights about on each and every side;
In his own house his power can't be denied; 1105
His meal is served before him by four knights:
Beuvon is one, with Claron by his side;
The third's Ernault and the fourth one is Miles;
Now Turpin speaks and hails him in this wise:
"May God our Lord, Who rules the seas and tides, 1110
And by Whose Grace you rule in all your might,
And may His son, Who died, then rose on high,
Safeguard King Beuvon's son and all his line,
Bless you and keep you--so King Carlon desires!
A great assault is turned on Charles this time: 1115
King Agolant and Aumon have arrived
With such a host that no one's seen its like;
They burn the land beyond Mount Bitter's heights;
The folk they slay and slaughter many a child;
King Carlon's force cannot match theirs for size; 1120
He summons you therefore to do what's right:
To go with him against this foe to fight;
If you do not, your honor's in decline."

68

When Girart hears the Archbishop talk thus
His anger flares and his face starts to flush; 1125
In full-flown rage he's quick with this rebuff:
"God rot your bones, Sir Priest, you've said enough!
You are my kinsman, you ought to show me love;
Yet you come here and speak like this to us!
I must pay homage to Charles, the midget's son! 1130
Pepin his father--now what a sight he was!
He could have rolled, he was so round and plump!
You could have played pelota with Pepin!
If Charles intends through Burgundy to come
He need not go as far as Aspremont 1135
If he wants war with blows a-plenty struck!
But you'll not live to tell him this, I trust!"
He holds a knife whose blade is far from blunt,
Whose edge is sharp and deadly dangerous;
He looks at Turpin and lifts this dagger up 1140
With firm intent to shed the good man's blood;
But Turpin's quick and moves to miss the thrust;
Then he himself moves forward with a lunge
To wrench the blade from Girart's grip at once
And cut this short ere he himself is cut: 1145
"You're crazed with sin, Girart!" he says at once;
"Your soul has slipped into the Devil's clutch;
You'll see your land destroyed as a result;
That thought, indeed, was foul and hideous;

You should kill heathens, but you're too old,
   I judge." 1150
Girart near goes berserk when this taunt's flung.

69

"You were too rash!" the Archbishop repeats;
"To aim your blade at me was mad indeed!
When Charlemayn observed and picked out me
As a young man of promise and degree 1155
It was two years since I was made a priest;
He dubbed me knight and now has sent me here;
For your rash act a rich reward you'll reap;
When the Pope hears the treatment I've received
He'll excommunicate all Burgundy; 1160
Your land is doomed as you can surely see;
No service sung, no sacraments received,
No man confessed or married can there be."
Girart replies:"Now if my memory's clear,
There are three thrones where Church and State do
   meet: 1165
Constantinople's one, you will agree,
Rome is another, and this city makes three--
Then there's Toulouse which also is my fief;
In my own realm I've priests of my decree
For baptisms or any Christian need; 1170
I do not need your Pope to sanction these;
I'll make a Pope myself, should I so please!
Whatever's mine, my wealth, my land, my weal,
Not one shelled egg thereof I'll ever yield
To any man--Lord God alone I heed! 1175
Your King Carlon I'll never love or fear;
Let him come here and kneel down at my feet!"
"You're mad, Girart!" chides Turpin as he speaks.

70

When Turpin hears and sees and it's made plain
That Girart will do nothing for Charlemayn, 1180
He says: "Come, cousin--listen to logic, pray!
From whose power comes your power and from whose
   Grace?"
"From God Almighty," Girart replies straightway;
"No other man has any right or claim."
Turpin pursues: "Come then, defend the same 1185
At Carlon's side against the Paynim race!
But there's one fact I feel you can't escape:
You will be ruled by someone, one of these days."
Girart hears this and almost bursts with rage;
He turns on Turpin and tells him, full of hate: 1190

"My lord Archbishop, I think you must be crazed;
Get out of here--and use your greatest haste,
For on my soul, which may the good Lord take,
If you say one more word, your neck will break!"

71

When Turpin hears the warrior Girart tell him 1195
That he will never bring Charles and him together,
He says to him: "You are disloyal and treacherous
To slander Charles and stubbornly reject him;
There's no prince living so noble and so steadfast;
I swear to you, by our Father in Heaven, 1200
If Charles is saved from this malicious enemy
Who have set foot upon his rightful heritage,
You'll curse the light of day when he seeks vengeance;
No town or keep he'll leave in your possession;
He'll wall you up within a tower forever 1205
Where light of sun or moon shall never enter;
You'll never be free to hunt with friends for pleasure;
Because of you women shall lose their menfolk;
You know full well, you wretched demi-devil,
That there's no man, be he so proud or dreadful, 1210
Whom our Lord God cannot reduce to wretchedness."
He turns about, this sentence having ended,
Rejoins his men and they ride off together.

72

Turpin rides off, he and his entourage;
His look is sad and he is sick at heart 1215
That there will be no help from old Girart;
They climbed the hills, through wood and grasslands
    pass:
Till they reach Paris the reins leave not their grasp;
They meet the army whose ranks swell proud for Charles;
Bretons have come and Norman knights have marched, 1220
Men from Anjou, from Maine and all of France,
With men so many from other lands and parts
The army's size is such as none have marked;
The flower of France and knighthood's best they are
In numbers more than ever in the past. 1225

73

Direct to Paris, that worthy town, they've come
And all assembled--Angevins and Normans,
Knights from Lorraine with Picardy joined up,
With Angevins, Manseaux and Tourangeaux,
Irish and English--the army's size is such 1230

No bard alive could number now the crush;
And what rich ranks! Their value is so much
Two silver marks would buy a helm for one
And for two spurs one bezant's scarce enough;
For other armor I could not guess the sum; 1235
With all these men will go Roland the young;
He killed Aumon, who was Agolant's son,
Won Durendal and won the Olifant.

74

Now they depart with naught to hold them back;
They start from Paris on horse in serried ranks; 1240
They'll stop at Laon, for so Carlon has planned,
To meet with knights who come from other lands;
They make their way till neath Laon they're camped--
Laon, where Estous and Roland, the young lad,
With young Haton and Gui are all held back; 1245
When these four see the army, Lord God they thank.

75

At Laon town up in the mighty palace
Sit those four boys in whom rests so much valor;
When they behold the army in encampment,
Hear bugles blown that echo round the valley, 1250
Hear goshawks cry and horses neigh for action,
See busy squires on errands through the campsite,
They cannot bear that they themselves are absent;
They hail the porter with words of fulsome flattery:
"Hi there, good sir, most worthy man and valiant! 1255
Let us go down and visit Charlemagne!
We'd love to see how knights bear arms for battle;
When comes the time that we ourselves may have them
We'll dub you knight, you have our word on that, sir!"
The porter says: "Don't sweet-talk me, you lads, now! 1260
Me, be a knight? I would not, that's a fact too!
They joust and fight and get hurt! No, it's madness!
I much prefer my life and little naps here;
I guard you boys and my job ends there, thank you;
Turpin pays me--I'll give him satisfaction; 1265
You're going nowhere, so no longer harass me!
You have the garden--go out and play in that, then;
You want stroke-play? Go stroke your falcons' backs,
    boys!
Leave to the King the travelling and the travail
Of making war against the Paynim savages; 1270
Let him avenge himself upon the Saracens."
The boys hear this and they are filled with anger;
Till dawn next day their efforts they abandon;

The army stirs and mounts horse in battalions;
In mood those boys grow bleak and ever blacker 1275
And Roland cries: "Well might our rage be rabid!
While Carlon leaves to fight the Paynim savage
We sit and watch entombed within this garrison!
Is it small wonder it drives us to distraction?
What? Are we prisoners that we endure such shackles? 1280
Or are we thieves or murderers for hanging
That the Archbishop behind stout bars must banish us?
Come lads! Once more let's talk to our brave janitor;
Let's supplement his precious pay with mantles;
Let's see at least if that might change his manner; 1285
But take as well a branch each from the apple-tree!
And if once more our pleas fail to attract him
We'll change our plan from flattering to battering!
Then, once outside, we'll have to leave here rapidly
So that no one can have a hope of catching us." 1290
"What you say should be done," say his companions.

76

Young Roland burns with rage and sorrow fierce
To see the army lift lances and raise shields
And Charles form ranks and make ready to leave;
He and his friends can no more curb their zeal; 1295
With four stout sticks in their mantles concealed
They greet the porter who's by the gate asleep;
High-born and strong Roland it is who speaks:
"Porter, good brother, God save you and safe keep!
Behold the King as he prepares to leave! 1300
Let us go down to him and we'll love thee!
For I know not if ever again we'll meet;
When we have seen him we'll come back here in peace."
"Get back up there!" the fell porter repeats;
"You will stay here, the Archbishop's decreed, 1305
Until Carlon has come back from the field;
You're wasting time to try and get past me."
Roland replies: "You lie, as now you'll see!
Lay on, brave lads, this can no longer be!"
With rapid hands the wretched rogue is seized; 1310
They hit him hard, their fists and sticks he feels;
Before five blows from each lad he's received
All of his bones are broken, he was so weak!
They leave him there spreadeagled in a heap,
Rush out the gate and make off at top speed. 1315

77

Roland runs off, escaping from Laon
With Estous, Gui, Berenger and Haton;

Behind those ranks they jog along and trot
Till Roland says: "My lads, is this our lot?
Like stable-lads are we to run along?" 1320
They look about and Bretons five they spot,
Men from the house of good King Salemon;
Four fine war-horses, a present from Carlon,
These five men have and proudly sit upon;
Each horse is wearing a padded saddle-cloth; 1325
Young Roland says: "We'll have these four--come on!
Nor shall we ask them first for what we want!"
His friends reply: "With the blessing of God!"
Square on his skull the first man feels the shock
And hits the ground, his legs sprawling aloft: 1330
"Let go," says Roland, "your horse from Aragon!"
He seizes it and swings himself on top;
He spurs his mount a second man to stop
And gives his neck a carefully aimed chop;
Down to the ground upon his knees he's knocked; 1335
He takes his horse and gives it to Haton;
Why spin this out? Those lads capture the lot;
Those Breton men don't argue, they scurry off
To tell their tale to Salemon the strong:
"Some band of rogues, in truth we knew them not, 1340
Have robbed us of our steeds from Aragon!
They fell upon us, then rode our horses off;
They took our steeds and left our heads a-throb;
Haughty they were and born of evil stock!
If you had seen them with their silk mantles on, 1345
Their smart tight tunics, their fur pelisses donned!
Yet bare they were in courtesy, by God!
They beat us cruelly, like donkeys that have stopped."
"Let's after them!" King Salemon responds;
The king makes haste with men one thousand strong; 1350
They catch them too on sloping ground and long;
For those four lads had found a falcon lost
Or fled some lord whose name I know not of;
The king looks at them and sees that it's Haton,
Roland the lad and Estous and Guion; 1355
He laughs out loud and says then to Oton:
"What noble thieves, indeed, my lord, we've got!
Behold young Roland with this silk mantle on!"
He runs to him without one moment's loss,
Kissing his chin in warm embrace and fond; 1360
Then Roland tells him how they escaped their bonds:
"We killed the porter, a good-for-nothing dog!"
The king laughs loudly then calls on good Sanson
And Erneis and Girart and Rogon:
"Look after these four boys!" says Salemon, 1365
And they reply: "With the blessing of God!"
Carlon with his great ranks rides on and on;

35

Now you will hear a fierce and stirring song,
How Charlemayn climbed up high Aspremont
And how he vanquished Aumon and Agolant. 1370

78

When from Laon King Carlon makes his way,
Alemans and Germans form ranks and take their place,
Knights from Bavaria, the Ardennes and Lorraine,
From Brittany, Le Mans and from Touraine;
Full fifteen dukes and seven kings he takes, 1375
One hundred counts and all those in their pay;
The world never saw so fine a cavalcade;
They'll all defend their lands and their estates,
So help them God, who on the Cross was nailed;
By Aspremont, down on the sandy plain, 1380
So many Turks and Persians lie in wait,
Indians and Moors and hordes of Afric race,
Armies of Lycia and those of Amorave,
Both black and white so many Paynim knaves,
High-born nor low their sum could estimate; 1385
Alemans and Germans will fight a fearsome fray.

79

Carlon rides on and now so far has ridden
With all his army from all their different kingdoms,
He reaches Rome, that worthiest of cities;
If you could see that company of princes! 1390
Not since the day of his Empire's beginning
Had knights so many assembled in such richness;
Large ranks have come to fight for their religion
Who owe Charles nothing by fealty or kinship;
The Pope sings Mass for all of them as Christians 1395
And Charlemayn the altar-table visits,
Honoring Saint Peter, ten marks of pure gold giving;
Beseeching Jesus, the Pope prays for their mission--
That Charles may seal his birthright with a victory
And by so doing exalt the name of Christendom; 1400
May he kill Paynims and cast out all the Infidels
Who've forced their way into his own dominion!

80

Let's leave awhile our fierce-faced Charlemayn,
Who's come to Rome and there a while will stay;
He prays for strength to drive his foe away; 1405
Yet ere they leave, a mortal price he'll pay;
Now I would tell of Duke Girart again,
Lord of Eufrate, a proud man, yea and vain;

It is no wonder his power is so great,
For he controls the whole Burgundian state, 1410
All of Auvergne and Gascony the same,
All of Cosence, that wide-bordered domain,
And Gevaudan, beneath his rule and sway;
He cannot rid his mind of that threat made
By the Archbishop, who spoke for Charles that day; 1415
So all his princes he summons in great haste
To meet with him in his ancestral place;
He sits there now, the old man fierce of face,
With Emmeline, his courtly wife and dame,
And his two sons called Renault and Renier 1420
And well-loved nephews, Claron and Beuvon they:
"My lords," he says, "my mind is much amazed
At Charlemayn, whom all of France obeys,
That he should dare to call on me for aid;
Were it not for God, who Final Judgement makes, 1425
And for whose sake Carlon this war does wage,
I'd ride out now and fight him on his way."

81

Girart exhorts his sons now and his nephews
And barons all about him there assembled:
"My lords," says he, "I've brought you up and fed you 1430
And see you now all handsome men and healthy,
While I, God's truth, a little old am getting;
This I command you: when I am dead and buried,
Hold naught from Charles in service or in territory;
His father was a dwarf--a sullen wretch he, 1435
Who robbed the poor and purloined from the wealthy;
In my own mind I am King Charles' better!"
His wife speaks then, the proud-faced Lady Emmeline:
"My lord Girart, what lies are these you're telling?
The King of France is powerful over everyone; 1440
This is God's law, His charter writ from Heaven;
Why do you tarry, you wretched, hapless fellow?
Did you not hear that Agolant the Emir
And his son Aumon good Christian blood are shedding?
They've crossed the sea and struck inland already; 1445
They are destroying the Christian Faith, I tell you;
Now you indeed with such black sins are blemished,
Who have burned churches and murdered men so many,
Such awful sins, Girart, you've steeped yourself in,
Go now to Charles and with your sword do penance!" 1450

82

Be still awhile, my lords, and give good ear!
A worthy wife is a blessing indeed,

Much to be loved, enjoyed and held most dear;
Be she a bad one, then shun her company!
Dame Emmeline cuts short her husband's speech   1455
And says: "Girart, let your bad humor be!
Call on your men to come from all your fiefs
And go to Rome and serve God faithfully!
Aid Christendom in its great hour of need
And fight with Charles against the Paynim breed!"   1460
"In truth," says Girart, "I'd rather cease to breathe!
And I say more--no worthy king is he
Who'd place his flag with Carlon's in the field!
Let us leave Charles to fight his foe in peace!
But call I will on those my men of liege   1465
And go with them fair France itself to seize,
Then stop Carlon from ever coming near!"
"God curse you, Girart, for your malicious streak!
You would die evil as all your life you've been;
Good men so many you have compelled to flee,   1470
And shamed good women and forced them all to leave;
That God still gives you breath amazes me,
Still lets you live and not die horribly,
Since all His laws you break and never heed."

                    83

Says Emmeline: "Girart, my noble sir,   1475
Consider now how you your God have served:
Was not Duke Alons put to death on your word
And did you not make whores of his two girls?
You never were happy or felt any real mirth
If you weren't killing people or causing hurt;   1480
You've not repented, but have each day grown worse.

                    84

"Girart, what will you do?" says Emmeline;
"A century back you took me for your wife
And each day since you've spent committing crimes;
You've robbed and burned and plundered all the time; 1485
Bad has grown worse; but as you end your life
What will you do as you grow old and tired?
Call on your men to come from all your shires
And help Carlon! Why think about it twice?
In fighting Paynims your penance you may find."   1490
Girart hears this and checks somewhat his pride.

                    85

When Girart hears the stern rebuke she gives him
He says: "Good wife, I'll not hide what I'm thinking;

I'd take my men and gladly go to Italy,
But I would gain no fame from any victory;   1495
It's Carlon's war, I cannot deny this much."
"I'd not hold back," his wife says, "for so little;
If it were me I'd summon all my princes
And leave for Charles and Aspremont this instant,
To fight for God with all of my ability;   1500
But first in Rome Saint Peter's I would visit
And cleanse myself of all sins I'd committed;
You're old, Girart, and your life's nearly finished."
Girart hears this and his heart stirs within him;
Right tenderly he heeds her word and bidding.   1505

86

Girart d'Eufrate hears his wife's words and heeds,
Calling to mind Lord God and what He means;
Now his old heart can't hide the pain it feels
And for his sins right heavy sighs he heaves;
He says: "My lady, I beg you let me be!   1510
With my Lord God it's time I made my peace."
With rapid hand his letters now are sealed
And sent away through all his lands and fiefs;
Princes are summoned, brave knights and many peers;
When they arrive Girart their liege-lord speaks: 1515
"Free men of mine, we must prepare to leave!
King Agolant has sailed across the sea
With his son Aumon, this news I have received;
With countless sums of Saracens he's keen
To capture France with Charlemayn's defeat,   1520
Then to stamp out all Christianity;
If he succeeds and beats Charles in the field
Then no one else for long shall be reprieved;
No one of us must now his wealth conceal,
But place it in this mission to meet this need;   1525
And if Lord God should bring me safe back here
Then I shall know whom hence I may hold dear."
Girart then summons his nephews to appear;
Beuvon and Claron these two were called, I hear:
"Brave boys," he says, "make ready with all speed!   1530
The time has come to knight you now and here
With my two sons for whom my love is dear."

87

Old Duke Girart dubs young Claron a knight;
A gold-hilt sword he girds upon his side;
With a stout lance whose tip is of sharp iron,   1535
Which bears a banner sewn with a gilt design,
He makes the lad lord of Auvergne entire:

"You own twelve cities now and are their sire,
One hundred castles too as I devise;
Within your realm twelve noble counts reside,   1540
One thousand castellans and knights likewise;
These all are yours if you heed this advice:
Don't trust a man whose brain is still a child's,
Nor trust a priest save at confession time;
If God grants you good thoughts in a true mind,   1545
You'll have no peer in all this realm of mine."

88

When Duke Girart has girt young Claron's sword
He dubs Beuvon without a moment's pause;
All Gascony he gives to this young lord
As knighthood's blade in tasselled sword-belt falls; 1550
A wife he gives him too, a maid high-born,
Whom Duke Lohiers had wooed and sought before
At Aix one time when Charlemayn held court:
But I'll not tell that tale today, my lords.

89

After Beuvon Girart next dubs Renier;   1555
He girds his sword, a most praiseworthy blade,
And gives to him all Gevaudan's estate,
Which is indeed a widespread, wondrous place;
These words of wit likewise Girart donates:
"Renier, my lovely boy, heed what I say!   1560
Be you a knight of loyalty and faith;
Believe sound counsel and act upon the same;
Keep to those men who'd die to keep you safe;
Heed not the man who changes day to day."

90

Ernault it is whom next as knight he dubs;   1565
On his left hip the sword is girt and hung:
"I've not forgotten you, my lovely son!
I give to you when my lifetime is done
All of Cosence, a kingdom rich enough;
One thousand lords will serve you there in trust,   1570
And four counts too, all princes of the blood;
Where you find loyalty, respond with love,
And be not mean with wealth such friends among;
Yet do not scorn the poor man who has none;
Never let money turn you from what is just."   1575

91

Now that Girart has doled out all his heritage
And given it to his sons and his nephews,
Throughout his lands his army he assembles:
Men sixty thousand endowed with the best weapons
And bravest hearts that he can bring together, 1580
Such are the troops he'll take to meet the enemy;
There you had seen fine gilt-edged shields so many,
So many blades and so many green helmets,
So many lances of good steel finely tempered,
The triangles of silk of countless pennants, 1585
And brick-sheened rumps of so many fine destriers!
Salt beef and wine in bundles are made ready
For one whole year; though they find nothing henceforth
They'll have enough for dinner and for breakfast;
Girart embraces now Lady Emmeline: 1590
"I leave, my lady, for this most holy melee
With Saracens, that race of heathen devils;
If in some way I've angered or offended you
Forgive me now, good Emmeline, I beg you!"
Duke Girart weeps and holds her to him gently, 1595
And then he goes, her soul to God commending;
Full many a tear he sheds at this farewelling;
Then he rides out with his great force of fellows,
And as he rides by his long beard he threatens
That Saracens shall rue the day they set out; 1600
The Christian Creed they'd flout, and they'll regret it!
Girart rides on from dawn till sun is setting
To follow Charles as fast as spurs will let him;
The King's in Rome, his army lodged in tents there;
Now Charles commands his army to make ready: 1605
They must all head for Aspremont directly,
Where Charles will fight the Paynims for his Empire.

92

Carlon commands his army to move on now,
And they obey, for none would tarry longer;
They pack up arms and sacks of corn and fodder; 1610
As they leave Rome Carlon surveys his convoy:
Full seven kings with royal crowns upon them,
And fifteen dukes and thirty counts in consort;
The Pope himself is there with a large following;
No king henceforth could summon such a congress! 1615
Behold so many helms there from Dordogne,
So many shields with fine gold-stud embossing,
So many flags held high in flapping columns!

Our Emperor throughout his host spurs strongly;
Acart of Reims he makes his rearguard officer, 1620
Together with Count Simon of Peronne;
The Saxon king alike shall lead these warriors
With Driu de Melans and Ernault de Fordione.

93

The vanguard troops of Charles, son of Pepin,
Are led by Fagon and good Duke Aubuin; 1625
With these alike are mighty Duke Elin,
King Salemon and young King Thiorin,
Hoel and Hues and Geoffrey Angevin
And Normandy's worthy Duke Anchetin.

94

In the front ranks of Carlon of La Chapelle 1630
Are Driu de Neele, a count of proven valor,
And Orbendele's duke, the good Frangalas;
How fine a sight is all their household cavalry!
If you could see them all astride their saddles,
Each one of them a matching buckler balancing! 1635
They'll bring bad news all right to those vile
    Saracens!

95

In the front ranks of mighty King Carlon
Ride mighty dukes: the powerful Milon
Rides side by side with wealthy Duke Sanson,
While next to him is worthy Duke Margon, 1640
Who rides abreast of good Duke Amelon;
From Hautefeuille rides the rich Duke Grifon
With his son next to him, called Ganelon;
Twelve dukes rode there and two kings, says the song,
With men in ranks full sixty thousand strong; 1645
Behold them all ride forth for Aspremont,
Who seek to find Agolant and Aumon!
They ask for nothing from him who leads them on
Save riches reaped from beating Agolant.

96

Carlon rides on, our Emperor the great, 1650
Surrounded by his dukes and all his train;
One hundred thousand men his flag acclaim;
He lifts his hand to bless them in God's name:
"Dear Lord," he says,"Who everything did make,
The sky, the earth, the seas, the lands and lakes, 1655

Confound, O Lord, this vile and savage race,
Who by brute force have entered my domain!
Guard Christendom, O Lord, and keep it safe,
And guard for me all these my vassals brave!
If You so wish that I survive this fray,   1660
With my own sword I'll pierce my side in faith."
So far they ride o'er hills and over plains,
Cross broken bridges and unknown waterways,
That Carlon's host cannot their ranks maintain;
Then they see Aspremont and its fierce face.   1665

97

So far he rides, Carlon our mighty Emperor,
Surrounded by those princes of his escort,
Till they make out fell Aspremont ahead of them;
And here they meet with poor folk seeking shelter
Across the Mount before the Paynim menace;   1670
The French up front ask these poor folk to tell them
Where they are from and whither they are headed;
And they reply that they are Christian brethren,
That over the Mount are hordes of Paynim felons;
That Agolant and Aumon are their generals,   1675
Whose boast is this: all France shall burn and perish
And Charlemayn shall be expelled and exiled!
The French reply: "Ne'er so, if we can help it!
See for yourselves the force that will prevent it!
Before too long they'll have us to contend with!"   1680
To hear these words a great joy fills those wretches:
"My lords," they say, "may God, Maker of everything,
Protect you all from these fell Paynim devils!
They're a huge force--we cannot say how many."

98

The front ranks hear the tale those poor folk tell,   1685
But in no way are their spirits depressed;
With twelve brave counts and two kings at their head
They would have fought straightway as they had said,
But they hold off as night starts to descend;
They set up camp upon a river's edge;   1690
O'er three leagues long of riverbank they're spread.

99

Carlon looks up and sees the night come down;
He tells his men to make camp and dismount;
Then in the morning, when dawn lights up the ground,
Throughout the army Carlon's command goes round: 1695
Four days they'll lodge in this spot they have found;

43

Each man must rest, his strength to re-endow;
Next Carlon calls his barons all about,
And they all come, peers, princes, dukes and counts
And the Pope too, their tactics to plan out: 1700
"My lords, give ear!" says Charles, fair France's crown;
"Lo! Aspremont, which we must now surmount,
The Paynim force to find and to confound,
Who, while we breathe, lay claim to land that's ours!
Therefore I say, if you too think it sound, 1705
That one of you should ride out even now,
This lofty mount to scale and then to scout
The Paynim force, its phalanx and its power."
A silence falls and no one speaks out loud.

100

"My noble knights," repeats King Charlemayn, 1710
"Which one of you for me will undertake
The lofty wall of Aspremont to scale,
The Paynim force to spy and estimate,
So that we may shock them and not us they?"
Still none of them moves up to voice his claim, 1715
Except one man, Ogier, the worthy Dane;
He rushes up, his mantle half-unlaced;
In front of Charles he kneels and lifts his face:
"My noble King, no longer be dismayed!
In your whole court no other knight I'd say 1720
Was better for this task than I, Ogier;
Who more than I could make your message plain?
I shall climb up Mount Bitter for your sake!
If I find Aumon or Agolant the knave,
I have good ways the wicked truth to gain 1725
As to just why your lawful land they'd take!
I'll show them well the error of their ways!"
"Ogier, step back," commands Carlon in haste,
"And say no more unless I call your name!"

101

Up on his feet now jumps seneschal Fagon, 1730
Duke of Touraine and cousin of Charlemagne,
Whose flag he bears and carries into battle:
"My lord and liege, give ear to me, Majesty!
I am your kinsman and am also your baron;
I hold Touraine and all its land in vasselage; 1735
I'm seneschal of your most mighty palace;
When war is fought I bear your battle-standard;
Whom more than I should you involve in planning?
I'll go for you and scale the walls of Aspremont;
I will observe those knaves Aumon and Agolant, 1740

The Paynim force, its power and its phalanx."
In haste Carlon commands: "Fagon, step backward!
Sit down and say no more about this matter!"

102

Up on his feet see Geoffrey of Paris jumping,
Grise Gonele*, a duke of dazzling courage;   1745
To Charles he says: "My lord, pray be not worried
That Paynims ever shall wrest from us our country!
Who would sing Mass at Saint Denis on Sundays?
Who would partake of the Sacrament's succor?
No ladies fair would come bringing their husbands,   1750
No young girls, either, attended by their lovers;
In Saxony I fought and much accomplished;
So, if you please, I'll scale Mount Bitter's summit
And tell these Turks and Arabs that you're coming!"
"Geoffrey," says Charles, "be not in such a hurry!   1755
You shall not go--it's not for you, this summons."

103

Good Aubuin then jumps up on his feet;
Duke of Beauvais, Beauvaisis is his fief:
"Enough of this, great King of France!" says he;
"I'll climb for you Mount Bitter's lofty peak,   1760
The Paynim force and phalanx for to see."
"You shall not go!" Charles, Pepin's son, repeats;
"I'll send no man of rank or high degree;
These Bedouins are treacherous rogues indeed;
I do not want you killed by these cruel fiends."   1765

104

"My lords," says Charles, "pray do not feel insulted;
I do not wish to send upon this summons
A nobleman with land and lives to govern,
Lest he be killed by these cruel-hearted cut-throats;
Have we not here any poor knight among us   1770
Who can defend himself if he meets trouble
And handle himself well in hostile company,
To take our message and say it with full courage
To Agolant, the proud and the presumptuous,
Who sees himself as heir to this my country?"   1775
These words scarce out, good vassal Richer jumps up;
The nephew of Count Berenger this one is
And is also the good King Didier's cousin;
A single man, he has no wife or young ones;

  * Literally "gray long-tunic"

He comes to Charles and kneels before him humbly: 1780
"Sir Emperor, behold this knight in front of you!
I have no lands, no heir nor any son, Sire;
If you seek a poor knight to do this summons,
I volunteer to take the risks and run them."
"My friend, well granted this!" says Charles abruptly; 1785
"And I say this--if you return among us
Alive and well--I'll give you so much money
Your lineage will be restored and flourish."
Duke Naimes hears this and his heart fills with worry;
For it was Naimes who raised this knight and
    nourished. 1790

105

Young Richer waits for Charles to give him leave;
The Emperor in haste hands him his brief;
Duke Naimes sees this and comes to Charles and speaks:
"My lord, this choice is badly made, I fear;
Richer is brave and his strength great indeed, 1795
And in your court none better holds a shield,
But, Charles, I brought him up; what woe for me
If he were killed by the fell Paynim breed!
I brought him up; my hurt would never heal."
"Naimon," says Charles, "I would not have you grieve; 1800
If he returns, a good reward he'll reap.

106

"Naimon, fine sir," thus noble Carlon hails,
"Richer shall go, God bless him and keep safe!
If he returns, his guerdon will be great;
But let us pray his words will be well framed, 1805
For Saracens are fierce and quick to rage."
"This troubles me, my lord," replies Duke Naimes,
"For in my house I've nourished him and raised;
He's fiercer than a lion when in a rage!
He'll start a fight with all of them straightway! 1810
We need a man with self-control and brains,
For these defeat both blusterer and knave."
"None goes but I, my lord!" Richer exclaims;
"I sought the right and got it from Charlemayn;
Steep Aspremont I'll climb, God grant I may!" 1815
"Let him be gone!" says Carlon to Duke Naimes;
Back to his tent for armor goes Richer;
With hauberk donned and rounded helmet laced,
On his left hip his sword, a worthy blade,
He mounts his horse, his lion-shield held straight, 1820
And leaves the camp, his letter safely placed;
To Aspremont he rides and comes apace;

God guard him now, in His most holy name--
For soon, my lords, his terror will be great!
Down from the rock a griffin fierce does gaze! 1825
Let me describe its awful look and shape:
A whole lance-length its body is, I'd say,
And thirty feet its length from nape to tail;
Broad-backed enough a donkey's load to take,
This fiendish beast portends an awful fate; 1830
Its eyes are red as burning coals aflame;
A three-foot beak it has from tip to base,
And when it flies such fearsome screech it makes
It can be heard an arrow's draw away;
High in the cliffs its nesting young ones wait 1835
While it seeks food across the sandy waste;
Now it sees Richer approach across the plain
And flies at him with such force and such pace,
Its fearsome wings attack the baron brave
Upon his shield with such a wicked aim, 1840
His straps and saddle just cannot take the strain;
He hits the ground and ere he's up again
The griffin strikes his Aragon destrier;
Its claws dig deep into the flesh and maim;
Its lungs and liver it rips and tears away; 1845
Down to its bowels it scrapes out the entrails
Then takes to flight to feed its young again;
Richer gets up, his heart filled with dismay;
He draws his sword and brandishes the blade;
He seeks revenge as his heart fills with hate, 1850
But the fell beast sits high upon the face;
Richer despairs, bewailing his sad fate:
"Dear God," he says, "by Your most holy name,
How may I now scale Aspremont this day,
Since I have lost my Aragon destrier? 1855
Behold the torrents whose waters rush and race!
Should I dive in, I know I'll never escape;
Yet shall I thus return to Charlemayn?
I fear the wrath of my liege-lord Duke Naimes;
To come back thus will earn me naught but shame." 1860

107

Good Richer's heart is filled with rage and rancor
That he should lose his horse in such a manner
When he had hoped to scale the slopes of Aspremont;
He climbs o'er rocks and sees the mountain rapids
And dives straight in, although he knows it's madness; 1865
He's borne downstream, tumbling this way and that way;
He would, in truth, have perished in the action
But for Lord God, Who helps the worthy vassal;
With both his hands he grasps a branch o'erhanging

47

And hoists and hauls with all his strength and valor; 1870
With both his hands he claws the earth and scratches
Until at last upon the bank he scrambles;
It's Providence has saved the loyal baron,
For mortal strength could not have cleft that channel:
"Dear God," says Richer, "our Spiritual Champion, 1875
Yet shall I thus return to Carlon's campsite?
What will Naimes say, my liege-lord true and valiant?"

108

Richer is swept downstream by that fierce current;
Harriers and hawks, merlins and other vultures
He sees in flocks, circling his horse above him; 1880
Now, lords, behold a wicked scorpion coming!
Its mighty claw grasps Richer as it lunges
And tears the spur from his foot as he struggles;
It falls to ground and he cannot recover it;
Nor may he stay, he sees that well enough now; 1885
Will he or not, he must haste back and hurry;
To Naimon's tent, not stopping once, he rushes
And tells the Duke the terror and the trouble
The birds of Aspremont have made him suffer;
How they have killed his Gascon war-horse under him; 1890
Naimes hears him speak and great dismay o'ercomes him:
"I thought you were," he cries, "a man of courage!
I brought you up and now I grieve because of it;
A craven coward in you it seems I've nourished!
You did not dare approach Mount Bitter's summit! 1895
You never even tried, you good-for-nothing!"
He takes the letter that Carlon gave the youngster.

109

Naimes frets so much his lips with anger tremble;
Richer his man he stings with slights envenomed,
Then he himself takes up armor and weapons; 1900
He dons his hauberk and laces on his helmet,
Then girds his sword, its hilt of gold nielloed;
Then he puts on expensive padded leggings;
His lance he grips, his strong grasp holds it steady;
His chamberlains don't wait for him to tell them: 1905
They dress Morel, Duke Naimon's noble destrier,
In panoply both pleasing and protective;
Morel is strong, with features well-developed;
Naimes mounts him now, the knight whom Charles most treasures;
His entourage rides out with him in escort 1910
And each one weeps for pity when he farewells them;
When Charles finds out, his heart with woe is heavy:

"My lords," he says, "behold me all bereft now!
If I lose Naimes, the knight whom I most treasure,
My happy heart will be exiled forever." 1915

110

Thus would I leave a while Carlon the bold,
And tell of Naimes, Bavaria's Duke of old;
Bearing the brief to Agolant he rode
Astride Morel and Aspremont approached;
All of a sudden the land freezes with cold; 1920
His horse's neck is covered soon with snow
And through his hauberk he is chilled to the bone;
The snow wets him right through from top to toe;
To that ravine he chooses now to go,
Whose stream it was down which Richer was thrown; 1925
Naimes sees the ice sheer off and drop below;
The water's width is the shot of a bow;
He rides two leagues alongside of these floes
Astride Morel to seek a crossing o'er;
He finds no bridge or boarding, neither shoals 1930
Which he might take to cross this fearsome flow.

111

Naimes takes a path which leads down a ravine
Along the edge of that dread, deadly stream;
He finds no ford, though high and low he seeks;
The worthy Duke no crossing-point can see; 1935
His anger swells and spurring hard his steed
He plunges in where the flow is most deep;
To God in Heaven he calls out in appeal:
"Mary most holy, sweet Virgin, Heaven's Queen,
Protect today, I pray, my horse and me!" 1940
So much does Naimes his Heavenly King beseech,
God sweeps him to a rocky outcrop's reach;
His horse has suffered much and shakes with fear,
And Naimes knows too how close to death he's been:
No one day's woe before had come so near; 1945
Now he dismounts, firm ground beneath his feet.

112

Naimon the Duke dismounts now from his destrier;
The horse has suffered much and stands there
    trembling;
The floating ice has pounded it so heavily
Its leather coat in many spots is shredded: 1950
"Morel, you saved my life," the Duke says tenderly;
"No beast e'er had your courage or your mettle;

If God, Who shapes all things, this much has destined,
That you and I return from this adventure,
I'll never sell you or give you up to anyone;   1955
For love or money you'll never be dispensed with!"
Duke Naimes remounts when he a while has rested.

113

Duke Naimes begins to climb steep Aspremont;
A little way he and his horse have gone
When to his right he looks and stares in shock;   1960
A huge ravine he sees, an awesome drop;
It falls more sheer than sea-cliffs do on rocks;
He turns Morel and rides on towards the spot:
"Dear God," he says, "here's a bad place to stop!
If it's through here that Charlemayn must cross,   1965
The Emir doesn't need to fear one jot!"

114

Astride Morel, Duke Naimes moves on upwards,
And all this while those birds keep watch above him;
Harriers and hawks, merlins and other vultures,
And eagles with huge beaks and scorpions hunt there;   1970
Fearsome screech-owls and vicious mountain buzzards
And crocodiles with smaller beasts and sundry--
All dwell among the rocks there in abundance;
Duke Naimes is still a long way from the summit
When lo, my lords, that wicked griffin plunges,   1975
The very beast which caused Richer to suffer!
Now when it sees the Duke towards it coming,
It flies at him with such a fearsome flurry
And strikes Morel with force and fall so stunning,
Deep in its flesh the claws take hold and clutch it;   1980
Against this beast what use is Morel's courage?
The fiendish beast swoops swiftly from its cover
And with Duke Naimes astride lifts Morel upwards;
Three feet they rise and then fall back abruptly;
Naimes turns his head and the fierce beast confronts
    him;   1985
He sways with fright and from the saddle tumbles.

115

The valiant Naimes with shock was badly shaken;
Morel his horse by that fierce bird was taken,
Who with its claws three feet aloft upraised it,
Then back to earth dropped both Morel and Naimon: 1990
"Dear God," he says,"by the Archangel Gabriel,

Our royal host cannot withstand these dangers!
The Emperor can't hope to pass this way now
Without suffering great trial and tribulation."

116

He sways and falls, but quickly jumps back on
And draws the sword which hangs by his belt-knot;
But as he speaks, the griffin once more drops!
Naimes deals the beast a blow so straight and strong,
A blow, in truth, blest by the will of God,
That both its feet he slices through and off;
In Morel's hair like stirrups twain they rock;
They are as thick as a foot-soldier's rod;
Each talon's tip would have contained, cut off,
A gallon-full of wine or water-drops;
Naimes takes one claw to serve as proof anon
And puts it in his pouch to show Carlon;
If any man cannot believe my song,
Go to Compiègne, where now that claw belongs;
The Duke remounts and as he moves along
He looks about and on a ledge of rock
That single spur of brave Richer he spots
And then his horse, to that fell griffin lost!
The Duke cries out: "In the blest name of God,
I blamed Richer and was, I see, quite wrong!"
The Duke advances, Morel moves up and on
Until they reach the ridge of Aspremont;
Naimes does not stop till he reaches the top.

PART 3

117

Duke Naimes has scaled Mount Bitter's lofty wall;
The night is black, the birds back in their haunts;
How fared he hence? Now listen well, my lords!
Naimes stops beneath a well-leafed tree and broad
Where he dismounts, both angry and distraught;
Then he lies down and sets aside his sword,
Quiet unaware of dangers still in store:
For close at hand a shelf of rock juts forth
Where a she-bear has left her cub newborn;
The wind gusts hard and clouds of hailstones fall;
No man alive would not have felt forlorn;
Duke Naimes himself is hard-pressed by the storm;
From top to toe he's sodden, numbed and raw;
Morel champs on his bit all night, poor horse!

Says Naimes: "Morel, it's you I'm sorrier for!
If I could find some food for you at all,
Though it should cost pure gold it would be bought;
God grant you reap a happier day's reward! 2035
For our lodgings tonight are of a sort
To give us not one moment's rest, I'm sure."

118

Naimes spends the night beneath a tree on Aspremont--
A cheerless night, in warmth and comfort lacking;
Between two rocks he beds Morel his stallion, 2040
Quite unaware this place is a bear's cavern
Where even now a cub sleeps in the shadows;
The wind blows hard, the hail pierces the blackness;
Naimes tilts his shield, the pelting stones to parry;
How he needs now his ermine-padded mantle! 2045
"O Lord," he prays, "Who saved Your servant Daniel
When in the lion's den his life was challenged,
Saved Jonah from the whale and ocean's fathoms,
And led the Israelites in that great caravan
That breached the waves and boatless cleft the
 channels, 2050
As You sent down to Earth the Angel Gabriel
With tidings glad to Mary, maiden matchless,
Hear my prayer now and look down on your vassal."
Duke Naimes is cold to death and trembles madly;
He can't pray more--his teeth rattle like hammers. 2055

119

In such a state Duke Naimes must spend the night
As no noble before him ever survived;
He'll not forget it for the rest of his life;
See now that bear returning at first light,
Back to her cub left in that lair behind! 2060
Naimes sees it come and marvels at its size;
The bear comes up, which fears Naimes not a mite,
And, jaws agape, it goes for Carlon's knight;
Naimes sees it come and calls to God on high,
Then draws his sword and moves forward to fight; 2065
The bear attacks and with its front paws strikes;
Good Naimes responds with sword-blow so precise
The bear's front paws in that one blow are sliced;
The beast, unbalanced, falls down and cannot rise;
If you could hear that she-bear's awful cries: 2070
The noise of them filled up the mountainside!
Drawn by the roars of that bear as it writhes
A second bear and a leopard arrive;
Both see Morel and move on him alike,

But good Duke Naimes, his cutting blade held tight, 2075
Strikes hard the leopard and its head leaves its hide;
The bear runs off, not daring to abide;
Duke Naimes remounts Morel and off they ride.

120

Duke Naimes rides down the fearsome slope of Aspremont,
Rides high and low through the length of Calabria 2080
Until he reaches Messina's coastal channel;
And there he sees so many ships and galleys,
And on the shore so many tents and camp-sites
And Turks so many making their heathen racket!
Not since Lord God made all the world and mankind 2085
And all the things that the whole earth inhabit,
Was there so big an army, God curse and damn them!
Naimes sees this host, his eyes tear-filled with sadness;
For he knows well what hurt they'll do and damage.

121

Duke Naimes has much endured and much has mastered 2090
When down the slope of Aspremont he passes,
Comes to the Strait and sees so many barges,
Sees sails so many set in bejewelled mastheads,
And on the shore so many tents and marquees;
The Emir's tent stands out by its rich markings 2095
And the carbuncle atop the entrance sparkling;
There he awaits strong King Boidant's army
And Jerusalem's King, the strong Moadas;
So great a host waits there to serve Tervagant
Their food's run low--it's sold on a black market 2100
Where the least handful fetches one silver mark-piece;
Their good pack-mules for lack of food are starving
And their war-steeds grow weaker and lethargic;
That godless breed eat their sick mules and chargers;
Aumon grows restless, and Agolant his father. 2105

122

While Naimes had left Carlon upon this mission
A Paynim knave of the Devil's religion,
Sent out to spy on Charles, his knights and princes,
His mission done, back across the plain had ridden
To Reggio town, that noble, southern city 2110
Where Agolant has come to parley with him;
He sees him now and scans the scoundrel's visage:
"Did you reach Rome?" the Emir asks him quickly:
"Indeed, my lord, and lengthy was my visit;
Carlon is coming with an army of Christians; 2115

In his front ranks, which ride ahead some distance,
There are twelve dukes and two kings in addition;
Wherever they camp they claim Carlon's dominion;
This force, I'd say, has forty thousand in it;
I've never seen such armor and equipment; 2120
There's not one hauberk that is not double-thickened,
And not one helm unstudded with gold insets;
When to the sky their lances are uplifted
It's like a forest--you'll not see one that's thicker
Or closer planted than this French vanguard is, Sire; 2125
One hundred thousand make up their next division."
Aumon hears this and eyes him with suspicion:
"Silence, you wretch! Your words are too long-winded!
It's clear to me that they have scared you witless;
You've said too much! Be gone from here this instant! 2130
Even if the French were made of steel fine-finished
They could not fight with us and be the victors!"

123

"Good son, leave be," says Emir Agolant;
"We cannot blame this man here out of hand;
But we can see if his fear's based on fact; 2135
Which one of you will volunteer, which man
Will go for us and climb Mount Bitter's back,
To estimate the Christian force and rank?"
Not one of them makes boast of doing that.

124

Salatiel at last to his feet rises: 2140
"My lord, Emir, since you yourself desire it,
I'll volunteer for Aspremont, to climb it;
With my best speed I'll ride until I find them;
If I meet Charles, be sure I shall chastise him!"
Gorhan replies: "Salatiel, be silent! 2145
A king and leader should not take this assignment."

125

When this is said, next speaks the king of Befany:
"King Agolant, your army is assembled,
But our supplies of meat are now all empty;
You have great fighters, but soon they'll starve to
    death here; 2150
King Moadas is still away in Femenie
And Boidant with his help is not present;
Up, King, therefore! Let us ride out together,
Neath Aspremont to fight upon the meadow,
Your noble force against Charles and his rebels! 2155

Strike down the pride of their upstart rebellion
And Christian Law within this land erected!
Through all of France let your law be respected
And may Mahom be worshipped at Saint Denis!"
Balan hears this and laughs--he cannot help it; 2160
He turns and says to the rich king of Femenie:
"This brave lord's talk of battle is too headstrong;
He knows not Charles nor the strength of his Empire,
Nor does he know what noble knights attend him;
Ere long, I swear, they'll start on such a venture 2165
Where good men's lives will recklessly be ended."
"Hush!" Gorhan says; "Father, say not I beg you
That Christendom shall ever withstand our vengeance."
Then to the King he says: "Don't worry, Emir!
I'll spy them out, my lord, if you will let me." 2170

126

"Emir, if it's your wish," thus speaks Gorhan,
"Behold, I'll leave straightway for Aspremont,
The Christian force to estimate how strong;
But let me take your white horse, Agolant,
Which two nights back was brought from Messina, 2175
Then I'd be sure of reaching King Carlon,
To ask him if he will or he will not
Renounce his realm and be your seneschal
And place his faith henceforth in Lord Mahom."
"Give him the horse!" calls out the Paynim throng; 2180
The King agrees and to his squires he nods;
They bring the horse, clad in a rich silk cloth;
A finer looking beast you could not want,
Its temperament unmatched, so says the song;
The squires make haste to put the saddle on. 2185

127

The squires make haste to saddle the horse quickly;
Its saddle-bows are gold, its saddle silver,
And from the saddle there hang two shining stirrups;
See Gorhan move to mount the courser quickly!
With hauberk donned and shining helm laced swiftly 2190
He girds his sword, its gold-hilt blade a-glinting;
Then he adjusts the heavy shield they give him,
With leopards three upon the front depicted;
When Gorhan mounts, his cutting spear they give him,
Which bears a flag, by three gold nails affixed there; 2195
His leave he asks and takes when it is given;
Then from the Queen, with love for whom he's smitten,
He takes his leave and says with laughing visage:
"I leave, my lady, but may Mahom be with you!

I must see Charles, to find out what his will is 2200
And to spy out the force of men he brings here."
"Go then!" she says, "to my God I submit you;
Great Tervagant protect you from all injury!
The world regards my love for you as sinful,
But you know well the way our love commits us; 2205
So, if you love me, to your worth now bear witness."
"Lady," he says, "it will be as you wish it."
He leaves the camp riding past the pavilions.

128

With happy heart Gorhan goes riding out,
Wearing fine armor, the finest to be found, 2210
Astride a steed whiter than any flower;
It is no wonder his confidence abounds:
A man of wealth he is and of much power;
He's valiant, brave, with courtly skills endowed;
At chess and draughts he wins bout after bout, 2215
Knows rivercraft, can hunt with hawks and hounds,
Knows more than hunters of woods and hunting grounds;
Articulate in speech, in counsel sound,
He is severe towards the forceful proud,
But sympathetic to the poor and castdown; 2220
His wealth's not there to hoard up and to count,
But to help out a man in his need's hour;
Gorhan is handsome and love sits on his brow;
The Queen's eyes rest on him in every crowd;
Now he climbs Aspremont, that rugged mount, 2225
While our Duke Naimes is making his way down;
They see each other and each hails each aloud;
Both men would hear from the other man's mouth
The news they seek and both have pledged to scout.

129

Gorhan and Naimes, as each moves on and rides, 2230
Approach each other upon the mountainside;
Duke Naimes speaks first and hails him in this wise:
"Pity, I pray, your lovely horse, sir knight!
If you ride on as I've seen you arrive,
Before you reach the summit of this climb 2235
Your lovely horse will scarcely be alive!"
Gorhan hears this and quickly thus replies:
"Who are you, sir, to give me such advice?
Are you a Christian, in Lord God's name baptized?"
"Indeed I am, in the sweet name of Christ, 2240
The One True God, whose Judgement Day is nigh,
Who whilst on earth by Jews was crucified."
"Indeed," says Gorhan, "your faith you've not denied;

Are you from France, that worthy land and prized?"
"From Carlon's seat at Laon," says Naimes with pride; 2245
"Charles has sent me to ask the Emir why
He has set foot and camped in his Empire,
Killing his people and setting land on fire."
Gorhan retorts: "Your trip's a waste of time!
By Mahomet you were badly assigned! 2250
Your journey hence I do not think you'll like;
That horse of yours, you see, has caught my eye;
If you can't find another, you'll walk for miles!"
"My lord," says Naimes, "it would be wrong to fight;
This challenge keep, I pray, a little while 2255
Till I have spoken to your master from mine;
So help me God, if you grant not this right,
I'll not accept such taunts spoken so wild."

130

"Sir knight of France," thus is he hailed by Gorhan,
"Your horse looks full of running, a real black
  courser, 2260
Light on its feet, but strongly built for all that;
Dismount it now! You shall not take it forward!"
Duke Naimes retorts: "It would be most uncourtly
For Carlon's envoy to be compelled to walk there;
I'll thank you, sir, to kindly hold your horses 2265
Until my message to Agolant's reported;
And if you still refuse this your accordance,
For sake of peace with you I'll say one more thing:
Take my black horse! But firstly give me your one!
In this exchange you would not be the poorer; 2270
But God curse me if otherwise I'll alter."

131

When Gorhan sees for all of his bravado
That he'll not have Morel for any asking
Unless he gives his white stallion to start with,
He says to Naimes: "Sir knight, be on your guard then! 2275
When I use steel I drive a harder bargain;
My price if I defeat you is your black charger."
Duke Naimes replies: "I'll not be in this market."
"Then you will be the poorer!" Gorhan says darkly;
These words delivered, he turns his war-horse sharply; 2280
He rides at Naimes and brandishes his lance-head;
The Duke himself is in no way faint-hearted;
He lifts his lance, rides hard and strikes Gorhan first;
High on the shield his strong thrust finds its target;
In the top corner Bavaria's Duke so hard hits 2285
The shield is buckled and the blow pierces past it;

The double hauberk's mail is cleft apart too;
The hole in Gorhan's shield where the lance passes
Is wide enough for him to put his arm through;
If Naimes should now strike his body unarmored, 2290
Gorhan would never report back to his master.

132

Gorhan knows well that his shield has been split;
He strikes Duke Naimes on his shield edged in gilt;
He shatters it and onward his lance drills;
The hauberk's strong, the chain-mail double-knit, 2295
And Gorhan's lance breaks off close to the tip;
They turn about and draw their swords forthwith,
Then drive their horses at each other full tilt;
If you had seen that fight and witnessed it!
Blow after blow on each man's helmet rings; 2300
No precious stone set hard and fast therein
Leaves not its setting, to take the blows each gives;
Their shields can take no more and fall to bits;
The very glue and gloss off each shield's chipped;
Naimes in full fury delivers such a hit 2305
On Gorhan's helm, on its gold-circled brim,
That the Paynim is stunned and his head spins;
His vision's clouded--a league away all's dim;
He would have fallen with the great force of this
But to his golden saddle he tightly grips; 2310
His horse, unchecked, bolts off into the hills;
Gorhan rides off, whether or not he will!
Naimes laughs out loud and calls out after him:
"Where are you off to, Paynim? You must admit,
The wings of your conceit I've somewhat clipped! 2315
What's mine is mine and not yours on some whim;
Though you charge hard my worth is higher still."

133

Duke Naimes is wise and well he realized
That if he had killed Gorhan there outright,
At Paynim hands himself he would have died 2320
Ere he returned to Charles with a reply;
Gorhan meanwhile, to consciousness revived,
Calls, to inspire him, his lady-love to mind,
Who that same morning sweet promise had implied;
He turns his mount, his naked blade held high, 2325
And spotting Naimes towards him swiftly rides;
But Naimes is waiting and strikes a second time;
Gorhan's so stunned he fears now for his life,
With sore regret that he was ever inspired.

134

So long the fight of these two knights endures, 2330
The give and take has so tired out the two
They face each other but neither of them moves;
They face each other but neither asks for truce;
Gorhan it is who speaks first to the Duke:
"Chevalier, brother,I beg you tell me true, 2335
Do all the Christians fight as well as you do?"
"Vassal," says Naimes, "I've never sought the proof;
But I am certain plenty fight harder too;
I say again, let us drop this dispute
Till with your King I have held interview; 2340
When I return, taking this selfsame route,
Which gives you time your mission to pursue,
If you desire to carry on this feud,
Upon my loyal oath I pledge to you
I'm not a man who ever would refuse." 2345
Gorhan replies: "I would agree,in truth,
But Paynims hence my honor would abuse."
"Sir, it will cost them dear," Duke Naimes rebukes;
"Whoever blames you is the sort of man who,
Had he crossed me, would have died in the duel." 2350
Both men discuss and talk the matter through
Till finally both of them have approved
That the Duke's plan is the one they should choose;
Gorhan says then: "Now that we have a truce,
I will escort you to where the Emir broods; 2355
For by yourself I fear your life you'd lose."
"Paynim," says Naimes, "I thank you for this boon;
A rich reward it will earn for you soon."
Thus they both ride towards the Paynim troops.

135

Gorhan and Naimes ride down the rims and rocks; 2360
Till Paynim ranks are reached they tarry not;
All see them come and rush to Agolant:
"Lord Agolant, true ruler of great rod,
Heap praise, Emir, upon your seneschal!
He is returned, already, from Aspremont! 2365
A knight of France on a black horse he's got!"
"That's why I love him!" King Agolant responds;
"He's helped me out in many a tight spot!"

136

Gorhan dismounts before Agolant's tent;
More than one hundred Paynims rush up to help: 2370
"Good men, hold back!" Gorhan calls out to them;

"Serve this knight first and to his needs attend!"
Apart from shields, no armor do they shed;
The Emir speaks and says before the rest:
"Speak up, Gorhan! Don't leave me here to guess! 2375
Is this knight here from the ranks of the French?"
"He is indeed, my lord," Gorhan says then;
"Carlon's best messenger, the truth to tell;
Our paths both crossed and thus it was we met;
Though this was chance, it cannot bode but well." 2380
"Is he your captive?"--"Indeed, in no respect!
What can I say, save that not many men
Could capture someone who showed such self-defence?"

137

The Paynims there all stare at Naimes meanwhile;
It's Gorhan's shield which most attracts their eye; 2385
Upon this shield, in its top corner high,
There gapes a hole through which a hawk might fly,
Through which your arm might pass, it is so wide!
Down to the hood his helmet too is sliced
And flaps about his shoulders on either side; 2390
The Paynims now, each man to each, confide:
"No lad did this, nor any stripling squire;
If all the rest of the French fight alike,
Then woe the hour that led us here to fight."
Now Agolant addresses Naimes and cries: 2395
"Vassal, tell me and do not try to hide:
Are you a wealthy man, are you a knight
With men and land to govern and to guide?"
Bavaria's Duke and ruler Naimes replies:
"I am liegeman to Charles, our King by right; 2400
Carlon it was who dubbed and made me knight;
I am his servant, his favorite porter I;
A short while back he made a small plot mine;
Now Carlon says that he'll give me a wife
For coming here and telling you his mind; 2405
But I owned not one penny's worth erstwhile."

138

Cries Agolant: "You Slavs and Saracens,
Lead off this messenger and guard him well!
Then in the morning bring him back to my tent
And we'll cut off both his arms and his legs! 2410
He'll be dismembered to show Charles our contempt!"
"Be not so hasty, Sire!" Duke Naimes says then;
"It ill befits a King brave and well-bred
To hurt or harm an envoy to him sent;
My lord Emir, let me complete my quest! 2415

The Emperor, in whose name I was sent,
Commanded me to ask of you yourself,
What sort of sin makes you come here in strength
To waste his land and murder all his men?
Would you rob Charles of his birthright and realm?" 2420
"Indeed I would! I'm here for nothing else!
Ere he had been baptized, had he instead
Come first to me his folly to repent,
I would have pardoned him and been his friend;
But now I'll give no king an audience 2425
Who does not come with his lands to present
And at my feet his will and weal to bend;
I'll disinherit him though he live yet;
Though in his prime, he'll meet a sudden end."
"My lord," says Naimes, "you've a long road ahead 2430
If you wish to achieve all that you've said."

139

Naimes stands before King Agolant the Infidel
And speaks to him both firmly and distinctly;
Now as he speaks, his message bold delivering,
Tells him what Carlon thinks and what he wishes, 2435
Behold Balan approach as Naimes continues;
He sees the Duke and knows him in an instant;
He knows the Duke both by his voice and visage;
Now with a smile to the good Duke he whispers:
"Chevalier, release your sword, I bid you; 2440
Give it to me and my pledge I will give you
That no one here shall find a means to kill you;
If anyone so plans or even thinks to,
I shall help you as a father his infant;
For I recall, nor could forget so quickly, 2445
The courtesy and great honor you did me
When I journeyed to France upon my mission;
Fear nothing then! It is Balan who bids you!
I will protect you, within my power, from injury."
Naimes hears Balan and offers him thanksgiving. 2450

140

While Duke Naimes stands before the Paynim Emir
Balan removes the good Duke's pointed helmet
And then undoes the hauberk he is dressed in;
Then he gives him a gown of ermine precious
And a fine mantle of silk with golden edges; 2455
Duke Naimes is strong, both handsome and impressive
As he speaks now: "Did you not hear my question?
Why are you here invading Carlon's Empire?
This land is ours to the Pillars of Hercules;

Yet you want Charles to come to you repentant? 2460
It often happens, I'm sure you've heard it, Sire,
And seen it too, that he who lusts for everything
Ends up by losing all that was his already.

141

"My lord Emir," Duke Naimes loudly repeats,
"Charles charges you and I alike entreat: 2465
Will you turn back or will you still proceed?
In your whole convoy there is no sumpter-beast
Who in three months, though making its best speed,
Could travel France, so broad its borders be;
Do you go there to conquer and to keep? 2470
Charles charges you to stop and fight him here;
Choose now the time and place that you shall meet
To fight out this dispute, just you and he!
I call on you to choose a day, Emir,
And should Carlon hold back and not appear, 2475
I'll give you France; this glove shall be the seal;
In every court your claim I'll guarantee.

142

"Emir, my lord," loudly repeats Duke Naimes,
"I have been sent to you by Charlemayn
To hear from your own mouth as you explain 2480
Just why you've come and camped in his domain."
Says Agolant: "To chase Carlon away!
And if I can lay hands on him or blade
He and his line will be forever shamed!"
"My lord," says Naimes, "God help him in that case! 2485
For three days hence, Emir, keep watch and wait;
Then you can fling your taunts at closer range."

143

King Agolant calls now upon Sorbrin:
"Have you not been to France, good Saracen,
To spy on Charles, the son of King Pepin? 2490
Do you not know this evil, wretched man?"
"Yes, by Apollo, I do, Lord Agolant;
I know all Carlon's men, Sire, that's a fact;
I saw and know Droon the Poitevin,
King Salemon, his nephew Thiorin, 2495
Hoel of Nantes, Geoffrey the Angevin;
I know Normandy's duke, good Anchetin,
And the duke of Beauvais, called Aubuin;
I also know the Archbishop Turpin;
Carlon's nephew I know, the young Roland, 2500

And England's King Cahoer, likewise a lad;
And all the lords the son of Pepin has;
But Carlon has a neighbor, a powerful man,
Girart d'Eufrate he's called by Limousins;
He is so rich in pure gold and in lands 2505
No less than thirty cities pay him their tax;
Were he and Charles related or friends by pact,
Those two together might well upset your plans;
But old Girart won't give Charles one brass tack;
He hates him more than stings hate theriac." 2510

144

The villain spy speaks on: "Emir, my lord,
There is in France no prince or vavasor
Nor any man, so boastful are they all,
Who does not think he can escape when caught;
Behold again this knight Gorhan has brought-- 2515
This messenger, who chides you and who taunts,
Who when you questioned him, said he was poor;
He said he was a porter,as you recall,
And Charles gave him some land that was but small;
Well, by Mahomet, who judges one and all, 2520
This man's Duke Naimes, of all Bavaria lord!
There's no man living whom Carlon dotes on more;
Above all others he is his counsellor;
If you desire to hurt Charles to the core,
Dismember him and render him a corpse! 2525
The French could feel no greater loss, I'm sure."
Balan grows angry as he hears Sorbrin talk
And straightaway towards the traitor stalks;
He taps his shoulder and to one side withdraws,
Then in his ear his own opinion pours: 2530
"By Mahomet, you weak son of a whore!
If I get hold of you outside this court,
This very day I'll flay you with such force
You'll never threaten a good man's life henceforth."
Aloud he says: "I am surprised, my lord, 2535
That you confide in villains of this sort;
He will teach you the tricks that he employs;
He tells you lies to earn a rich reward;
For I myself know Naimes, Bavaria's lord;
In all of France no finer knight holds sword; 2540
Naimes is no more this man than cheese is chalk;
Can you believe that Charles with all his scorn
Would send to you his chiefest counsellor
Or any man so vital to his cause?
This fellow here is some valet, I'm sure, 2545
Some sort of lackey who does Charlemagne's chores;
Carlon's no fool; he never would have thought

To use a duke or prince as his envoy;
Give me, Emir, this wretched liar of yours
And I will drown him in yonder waterfall." 2550
Thus Balan talks, says this and that and more
And snatches Naimes this time from danger's claws.

145

"My lord, listen to me!" continues Balan;
"Do not believe the words of every flatterer;
Let your behaviour always befit your rank, Sire, 2555
As all the princes have within your family;
When envoys come to speak with you, sit back, Sire,
And let them speak without responding rashly;
Then if they fling at you some taunt or madness,
Just laugh at them as Charlemayn laughed at me; 2560
No taunt or insult that I tried to throw at him
In any way made Carlon show his anger
Or hastily reply with word or action;
Do likewise, Sire, to rule in courtly manner."
"I shall do as you say, Balan," says Agolant; 2565
"Lead off this man to your own lodge and campsite!
And if he wants a gold-sewn cloth or taffeta,
A he-mule, she-mule, a war-horse or a saddle-horse,
Give them to him! Like Carlon I'll be lavish."
Balan replies: "Your will be done, your Majesty." 2570
These words delivered, Naimes leaves with Balan gladly.

146

So long speaks Balan to Agolant the Emir
That he saves Naimes, securing his protection;
Now as both leave, the Paynim calls out gently:
"Envoy, good brother, don't think I am forgetting 2575
That Charles has challenged me and I've accepted;
When you return to him make sure you tell him
That we shall meet down in Mount Bitter's meadow
Three days from now, the earlier the better;
For a long time my army's been assembled 2580
And my supplies of meat and corn are empty;
So tell Carlon to make sure he is ready;
And mark you make this message clear and stress it:
Not since the hour he was as knight invested
And girt a sword on his left hip and held it, 2585
Will he have fought so fierce a battle ever
Or Paynims seen so many in one melee!
Yet if ere then his conscience was to tell him
That his baptism in Christ's name was an error,
And he renounces his wicked Christian heresy, 2590
I think I still might show Carlon some clemency,

Provided that he worships Mahom henceforth."
Duke Naimes replies: "I have heard all you've said, Sire;
But Charles, I'm sure, would rather be a dead man!"
With these same words, just as I have expressed them,   2595
Good Naimes departs, leave having been requested,
At Balan's side, with whom the Emir sends him;
They head straightway to where the Paynim's tent is;
No man was ever served as Duke Naimes then was:
What lovely clothes he gives the Duke to dress in: 2600
Robes of pure silk with fine gold filamented!
They go to eat and he seats the Duke next to him;
In cups of gold he pours him wine a-plenty;
A king serves Naimes, to all his needs attending:
Gorhan it is, called back from his defence-post;   2605
Balan leans over to the Duke and says then:
"Most honorable sir, I bid you welcome!
In your own land you honored me, your enemy;
Until I die I'll honor and respect you;
Wherever I am, you can count on my friendship;   2610
In friendship, too, greet Carlon with my blessing;
When this pitched fight is fought at last and settled
I would then be baptized in his own presence."
Duke Naimes hears this and tender thanks he renders;
The Emir's Queen, meanwhile, hears of the tension   2615
Between her husband and Charlemagne's envoy;
She sends her page to tell Balan directly
To bring into her tent this foreign Frenchman;
She wants to see him; so Balan acquiesces:
"Duke Naimes, fine sir, I'll not conceal this message;   2620
The Queen asks for you and in her tent expects you;
Let both of us as friends go there together."
"Indeed," says Naimes, "I willingly consent to it."
So off they go to where her tent's erected;
The Queen stands up to greet them as they enter;   2625
She bids them sit and Naimon sits down next to her;
The Duke is handsome, his body well-developed;
His eyes are bright and comely his complexion;
He's somewhat bruised where his hauberk has pressed
    him,
Yet these same bruises enhance him more than blemish;   2630
The Queen sees him and loves him in that second;
Her heart is fired, his beauty makes her tremble;
Her passion's flame burns fierce and with such frenzy
That silently she whispers to herself then:
"Hey Mahom, lord, if your great power could ever   2635
Bring him and me much closer both together,
Say side by side in a good bed well nestled,
In pleasure's terms it would be worth an Empire!
Lord Agolant would no more rate a mention;
This lord is in his prime, the other senile!   2640

Agolant's body is like a ravaged relic,
While this knight's body has reached its peak
    perfection!"
She hails Duke Naimes in tones of sweet affection:
"Frenchman," she asks, "don't lie to me, I beg you,
But on your word as a true Christian gentleman,   2645
Have you a wife back home in Carlon's Empire?
You are most handsome! Are all the Christian menfolk?"
"I've never sought the proof," says Naimes correctly,
"But I am sure that handsomer are many!
Have I a wife? You've asked me and I'll tell you;   2650
I have not, lady, nor ever had the intention,
For I have pledged my life to Carlon's welfare."
When she hears this the Queen is most contented;
In secret now, her hand to Naimes extending,
Her royal ring she takes and to him tenders: 2655
"Naimon," she says, "I give you my affection
With this my ring of gold the finest tempered;
Guard this ring well, and it will bring great
    benefit;
If once you lose it, it will stay lost forever;
I'll tell you why this ring is to be cherished: 2660
It will protect you from witchcraft and from devils;
You'll never be poisoned by any food or beverage;
Whatever wealth you win, whatever treasures,
Will never be stolen nor lost of them a penny;
Its wearer never in battle will be bested,   2665
Nor fall a victim to wicked plot or treachery;
This ring has power to guard you and direct you;
I'll tell you why I've given you such a present:
When you return to your homeland, all henceforth
My joy will be and my private remembrance   2670
That I've a lover among the Christian menfolk;
And if I thought that you loved me yourself too,
The rest of life I'd count a lot more precious."
Says Naimes: "My lady, your honor so indebts me
I'm lost for words to give my thanks expression."   2675
Naimes asks for leave, which the Queen grants
    regretfully;
The Queen sighs deeply when our Duke Naimes has left
    her;
With tearful eyes she lifts her gaze to heaven.

147

Duke Naimes departs, his leave asked for and given,
And both return to Balan's own pavilion;   2680
Balan brings forth all the wealth he has with him:
Goblets of gold, expensive silks and linen,
Horses and money and all sorts of gold dishes

And then he says: "Choose anything you wish for!"
But Naimes replies: "Do not be too insistent! 2685
What's yours is yours; I seek not wealth or riches."

148

When Balan sees that Naimon is quite adamant,
And will not take his gold or metal chalices,
He tells his squire to go and fetch his stallion;
Whiter than snow or crystal is this champion; 2690
Its head is sleek, its blue-sheened rump is dazzling;
Its reins are gold, wrought finely and enameled;
Gold too the saddle-bows, of highest carat;
The horse is draped in a rich silken blanket
And by the squire attended as it stands there; 2695
Balan takes Naimes by his taffeta mantle
And says: "Behold, good Duke and gentle baron!
This stallion runs so swiftly hills and valleys,
No other horse can make such pace and match it;
No other horse can do what this horse can do! 2700
No mortal man should climb into its saddle
If he's not bold, adventurous and valiant!"

149

Balan says on: "Lord, listen to me, pray!
On my behalf take this to Charlemayn;
It's his to have on this agreement, say: 2705
If God promotes the plans that I have made,
In Him I'll trust and Christian Law obey;
But for the length of this ferocious fray,
While in the battle, I cannot change my faith;
Now mount this horse and I'll lead you away." 2710
So Naimes departs and takes the destrier;
The Paynims watch and ill at ease exclaim:
"Look at that Frenchman! How arrogant his face!
How he becomes the richness of his train!
If all the French are of such mighty make, 2715
None of our mules or palfreys will be safe!"

150

Duke Naimes departs and Balan rides out with him;
Not taking though the route that brought Naimes
        thither
They ride instead along the camp's perimeter
Towards a tower which Agolant has built there; 2720
A pass it guards to land beyond Mount Bitter!
The tower is held by Aumon at his bidding--
One hundred thousand Turks he took there with him;

Balan leads Naimes and guides him past their pickets;
Onwards they ride till Balan in the distance 2725
Points to the valley with Carlon's army in it!
They say farewell, exchanging friendship's kisses:
"My lord, Balan," says Naimes, "I pray you, listen!
"It's good and right and God Himself does bid us
To render friendship where friendship has been given; 2730
Trust now in God and Lord God will deliver you;
Then come to us as soon as you are willing;
The Pope himself will baptize you a Christian."
"I would go with you now," says Balan swiftly,
"But Agolant has raised me from an infant; 2735
He dubbed me knight, gave me a crown of kingship;
To fail him now and go no further with him
I would be wrong; my heart would find me guilty;
I would not have it said by the least villain
That I failed my liege-lord in this commitment; 2740
And yet I know how this dispute must finish,
For in the end I know we cannot win it;
Greet Charles for me and all the barons with him."
Naimes hands Balan a crucifix of silver,
Which previously the Pope to Naimes had given; 2745
The Paynim bows and takes it with humility;
While he has this he will not be death's victim;
Naimes bows to him, then turns and leaves him quickly;
Till back with Charles he'd not delay one instant.

151

The valorous Duke Naimes goes onward riding 2750
And does not stop till French ranks close behind him;
Behold Carlon, in his great tent abiding,
Unsheath Joyeuse, whose honor he delights in,
And show the blade atop the scabbard shining!
Charles draws the tassels, full many a day left idle, 2755
And puts on new ones of delicate designing;
When he looks up and sees Duke Naimes arriving,
Beholds his armor in all its shining brightness,
And sees that horse, than any flower whiter,
He lifts his hands on high to the Almighty: 2760
"Sweet Lord be praised!" the son of Pepin cries out;
"You have returned to me my best and wisest!"

152

When Carlon sees his messenger Duke Naimes,
He cries aloud: "Sweet Lord, be thanked and praised!"
Before the rest he comes to lend him aid 2765
And as his squire helps him disarm straightway;
When the good Duke dismounts his destrier,

The King moves up his helmet to unlace:
"Naimon," he says, "have you returned unscathed?"
"Indeed I have; I never felt unsafe,   2770
Save when I climbed fell Aspremont's steep face;
I was so wrong to blame my young Richer;
I found his spur upon Mount Bitter's wastes
And the bones of his horse picked clean away.

153

"I'll not deceive you, Sire," Duke Naimes reports;   2775
"You cannot hope to scale Mount Bitter's wall;
This fearsome fell is so steep and so tall
It seems to lead right up to Heaven's vault;
The night I spent thereon was rude and raw;
From hail and snow I suffered hurt so sore   2780
I never slept till day began to dawn;
A wondrous bird attacked me and my horse;
Three feet aloft towards its gaping jaws
It bore us up and then it let us fall!
I slew this beast with one slice of my sword,   2785
And have brought back to you its mighty claw."
Naimes brings it forth to show the Emperor;
Charles sees it now and he is filled with awe;
To all his knights about he shows it forth.

154

Fierce-faced Duke Naimes speaks on and says: "True
    Emperor,   2790
Thanks be to God and to that noble messenger,
Who three months back by Agolant was sent to us,
I have come back to you alive and healthy;
I have told the Emir of your intentions;
But, Sire, do you recall that wretched beggar,   2795
That foreigner you entertained and welcomed
For one whole year, who feasted at your pleasure?
He was a spy for Agolant the Emir!
When I had said my piece and it was ended,
He met his master to counsel and to tell him   2800
That Naimes, Bavaria's duke, was I this envoy,
The one man whom above the rest you cherished;
And that should he wish mightily to vex you
He ought to cut both my arms and my legs off!
There is no doubt I would now be a dead man   2805
Had Balan not opposed the villain's evidence;
He saved me from their clutches by a hair's breadth,
    Sire.

155

"Carlon," says Naimes, "my death was very near,
When in the tent I saw Balan appear;
He told Sorbrin the spy he would indeed 2810
Tear him apart if more he interfered;
Then he sought leave to host and care for me
And took me back to his lodgings to sleep;
What can I say? When it came time to leave
He bade his squire to bring out this white steed; 2815
It is so swift no other has its speed;
Pursuing or pursued it has no peer;
It runs all day without a rest between;
Accept this gift sent from Balan to thee
As a sure sign that he in God believes; 2820
Yet he would not leave now his lord Emir,
Who brought him up and crowned him for his deeds;
He'll not desert or fight his lawful liege;
But if your force can win it in the field
And he escapes from death and from defeat, 2825
He'll come to you rather than turn and flee;
For he yearns to embrace the Christian creed."
"Sweet Lord," says Charles, "may You my witness be;
If he should come and join us Christians here,
One hundred knights will serve him as he please! 2830

156

"Naimon," says Charles, "pray now, keep nothing hidden!
Did you spy out the Saracen contingent?
What do you think? I must have your opinion;
Can our small force wage war with theirs and win it?"
"In truth," says Naimes, "they are amassed in myriads; 2835
For every Frenchman there are one hundred Infidels;
Yet their real strength I do not reckon this much;
I'll tell you why I have this firm conviction:
When they set out upon their murderous mission
They came by sea, fierce-faced and in high spirits, 2840
And landing thus they met with no resistance;
Now, three months later, their bread and corn are
    finished
And all these men have lost their vim and vigor;
They kill their horses and on the raw meat nibble;
And all the time they grow thinner and thinner; 2845
Who can stay hard when hunger howls within him?
If you attack with them in this condition
Their greater force will favor them but little;
I saw myself and read it in their visage
That most of them have lost their fighting spirit; 2850
Mount up, Carlon! Why waste another minute?

If your own knights and all these others with you
Turn them about and force them out of Italy,
Their wealth is yours--so much pure gold and silver
Your poorest kith and kin will all be rich men.   2855

157

"Great King, my lord," says on Duke Naimes the
    doughty,
"There is a pass where we may cross this mountain!
I know the way and well may be your scout there;
It leads to where the Emir's built a tower,
Which is well guarded, both within and without it,   2860
By his son Aumon and Slavs one hundred thousand,
All hand-picked men with which he has endowed him;
Like a wild boar in his blood-lust is Aumon;
If we attack just him, his tower surrounding,
We could defeat him, of that I have no doubt, Sire;   2865
He is so proud, I have heard it recounted,
He would not send for help nor will allow it."
Carlon hears this and calls his knights about him,
His kings and peers, his barons and his counties;
The Pope alike attends to offer counsel;   2870
Carlon the great greets them with this announcement:
"My lords," says he, "too long are we dismounted!
We must ride on, and shall at dawn's first hour!"

158

Carlon calls up good Aubuin and Fagon,
Good Duke Elin and valiant Duke Sanson;   2875
Then Thiorin with his uncle King Salemon,
Hoel of Nantes and good Geoffrey the Angevin,
Huon from Mans and from Blois worthy Anchetin:
"My lords," he says, "my brave and noble paladins!
In your good care I place my pride--my vanguard,   2880
Men sixty thousand in one noble battalion;
Without exception they are good men and valiant;
May God, who changed water to wine in Galillee,
Fill your hearts' brim with courage for this action!
You'll ride at dawn against Apollo's vassals,   2885
Who seek the death of blessed Christianity;
With your steel blades you shall the first attack them;
I'll follow you as quickly as I can do
With my one hundred thousand soldiers and cavalry;
This rancid race will rue the day they landed."   2890

159

The King calls next on good Duke Amelon,

On Count Anthelme and Poitevin's Droon,
Whose ranks are filled with brave Burgundians:
"I want your force to be ten thousand strong;
Guard our right flank when we ourselves move off;   2895
Our left will be maintained by Count Grifon
In company with his son Ganelon;
Take with you also the Frisian Gondelbuef;
Keep to our right, yet to our sight not lost;
In front of us our squires shall ride along   2900
With all our weapons in carts and wagon-lots
And all the food that we shall need anon;
At dawn, God willing, we'll fight these heathen dogs."
They all reply: "With the blessing of God!"

160

At break of day, when dawn's first light is spreading,   2905
Full forty counts, their helmets donned already,
Have formed the vanguard in a phalanx of splendor;
No man therein has not hauberk and helmet;
Thus well arrayed with armor and with weapons
The vanguard waits, alert and at attention;   2910
Then the horns sound and they move off together;
Their pace is brisk, both purposeful and steady;
They cross the land, advancing on the enemy;
When they are gone Carlon his host assembles,
One hundred thousand men of mighty mettle;   2915
Behold their lances so many raised to heaven,
That bear, with gold nails fixed, so many pennants!
You've never seen a forest planted so densely
As this forest of lances soaring and spreading!
Up hill, down dale, this mighty wedge progresses   2920
Till by a river they once more reassemble,
One half-day's ride from that strong tower erected
By the Emir as part of his defences;
The land about is razed and robbed already;
No blade of grass nor ear of corn is left there;   2925
Had Charles not brought supplies they would have
    perished,
For those fell Turks have robbed the land of
    everything;
Carlon sees this and almost leaves his senses.

161

When all are lodged, Bavarians and Alemans,
Bretons and Normans, Frisian and Picard landsmen,   2930
Men from Lorraine and fierce-faced knights from
    Brabant,
With fall of night, as daylight starts to vanish,

Without a sound or any fuss or clamor,
Twelve counts who bear the King's flag into battle,
Who are those knights in charge of Carlon's vanguard, 2935
Set off at once from the Emperor's campsite
With half their van, some thirty thousand vassals,
All well-armed men, experienced and valiant;
Their quartered shields imagine if you can, lords,
Their many burnished helms, their blades
    steel-fashioned! 2940
Straight for that tower they ride on their strong
    stallions;
Beneath some olive trees, hard by a rampart,
They halt and wait beneath the branches' shadows;
For they intend to fall upon the Saracens
And, if they can, inflict swift death and damage. 2945

162

Beneath the olive trees those Frenchmen hide,
Their shields drawn up, their lances all held tight;
Without a sound they form up in their lines;
Now see them gaze across a valley wide
As they behold a wondrous dust-cloud rise! 2950
Aumon it is, of Pagandom the pride,
Who has commanded a raiding gang all night!
He's taken towns and country-keeps alike;
He's hacked the head from many a lawful squire
And slit the breasts of their defenceless wives; 2955
He's given their girls, all daughters of fine knights,
More than three hundred, or so the charter writes,
He's given them all to the scum at his side
Then bound them all in chains, criminal-like;
These girls cry out, lamenting loud their plight: 2960
"Ah, Charlemayn! Come and avenge this crime!"
For gold and coin they're bought and sold meanwhile.

163

Aumon the king, the powerful and strong,
From foraging returns with all his mob;
They've taken towns and keeps and castles robbed, 2965
Killed many a man and children's heads cut off
And captives chained whom now they lead along--
Women and children all trussed and tied in bonds,
Those whom they spared from killing on the spot;
Hear them cry out, lamenting loud and long: 2970
"Ah, Charlemayn! Are we so long forgot?
Where is your aid? What are you thinking of?"
"Your words are wind!" the foul Paynims respond;
"Look not for help from your liege-lord Carlon!

```
He's not the sort to meet us here head-on!                    2975
Look not for him, for he has turned and gone!"
Such are the words of that pernicious throng
As they approach, each man from toe to top
With food, with bread, with meat and wheat
    well-stocked;
In front of them they bear four gods aloft,                   2980
Each one of them supported on a block;
Their flanks and shanks are all pure gold-embossed;
Their great mouths leer like evil things begot;
Those Paynims, though, bow down and sing them songs;
They dance and prance and sound their drums non-stop;         2985
In wondrous wise, with conquest all agog
They shout out loud, they bark and yap like dogs:
"Hey! Good my lord! Why stay your hand, Aumon?
Will you not now ride forth from Aspremont?
You have held back too long, Sire, by Mahom!                  2990
Why did you not take Rome much earlier on?
Saint Peter could long since have been defrocked
And you yourself installed with proper pomp!"
"Control your zeal!" Aumon straightway responds;
"I've said I'll never return, and I will not,                 2995
To Africa till France respects my rod!
I ask for no more men to do this job
Than you men here who are my chosen squad;
The day we reach Saint Bernard's Pass and cross
You'll have your fill of ladies fair and fond;                3000
Each man shall have two score or more thereof
And all the wealth and riches he could want!"
Thus speaks Aumon, the son of Agolant;
Those paladins, meanwhile, all this have watched
As there they wait, well hidden in that copse                 3005
With thirty thousand men, their armor donned;
The raiding gang they see, while thus ensconced,
Parade their gods in joy and lead along;
They hear alike those captives' wretched sobs;
My lords, ask not if this stirred up their wrath!             3010
"Look there, brave men!" each says to each anon;
"God brings to us what we have sought so long;
Whoever lets them escape to do more wrong
Cares naught for Christ nor loves the Lord our God!"
```

PART 4

164

```
The Paynim raiding gang is in high spirits                    3015
As all return well-stocked with wheat and victuals,
With cloths of silk, pure gold and finest silver;
```

They bear aloft the gods of their religion;
Those captives weep on whom they take no pity;
Aumon is boastful: "Paynims, we're sitting pretty!   3020
Now we have gained more than enough provisions;
We'll capture France, I know we will, and quickly!
How slowly comes great Charles to contradict us!
He has turned tail and fled in my opinion!
I'm off to Rome, right soon to be crowned King there!"   3025
Such words speaks Aumon and others in derision,
While all the time those paladins are listening;
Huon of Mans it is speaks to begin with:
"My lords of France, let us act now with wisdom!
See here Aumon who leads a large contingent!   3030
A mighty load each Saracen has with him;
If we strike now with skill from our position
We'll cut them down before they know what's hit them;
Let us charge now, courageously and swiftly,
And take from them the bread and wheat they've
    pillaged;   3035
This day Lord God a handsome present gives us--
Let us accept it and ride at them this instant,
And may the strongest take as much as he wishes!
If we strike now and can achieve this victory
The booty's such no army ever won richer;   3040
And whomsoever God deals death in His wisdom,
Accept it gladly for love of Him that wills it!"
All thirty thousand respond with quick conviction:
"We'll strike them hard! To God's will we commit us;
Though we're outnumbered, three Paynims to one
    Christian,   3045
We'll not be stopped from doing Lord God's bidding."
With these same words they move, fierce-faced and
    willing,
Then quicken pace, then charge those Paynim villains!
Those who have flags raise them and the wind lifts them;
Those who have swift war-horses dig their spurs
    in them;   3050
Aumon the Afric hears their noise in the distance:
"Who can these people be?" he asks his minions;
"Perhaps it is my uncle, good King Moysant?
King Esperrant perhaps or King Boidant?
They've come to thank us! Their sheer delight
    this din is!   3055
For we all know and it cannot be hidden,
How great's the need for the wheat we are bringing!"
But then one Justin, an oriental prince, says:
"Sire, by Mahomet, in truth I tell you this much:
Paynims never rode as these are riding hither,   3060
Nor ever bore such arms or such equipment!
This force is French,with troops thus dispositioned!

From Charles they've come, I do not doubt one minute,
Nor are they far, my eyes and ears bear witness!
Paynims, to arms! These men are out to kill us!   3065
We'll have to fight right soon in my opinion!"

165

Aumon the king, his head in helmet laced,
To see our men approach in such array,   3070
So many flags unfurled and skywards raised,
So many burnished helms and shield gold-laid,
Calls on one Hector, the king of Val Penee,
Into whose hands he's placed his oriflamme:
"Hector," he says, "can you see to make plain   3075
Which host it is full-armed that comes this way?
I know them not nor why they make such haste."
"Why hide the truth?" his flag-bearer exclaims;
"The mounted van this is of Charlemayn!
Sound out your olifant without delay,   3080
Your troops to rally, who everywhere have strayed!
We'll have to fight and fierce will be the fray."
"In truth," says Aumon, "the day will never break
Wherein for such a force as here displayed
I'd deign to blow my horn and ask for aid!   3085
Our honor and our faith would be disgraced."

166

Aumon is fierce, imperial and strong;
If he believed in our heavenly God
No better man there'd be of royal stock;
He looks ahead, then down, and all along   3090
He sees approach the twelve counts of Carlon,
With thirty thousand, fine destriers atop,
All bearing lances, strong Poitevin steel rods,
And many banners of silk and cendal cloth;
He calls upon Malduit the Pincenol: 3095
"This force of men comes not from Agolant;
These men are French! They've come to Aspremont
To look for trouble! Let's give them all we've got!
Line up my ranks and we'll supply their want!
Their force is small, I fear them not a jot!   3100
Their arms and horses will be ours ere we stop."

167

Aumon is fierce and strong--but is it a wonder
When he is with one hundred thousand cutthroats
And our French force but thirty thousand numbers?
"In truth, says Aumon, "Mahom must really love me!   3105

Whatever I want he gives to me in double!
For, after food, good weapons were our worry,
And these have plenty--but not for long, I trust men!
His best interpreter Aumon then summons:
"Ride out to that French force that's in such hurry   3110
And tell them to surrender without a struggle!
They need not fight; just tell them to give up now
And I will let them go and will not touch them;
But they must leave their weapons ere they run off,
Drop all their bows and spears and swords and
    bucklers!   3115
But should they try to ruin them for us here
They will pay dearly--their heads will all be cut off."
Aumon's envoy rides out with these instructions;
He comes to them and in a wild voice thunders:
"You knights of France! Rage will avail you nothing!   3120
Drop all your weapons! Thus mighty Aumon summons."

168

"Give ear to me!" the Paynim says with scorn:
"Aumon the Afric, all Alexandria's lord,
The best king to gird sword, invites you all
To give up now and his mercy implore   3125
To take your weapons and not your lives withal!
It would be useless to try to match his force;
Lay down your arms before him now, therefore,
And do not try, he says, to beg for more,
Unless you want your necks stretched neath his sword!   3130
If you agree, let each dismount his horse!
Lay down your arms, then flee both rich and poor!"
"Is he too scared to fight?" the French retort;
"We want to fight and he is in default;
Our blows will soon show him he's judged us false!   3135
Tell him we'll stretch his neck if he is caught!"

169

Aumon's envoy returns, God curse the fellow,
And says to Aumon: "For battle, sire, make ready!
The French said this, believe me when I tell you,
They've no intention of laying down their weapons   3140
And no desire to leave--this much they said, sire;
They want to fight and will attack directly;
You'll have to sound your olifant for help now."
Aumon replies, his anger giving vent to:
"Mahom, my god, curse me if I will ever!"   3145
He arms his men and sets up his defences;
Now see the French attack them with a vengeance!
Hark to those bugles as both sides come together

And all around the noise of battle echoes!
If you could see the lusty blows those men gave, 3150
So many shields spliced through and ripped to shreds there,
So many breast-plates shorn and torn past mending,
So many men unhorsed and falling headlong,
So many horses run through the ranks unchecked then!
So many Turks struck down and lying dead there! 3155
Aumon sees this and thinks he'll leave his senses;
He draws his sword, the cherished blade Durendal,
And in high rage strikes huge blows at the Frenchmen;
The man he strikes knows that his life has ended;
'Gainst Durendal vert helms give no protection; 3160
The man he hits knows that all joy has left him;
The ranks all shudder when he rides out and rends them;
Whoever fought and lived through that dread melee,
All of his days henceforth would not forget it.

170

The first assault upon Aumon is manned 3165
By Hugh of Mans, Geoffrey and Anchetin;
Four thousand men each rallies round his flag;
Duke Anchetin spurs his mount down the sand
And strikes the shield out of Pincenart's hand;
This Paynim's king of a strange heathen land 3170
Which knows not cold, nor rain or hail e'er had;
Through arms and armor Anchetin's lance-head rams
And flings him dead neath a tree's overhang;
Huon of Mans for his part strikes Gillefroi,
Aumon's own cousin and just as arrogant; 3175
Hugh's lance cuts through sword-like from front to back
And flings him dead down by a briar-patch;
Brave Geoffrey strikes a Turk from Argenoi,
Who taunts our faith each time his tonsils flap;
Now with his lance good Geoffrey pays him back; 3180
He splits his spleen, his heart and liver cracks
And flings him dead and mute where Aumon stands;
The king sees this and thinks he'll go quite mad;
He lifts up Durendal with its gold sash
And strikes Guion from the valley Harvoi; 3185
He splits his skull and speeds his soul with that,
Then strikes down dead Engerrant of Saucoi,
Guy of Orleans and Gerin and Eloi;
The French see this and fear invades their ranks;
Dismay runs through even their boldest man; 3190
But still they come and keep up their attack;
Behold, my lords, the start of such a clash
Seven thousand men spill all the blood they have!

171

Four barons lead a second wave of troops;
In charge of all is Sanson, mighty duke, 3195
And Frisia's lord the noble Gondelbuef;
See all their flags a-billow neath the blue,
Gold helms so many and shields lion-crested too!
These join the fray swift violence to do;
How many men fell there in their lives' youth! 3200
How many darts, how many arrows flew!
King Gondelbuef to strike King Cardion moves,
Capharnaon in the Far East he rules,
While Duke Sanson one Ostermart pursues;
For all the hurt and harm done by these two 3205
They're lifeless laid straight in their sandy tombs;
If you could see the fighting that ensued,
The hammering on helms of sword-strokes cruel!
Whoever fell to ground bade life adieu.

172

The fighting's fierce, the cries of men are chilling; 3210
There you could see such vicious blows delivered,
Hard helmets halved and shields shorn into splinters
And Saracens so many the hard ground hitting!
Many are dead and therein lies no mystery;
Behold so many struck straight down through the
    middle, 3215
Stretched out in death the bloody landscape littering!
Horses run here and there, their harness slipping;
Yet there remain so many of those Infidels,
Thirty or more there are to every Christian;
If God shows not His power, and very quickly, 3220
Not one of them shall Charles see hence in this world.

173

The shouting's wild and deafening the clamor;
Aumon's flag stands at the base of the valley,
Borne by King Hector, son of the Paynim Lanpal;
How many French are felled around this standard! 3225
But still they come and lock in deadly battle;
And there's Aumon on his ebony stallion,
God curse his soul and send it into blackness,
Holding aloft Durendal, blood-bespattered;
Amidst the press how firmly Aumon stands there 3230
Shattering shields and helmets of enamel,

Breaking those bucklers clean through their
    center panel;
Saddles and stirrups and horses, too, he slashes;
The French curse him and in God's name they damn him.

174

The press is thick, the cries of men are fearsome;   3235
There are so many of those pernicious heathens
Our men are shaken and their heart starts to leave them;
They call on God and Jesus our Redeemer;
With "mea culpas" their souls they pledge to Jesus;
The Paynims yell: "Mahom, Tervagant, keep us!"   3240
Then they close ranks to fight with more cohesion;
If you had tossed your glove their helms o'erreaching,
It would not have come down for one good league's
    length;
See now that Afric gang, as Aumon leads them,
Defend themselves anew with blows so evil   3245
That many a child was orphaned ere that evening!

175

The battle's fierce, the shock of arms is great;
Behold Geoffrey of Paris break through the fray!
He lifts his shield gray-brown and draws his blade,   3250
Then strikes a Paynim, Escrimis was his name,
Who of our men full many has waylaid;
He splits his helm, his forehead and his face
And flings him down at his feet on the plain;
Those Paynims shriek, blood-lusting at his fate;   3255
What use is now a vair or fur-lined cape,
A purple robe or mantle sable-made?
Behold, my lords, as weak men weep and wail
And brave men laugh, grow stronger and more brave!
In whom Lord God a noble heart has placed,   3260
In him may his friends trust and place their faith.

176

The shouting's great and deafening the battle;
Amidst the press behold Huon of Manseau,
His quartered shield held high, his bright blade
    brandished!
In all our ranks there is no knight more handsome;   3265
Not since the time of Abel or of Absalom
Has fairer prince of ours put on a mantle;
He strikes one Rodoant, son of King Cadiel,
Aumon's own cousin, one of his band of bachelors;
He splits his helm, his skull and brains he splatters,   3270

Then one more youth he kills in similar fashion;
The Paynims reel and mighty is the massacre;
Aumon sees this--ask not if he was happy!
When he beholds his men beset so badly,
To Jupiter he swears, alike to Mahom,   3275
That he will make these Christians rue their rashness!
Durendal flies, its razor edges flashing
As in the press he cleaves the French at random;
One's throat he slits, another's face he gashes;
With Durendal he scars full many a vassal;   3280
He gouges them and leaves their bowels hanging;
Through straps and skin their bones he strikes and
     smashes;
No chain-mail coat or helmet can withstand him.

    177

How strong that fight, how full of dread that scene!
See Salemon, a king of high degree!   3285
The seaward land he rules of Britanny;
At Boidant to tilt he turns his steed;
His rod rams home and runs right through the shield;
A whole lance length he flings him on the field;
Five hundred Paynims run up to help their liege;   3290
If you could see our men lay into these!
From what I know you would be brave indeed
If you could watch the sights this fight revealed.

    178

Amidst the press behold a fierce-faced king!
Hector's his name and Aumon's flag is his;   3295
On this same battle's eve he gave it him,
So he's right keen good Christian blood to spill;
See too Richer, who rides with his French kin,
That same brave knight who Carlon's message did,
And now as keen good telling blows to give;   3300
He'd not spare Turks and strikes that way and this
Till he sees Hector lopping French lives and limbs;
He'll hate himself until he pays back this;
He spurs at Hector, who stops not from his kill;
Upon his shield his lance-head lands full tilt   3305
And shatters it, then through the chain-mail rips;
Right through his body Richer's strong lance-head
     drills
And from his saddle-bows the felon's flipped;
Aumon's great flag drops from the dead man's grip;
As Aumon speeds to save the flag and lift,   3310
See Berenger ride up to where he is
With Aliaumes and Driu the Poitevin,

With good Girars, Renier and Thiorin
And men more than four thousand of our French kin;
Aumon retreats, whether or not he will; 3315
Through force of arms the battle-field he quits;
If you had seen those Paynim ranks all wilt
And them all fleeing and taking to the hills!
They all escape to save their Paynim skins
And their four gods they leave like orphaned things; 3320
Aumon himself, when he sees he can't win,
Surveys his loss, then his retreat begins;
Richer gives chase, and stalks him without stint,
Crying this challenge: "Turn back and fight to live!"
The Paynim hears, his heart cut to the quick, 3325
For he would love to do as Richer bids,
Repair his loss and sweet revenge inflict;
But of our men three thousand seek him still;
He's forced to flee and hide in a deep ditch.

179

How strong that fight, how fierce that struggle was! 3330
Behold Richer still spur his mount along;
With hate in heart he still pursues Aumon;
Those Afric troops, to see his great flag drop,
All turn in flight with no more heart to stop;
They leave Tervagant, Apollo and Mahom; 3335
So does Aumon; with three more kings he's off;
Richer gives chase and many follow on;
On each man's lips is just one prayer to God:
"May we catch Aumon and lead him to Carlon!"

180

Aumon rides off despairing and ashamed, 3340
Who thought himself the match of any made;
My lords, pride and ability are vain;
No man though he have both many a day
Won't know an hour when they both slip away;
To that strong tower new-built Aumon escapes, 3345
And when he sees its first drawbridge and gate
It gladdens him more than all of his gains;
Richer, on honor bent, still rides apace,
But when he sees he must give up the chase
He hurls his spear with all the strength he may 3350
To strike Aumon between the shoulder-blades;
He strikes instead Aumon's black destrier;
Through rump then heart the iron rips its way;
Aumon falls off and if Richer makes haste
King Agolant will lose his heir, I'd say. 3355

181

The French have won the first fight of this war;
Those Paynims flee defeated and distraught;
Our thirty thousand hit them with such a force
Those raiders reaped more than they bargained for!
Outside that tower hark to their mighty roar! 3360
Aumon has fallen, you've heard as much my lords;
His burnished helm into the ground has bored;
Those in the tower rushed out when this they saw
And guard him now as their great draw-bridge falls;
They take him in, divest his armor all 3365
And unclasp Durendal, that burnished sword:
"My lord, that was too close to being caught!"
"Indeed," says Aumon, "my gods have played me false;
Afield they lie, all feckless and forlorn;
He is a fool who'd trust in them henceforth; 3370
They have betrayed my troops and our great cause."

182

Our valiant knights, how well they fought for Carlon!
They put to flight Aumon and all his army
And conquered too those gods of theirs: Tervagant,
Great Jupiter, Apollo and proud Mahom, 3375
All four of them with finest gold a-sparkle!
So much red gold and silver's for the asking
Those French will all be richer men thereafter.

183

The French move off, the victors in this melee;
Never before have so few beat so many; 3380
That night they spend in the cold open meadow
And the next day, when dawn's first light is
      spreading,
Carlon arrives, their rightful lord and Emperor;
His ranks join up and cross the ford together;
Hard by a fount beneath a grove o'erspreading 3385
Carlon calls halt and his tent is erected,
And all the rest around him set their tents up.

184

Hard by a fount which from the flow escapes
Carlon makes camp, our Emperor the great;
His thirty marshals erect his tent straightway; 3390
On its gold pole, its top crystal-engraved,
The golden eagle is proudly set in place
And shines all round like a star of the day;

Those paladins, twelve counts of inborn grace,
Those thirty thousand who fought in that first fray, 3395
Ride down the valley with all their booty gained;
They bring back Mahom up on his platform raised,
Beating his flanks and sides with sticks and stakes.

185

Droon the Poitevin rides down the valley
With Thierry and Brittany's King Salemon, 3400
Hoel and Huon, alike Geoffrey the Angevin,
Richer, Elin and Normandy's Duke Anchetin;
Those thirty thousand, all bold unflinching vassals,
Who stormed Aumon and killed so many Saracens,
Ride down before Carlon, noble Pepin's son; 3405
They place before him both Apollo and Mahom,
Those heathen gods, Jupiter and Tervagant:
"Carlon, son of Pepin, you should be happy!
For yestermorn we met Aumon in battle
And fought it out with his ungodly savages; 3410
Thanks be to God, the true Father of Mankind,
We've somewhat clipped the wings of their great
     arrogance;
One hundred thousand Turks have learnt God's value;
They fled from us, their plunder all abandoning;
Had it not been for that tower built by Agolant 3415
You'd have Aumon, here in your tent of samite;
Behold, Carlon, the bread and wine we've captured
And finest gold borne up by thirty pack-mules!
We've brought Mahom and fell Apollo back too."

186

Those twelve counts say: "Rejoice, son of Pepin! 3420
We have just fought with the Emir's proud prince!
Were it not for that tower built on the cliff,
Aumon, Agolant's son, would not now live;
Full thirty mules of gold he thought was his
We've brought you back to use as you see fit; 3425
Their victuals too, their wheat and bread we bring,
And those four gods the Paynims believe in."
Carlon praises the Lord when he hears this:
"Brave men," he says, "I would keep none of it;
Let it be yours to do with as you wish, 3430
Who spilt your blood for it and lost your limbs;
Whatever you conquer will be yours every bit;
Not one glove's worth I'll keep and never will."

187

"Brave men," says Charles, "I bid you keep your
   wealth;
It should be yours since you won it yourselves;   3435
For it was you were maimed for it and bled,
The blows endured for my love and respect;
Not one die's worth do I want or expect;
Buy back your lands with it, you poorer men,
If coming here you lost inheritance;
Using this gold marry your children well;   3440
France will be richer and thus will I myself."

188

A righteous joy fills Charles to his heart's limit
When he beholds those gods the Paynims cling to;
He cries: "Get iron mallets and fetch steel pickets!   3445
Destroy these gods, tear them apart and strip them!"
If you had seen those lads run from the kitchens
All wielding rods and heavy truncheons swinging!
If you had seen the way they struck and split them--
Those idols could not save their tin-pot skins then!   3450
Charles gives this gold to all the barons with him;
He gives an arm to Druon of Berrichon;
King Salemon receives Mahom's left rib-cage
And Anchetin the thigh and waistband with it!
To Berenger the right shoulder is given;   3455
But Mahom's head is given to brave Richer,
Who felled the flag and paved the way for victory,
Then chased Aumon and tried so hard to kill him;
Thus those tin gods are tortured and distributed
And insult added to haughty Aumon's injury;   3460
Now Carlon's army has plenty of provisions;
One denier buys four loaves, so much food is there,
And just one loaf will serve two knights for dinner;
For one whole ox two sous are quite sufficient;
There is no horse, however he so thin and piteous   3465
That one denier of barley now won't fill up;
The Saracens meanwhile have naught to nibble;
Blackmarketeers can ask whatever they wish to;
For just one loaf are fifteen bezants bidden;
Alike ten sous for leg of lamb are given;   3470
They wait on Aumon to bring them some deliverance
With all the meat he promised he would bring them;
Let them enjoy all that he takes back thither!
No Paynim mouths shall he feed with his pillage--
That food's in big Bavarian throats this minute!   3475
Now, lords, I'll leave awhile Carlon fierce-visaged
And tell you more of Burgundy's Duke Girart,

Who set out from Vienne with all his kinsmen;
Some sixty thousand my lord Girart leads hither,
Many on horseback and all with new equipment; 3480
His flag is borne by Ernault and Renier
And Beuvon and Claron, the sons of Milon,
In company with twelve counts of his kingdom,
Who for their land to Girart are submissive
And fight for him when he needs their assistance; 3485
Like a true prince he speaks and they all listen:
"Brave men," he says, "let all your thoughts be this one:
How may we climb fell Aspremont the quickest?
If Carlon's there already we are all villains!
Now is the hour to seek your honor's increase!" 3490

189

White-haired Girart spurs his horse on and on,
Leading his men some sixty thousand strong;
So hard he rides and journeys for so long
He and his troops move up fell Aspremont
One league away, or so the geste allots, 3495
From that great tower built there by Agolant;
Girart that night makes camp upon this spot,
Refusing fiercely to make camp further off;
Aumon sees this and he is filled with wrath;
He orders rear-guard troops to move across, 3500
And many come replacing those he lost;
He'll fight Girart come day, he swears Mahom:
"I will surprise my father," pledges Aumon.

190

Aumon rides out with many of the enemy;
No better man than he would have lived ever, 3505
Had he believed in the One God of Heaven;
He and his men ride out with fierce intention,
For Aumon's thoughts are set on awful vengeance;
But old Girart is quick to stir himself too;
He calls on Claron and on Beuvon together 3510
And quickly summons his sons Renier and Ernault
And says to them: "Now listen, sons and nephews!
Here comes Aumon, for so my judgement reckons;
I want you four to ride out before any
With a small group, four thousand of our best ones; 3515
I want to see how you make out against them
And how I should deploy the others henceforth."
Those four reply: "We'll do whatever you tell us!"
Then they leave camp in rich armor resplendent;
If you could see the rich armor those men had 3520

As they rode hard in fell Aumon's direction!
If you could hear the noise when they met head-on
Of shattered shields and heathen sinews severed!
With arrow-shafts the sky above was heavy.

191

Great is the clash, the clamor and the struggle; 3525
Especially fierce the charge of the Burgundians;
See Claron now, spurring before the others,
His lance full-tilt, his flag unfurled and fluttering!
He strikes Malpriant, advisor to Aumon he,
Rips his chail-mail, his liver and his lungs too 3530
And flings him dead down in the dirt and dust there;
See Beuvon next charge Margon at the double!
His chain-mail rips--it gave him little cover;
His guts are churned from his heart to his stomach;
Ernault strikes next a king, Escorpion he, 3535
An Afric prince, a man whose wealth is wondrous;
He flings him dead--what help to him was money?
Renier attacks a Turk called Matefelun;
Prince Aumon's seneschal this fellow once was;
He runs him through amidst the cut and thrust there: 3540
"God!" says Girart, "What a good boy I've nourished!"

192

As Girart sees the progress of the fray
He calls on one Anseis Fauqueblé:
"Do you know what I'm thinking?" old Girart says;
"Although I have outlived my useful age,
To see these boys of mine I'm young again;
These lovely lads I've nurtured and kept safe;
Let's help them now for sweet charity's sake!"
Thus Girart speaks and scarcely this speech made,
Hark to Aumon yell out in his heart's rage: 3550
"What are you at, you Slav and Saracen race?
Avenge your gods which are stolen away!"
Those Paynims surge and Girart's boys give way,
With those five thousand men in their charge placed;
Back to Girart they ride without delay; 3555
When Girart sees how they have run away
He shouts at Claron these words of taunt and blame:
"Nephew of mine, now you show your true face!
In looks you may among God's fairest rate,
But it is not God's wish that you display 3560
An inward strength to match your outward grace!
You peasant boy! You coward-proven knave!
You are no son of Count Milon the brave;
How badly you have taken my place today!

Since the first time I ever drew my blade 3565
I never fled from any fight engaged;
Though all about me fled I always stayed."
As thus he speaks Girart is so enraged
He throws a spur, at Claron's visage aimed;
The lad ducks this, but he is struck by shame; 3570
His wounded pride then sets his heart aflame;
He says to Beuvon: "He's right, in good God's name!
In that first fight our cowardice was great;
May God curse us if we should flee again!"
They charge once more, their battle-cry upraised. 3575

193

The clash is loud and deafening the clamor;
Girart is old but still brimful of valor,
A fearsome fighter and skilled in warfare's tactics;
Without delay he lifts his battle-standard
And he and all his men plunge into battle; 3580
If you had heard those cries of taunt and anguish,
Seen helmets crushed and floral bucklers shattered!
See Girart now a Paynim king attacking,
From India he, king of Kashmir I fancy!
Girart's lance rips his good chain-mail to tatters 3585
And flings him dead between five hundred vassals;
Girart cries out "Eufrates!" like a fanfare:
"Strike on, my lords, gain honor in this action
While Charlemayn, king of the Franks, is absent!
Once he arrives all of our fame will vanish; 3590
If we can breach and break the Paynim ranks here
And place ourselves between them and their battlements,
They'll have no safe retreat and then they'll scatter."

194

Girart d'Eufrate is a valiant campaigner,
More skilled in tactics than any man created; 3595
What he does now completely tricks those Paynims;
He rides up close to Aumon's tower and stays there, 3596[b]
Hid in a valley with seven thousand brave men;
So, suddenly, between themselves and safety
Those heathens hear the mighty roar "Eufrates!"
If Aumon wants to rest his bones there later 3600
A mighty hostile seneschal awaits him!

195

Girart knows well how to outwit an enemy;
What he does next completely fools those felons;
He moves straightway to where proud Aumon's tent is

And with his men hacks it to ground and shreds it; 3605
He shows no mercy to any of its sentries,
He kills them all, in his proud rage relentless;
Towards the tower Girart's men run unchecked then;
They storm and take it and Girart hoists his pennant;
It is his father King Beuvon's ancient ensign; 3610
A flag of gold, like coals it flames to heaven;
Aumon beholds it and his heart starts to tremble;
He points it out to King Angalion next to him:
"For love of Mahom, look over there!" he beckons;
"We've lost our tower, our stronghold and protection; 3615
Behold that flag that flies above the rest there!
It is not one of ours, that I can tell you;
The tower it tops we nevermore shall enter."

196

When Aumon sees old Girart's burnished banner
Blazing like flame atop his tower's rampart, 3620
He knows it's lost and will not be recaptured;
He looks about him and sees all his men scattering;
With hate in heart he grips Durendal's handle
And strikes a Frank and splits him in his anger;
Then on he stalks, killing Bernart and Asselin; 3625
On our French youth Aumon wreaks awful havoc;
Renier sees him, a young and sturdy vassal;
Should he not seek him out and offer challenge
Girart his father will set at naught his valor.

197

Renier de Genvenes, brave son of a brave forebear, 3630
When he sees Aumon dealing our men such slaughter,
Seeks swift revenge, and spurs his war-horse forward;
He swings his blade and strikes a blow so forceful
It rips right through the mail on Aumon's hauberk;
On his left side a telling blow he scores there; 3635
Vermilion blood from a deep wound goes pouring,
But Aumon lives, nor does the blow unhorse him;
He turns about, his face with rage contorted,
And holds Durendal high, at Renier pointed;
On his gold helm a lethal blow he launches; 3640
Good Renier swerves, but the blow strikes his
    war-horse;
Its head is severed and on the grass goes falling;
With Renier down another blow employed then
Would have made both Aude and Olivier* orphans.

* Roland's betrothed and closest companion in the
Chanson de Roland.

198

In wondrous wise is Aumon proud and fell; 3645
He wants naught else but to see Renier dead;
But up rides Claron and Beuvon red of head,
Girart and Gui and noble-born Antelme
Together with more than seventy men;
They rescue Renier, but it takes all of them, 3650
For Aumon has great courage and great strength;
He's fierce and fearless and an expert in death;
He swings and swings Durendal razor-edged,
Which cuts through iron like a knife cuts bare flesh;
He ends the lives of many of our French. 3655

199

Aumon knows well that his life is in peril;
He's lost this fight and many of his fellows;
In swift escape a steep slope he descends now
With all the Turks that this defeat has left him;
He sheathes sharp Durendal, its blade blood-reddened, 3660
Cursing Mahom and Tervagant together;
He does not deign to blow his horn for rescue,
Though Agolant would come straightway to help him.

200

Aumon escapes, his heart both sad and angry;
Red-haired Girart returns now to his camp-site; 3665
He and his men have fared well in this battle,
Booty have gained more than enough to carry;
Aumon has nothing save a heart full of sadness;
Of seven kings two lie dead in that valley;
Of Paynims killed no one could tell the tally; 3670
Those who are left now beat their breasts in
    anguish,
Beseeching Aumon: "My lord, what's now to happen?"
Aumon retorts: "You wretched, irksome rabble!
Where are they now, those feckless, fawning
    flatterers,
Who back at home in my palace in Africa 3675
Swore they would hand me France upon a platter,
While in my rooms they sported in sweet dalliance
With my young maidens so yielding and attractive,
Who gave them lovers' kisses for all their valor?
You had no doubts when my best wine you drank then! 3680
Then you were heroes who soon all France would
    vanquish!
Cities and towns would crumble to your challenge!
Now you're surprised the French don't run in panic

But strike you hard with lances and attack you;
I was a fool to fall for your wild bragging; 3685
On your advice I set out on this action;
Now all my life I'll never more be happy."
Proud Aumon weeps for misery so matchless.

201

Aumon escapes who's lost and suffered much:
"Alas," he cries, "my happy days are done!" 3690
He calls to him both Barré and Butrun,
Salmaquin and his nephew one Lauridan:
"Go to our army, but not to Agolant,
And from me tell my seneschal Gorhan
To come and help me with his father Balan, 3695
Triamodes and good King Esperrant,
Brave King Cador and noble Moysant,
Salatiel and valiant Boldant;
My heart, tell them, weeps like the canker's pus;
For I have lost Mahom and Tervagant. 3700

202

"Do not delay this message to impart it!
Make haste and ride to these heads of our army
And tell them all of my shameful disaster!
For I have lost both Mahom and Tervagant,
And lost my tower with all it had well-guarded, 3705
And lost the lives of those I was in charge of;
I need their help, tell them, and need it fast too!
But tell them too, and say that I command them,
Not to inform King Agolant my father."
His men there say: "We shall do as you ask us." 3710

203

Those envoys four swing straight astride their horses;
They gallop hard, up hills, down slopes and forwards
Until they reach the Saracen headquarters
Where they dismount outside the tent of Gorhan;
Pagandom's leaders they find assembled, talking, 3715
Who ask straightway for news of noble Aumon:
Has he left yet and come down from his fortress?
Behold their shock when told of Aumon's torment,
How first Aumon was toppled from his war-horse,
Then almost drowned escaping through swift waters; 3720
How he has lost the mighty tower and fortress
And in the fighting his Paynims were all slaughtered:
"He seeks your help--he has no other choice now;
But tell his father nothing, this he implores you;

Pagandom's gods have been reviled and tortured; 3725
This is no lie, the Franks with great rejoicing
Dragged them down Aspremont amidst foul taunting;
Proud Aumon weeps as never before we saw him."
When they hear this those Paynim chiefs start roaring;
Their robes of taffeta they rip and claw at: 3730
"Shall we stand here and grieve," Gorhan exhorts them,
"While the best knight in Pagandom calls for us?
No better lancer lives! Come, let us all go!"
The army stirs as this news spreads abroad now;
The camp resounds with four thousand brass cornets 3735
As news of Aumon's plight and plea are broadcast;
Those Turks camped high and low prepare for warfare,
Stock up their weapons with sticks and stones assorted,
Bring out their bucklers and don their helms and hauberks;
Behold those rows of saddled horses snorting 3740
As they leave camp those savage souls supporting!
Five hundred thousand heathens are on horseback.

204

The Paynims leave and from their tents go forth;
Five hundred thousand Turks are armed for war;
They ride in ranks yet make great speed withal; 3745
Balan the king himself leads a small force
Of sixty thousand who scout well to the fore,
All valiant men prepared to fight and fall;
May God help Carlon and his brave barons all--
This day will see a fearsome battle fought! 3750
Balan the king looks up towards his corps,
But, heard by none, speaks quietly his thoughts:
"God, giver of my life," thus he exhorts,
"As You in truth are Heaven's One True Lord,
Who dwell on High in Trinity adored, 3755
By Your good Grace this favor I implore:
Let not the soul from my body be shorn
Ere I have been baptized and thus reborn."

205

Triamodes leads out the next contingent;
Paynims so many ride forth in phalanx with him, 3760
Some sixty thousand of the Devil's religion;
This group stands out by its superb equipment;
So many helms and breast-plates all a-glinting
And golden flags in the breeze all a-billow!
Triamodes speaks loudly and they listen: 3765

"Now is your hour, my worthy Paynim kinsmen!
Let us avenge Tervagant and Mahom swiftly,
Whom Charlemayn has dragged away and pillaged!
Your bloods should boil in anger at this insult!"
They all respond: "We will do as you bid us;　　　　3770
If you can lead the way so far and bring us
To where the Franks are at this moment hidden,
None shall escape, the great ones nor the little!
Carlon himself, the mercenary villain,
We'll drag in chains over every hump and hillock!"　3775

206

Boidant leads the mighty third battalion,
And at his side the fearsome King Salatiel;
Men sixty thousand ride with them ripe for action;
So many helms inset with stones are flashing,
So many spears there are with pennants flapping!　　3780
From burnished helms there issues such a dazzle
The ground's aglow and so is all the landscape;
Both these kings swear, themselves ablaze with anger,
That should they meet with Charlemayn in battle
They'll drag him back down Aspremont in shackles!　3785

207

The fourth battalion's led by King Cador
And Amandras the king of Tintagor,
An eerie land where daylight never dawns,
And King Lanpal, the father of Hector;
In this division are all Persians and Moors,　　　　3790
All Agolafrians and Luicianors;
Men sixty thousand make up the leading corps;
So many bay and sorrel steeds of war
They sit astride, and as they ride they taunt
That they'll hang Charles upon a sycamore　　　　　3795
And violate and mutilate his corpse.

208

Two royals lead the mighty fifth battalion:
Emir Butran and Rodoan, son of Cadiel;
This fearsome force boasts sixty thousand vassals;
If you could see those fiends astride their stallions, 3800
Their many shields and helmets crystal-patterned,
Their many flags of pure silk and of taffeta!
Carlon the great they threaten from their saddles:
His birthright France they'll take from him in capture.

209

Two fearsome fighters the rearguard ranks dictate; 3805
Kings Esperrant and Amargon are they;
Both ruthless men, both filled with pride and hate,
Their ranks are stocked with sixty thousand knaves;
Thick padded jerkins their carcasses keep safe
As their rich helms reflect the sunlight's rays; 3810
Full many a lance and pennant they display,
Full many a spear and many a leaden mace;
These two kings bear proud Aumon's flag this day;
Lords, see them now its pole of gold upraise,
An image of Mahom atop it placed! 3815
By trickery, in some deceptive way
They make it talk and loudly now it brays:
"Ride on, ride on good knights and barons brave!
Great Charlemayn shall soon be put in chains!
At Saint Denis Aumon shall take his place!" 3820

210

They ride and ride those ranks in haste until
They meet Aumon, whose heart with sorrow fills,
Whose breast with shame and anger trembles still;
When he sees them, his princes and his kings,
He weeps unchecked and greets each with a kiss 3825
And tells them all the evils and the ills
Those Burgundians of ours and Frenchmen did;
How twice in battle they have defeated him,
His plunder robbed and all his Paynims killed:
"I've lost my wealth and tower atop the hill; 3830
Now Charlemayn can pass this way at will!"
His Paynims say: "Sorrow no more at this!
All you once had we shall retrieve forthwith."

211

Aumon sighs hard, whose heart in anguish beats;
His kings and princes now all about him heed 3835
His loud complaint: "My lords, how great my grief!
The other day we went to plunder wheat;
I've lost my tower and lost our gods all three!
One hundred thousand men rode out with me,
Bearing our gods right gladly and with glee; 3840
We found much food, more than I've ever seen;
Then thirty thousand Franks of France appeared;
Of Carlon's van the hand-picked best were these,
Who fell on us with great force and great speed;
We were surprised and could not hold the field; 3845
One knight they killed was Hector my first Peer;

So many died for whom my heart now grieves!
Although I fled I'll never escape this deed!
With wrath and rage my breast so brutal heaves
It will no more bear flower or leaf carefree,   3850
Or nurture words fit for a lover's ear;
No more shall I the lay or harpist hear,
Nor hunt with hawk and dog at my heart's ease."
"Do not despair!" those Paynims all repeat;
"Tomorrow, Aumon, even while you still sleep,   3855
We shall have Charles a-trembling in his fear;
He shall be stripped of all his towns and fiefs!"

212

"Lords," says Aumon, "I raged with anger wild
To see our gods knocked down and so reviled;
But those fell French pursued me with such spite   3860
That in a ditch I dived to save my life;
Why did I never heed my father's advice,
Who told me once to cultivate the wise,
To love the worthy and cherish the upright?
I've bred instead so many craven liars   3865
That my own name and fame have now declined;
But should I ever return to my Empire
I shall destroy them and shame all of their kind,
Or exile them until the day they die."

213

Thus Aumon talks and leads these reinforcements   3870
To half a league from where Girart is quartered;
Girart's own troops can hear the raucous war-cries
Those Paynims yell as their horns urge them forward;
The news of this to Girart is reported:
"My lord Girart, fierce valiant-visaged war-lord,   3875
Aumon returns with so many fresh forces
No man alive could reckon or record them;
For two full leagues the land with them is crawling;
They're everywhere, behind us and before us;
Hark to their shouts! How loudly now they taunt us!   3880
One thing is certain, we'll all be dead come morning;
In truth, my lord, their ranks are so enormous,
If all our men were meat well-cooked and salted,
They'd slice us up and eat us in one course, sire!"
Thus Girart answers: "Be not afraid for all that!   3885
Free men of mine, your fate stands waiting for you;
God has unlocked His paradise's portals
And from His joyful throne He gently calls you;
We have all come to the day we were born for;
Those whom with death the Lord today rewards here   3890

Should bless the hour their mother's womb first bore them!
And he who lives--that man has my assurance
He will receive so much of my own fortune
The like of which he never saw or thought to;
If it's God's will that we survive this slaughter, 3895
My riches and my rooms will all be yours, men;
My maidens too, all noble-blooded daughters,
Will be all yours to love and take your choice of
And marry, should you wish, with my accordance,
With each a dowry befitting their importance." 3900
His men hear this and bow deeply before him:
"My lord Girart, all who stand here are loyal;
We will defend you and with our swords fight for you!"
Without delay they don their helms and hauberks;
Behold their shields, wheel-patterns all adorning, 3905
Lances so many, bold flapping flags supporting,
The brick-sheened rumps of so many war-horses!
Old Duke Girart now calls his ranks to order;
Down in a dale they wait for mighty Aumon.

214

Girart d'Eufrate is a very brave man, 3910
Too proud to fear the Saracen attack;
He calls to rank all his Burgundian band
And hoists the Saint Maurice, his household flag,
Which his men know, when he flies it like that,
Means he will fight and not take one step back; 3915
But I must back to Charles, King of the Franks;
A better Prince than he no land e'er had;
No braver King than he e'er governed land;
Behold him now as he lines up his ranks!
Men sixty thousand he places in his van, 3920
Led by Ogier and Naimes at his right hand:
"Advance with God!" says the son of Pepin;
"And if your force must fight the Saracens
I shall bring aid as quickly as I can."

215

Behold, my lords, great Carlon's noble vanguard, 3925
Full sixty thousand, the flower of France's manhood!
Duke Naimes was there, alike Ogier and Salemon
And Thiorin and the seneschal Fagon;
Twelve dukes were there, this is a fact established;
See if you can the many waving banners 3930
And noble armor of all our noble barons!
Across the plains they ride now at a gallop
Till Girart's force they spy in rank on Aspremont

As he prepares to meet Aumon in battle;
So many flags they see and helmets flashing 3935
That Carlon's men are sure it is the Saracens:
"Men, we must fight," they say, "so let us gladly!"
Some cautious say: "Send first for Charlemagne!
He is our liege and we are all his vassals."
"So be it then, my lords", King Salemon sanctions. 3940

216

"Richer, you go!" King Salemon requests him;
"I know of none whom Carlon more does cherish;
Tell Charlemayn to hurry now and help us;
Tell him it's time to join his ranks together;
Aumon the proud, the fierce, is here assembled 3945
To fight him now if his resolve is ready."
Richer responds: "I would not be so wretched!
I'll never take such a cowardly message
And lose my soul for my body's protection;
My self-esteem and honor would be ended; 3950
Tonight I'll lodge with all God's Saints in Heaven;
Your message needs another's lips to tell it."

217

King Salemon then calls on Amauri,
A count of Berry, a knight of high degree:
"Brave knight, you go!" King Salemon repeats: 3955
"Aumon, tell him, to us is come so near
That all his host in fearsome phalanx here
Is spread across Mount Bitter from reach to reach."
Says Amauri: "I would not be so weak!
On flowers in Paradise tonight I'll sleep 3960
With all God's Saints to keep me company;
Whoever goes Amauri will stop here."

218

King Salemon calls on Godefroi, entreating:
"Count of Boulogne, you are brave and esteemed such;
Will you then go to Charles our King and liege-lord 3965
With news of Aumon and how many his heathens?
Tell Carlon and his troops his vanguard needs him!"
Godefroi retorts: "In faith, I'll not go either!
While I've good arms and a good horse beneath me
Why would I not strike mighty blows for Jesus 3970
And pay to God the debt of all believers?
Body and soul I'll give Him here quite freely,
Prepared to die for Him as He for me did;
If you so fret to save your mortal being

Then go yourself, since you appear so fearful!" 3975

219

King Salemon again turns and requests
The lord of Tours, the worthy Duke Antelme:
"You go to Charles," he says, "and get us help!"
But Antelme says: "Your fear makes you forget;
Our fiefs and fortunes are nothing in themselves; 3980
We are God's vassals and serve as He sees best;
If you so fret to save yourself from death
You go to Charles, who seem so scared yourself."
Then Turpin speaks: "My lords, this feud must end;
I'll gladly go for all of you," he says. 3985

220

Archbishop Turpin brings wisely to a finish
The quarreling about Carlon's assistance;
He goes himself, spurring his war-horse quickly
Without a pause down valleys and up hillsides
Until he comes to Charlemayn's pavilion; 3990
He finds Carlon on Aragon silk sitting,
His gonfanon atop his lance-head clipping;
Turpin speaks out before Charles even bids him:
"God bless King Charles, Defender of the Christians!"
"And God bless you and pardon you Archbishop! 3995
You are no friend to that horse you've just ridden!
Behold its flanks with blood all freely dripping!
What news of my good barons, friend, do you bring me,
And my brave vanguard--tell me, how goes it with
    them?"
"We have seen Aumon," says the Archbishop swiftly, 4000
"And in his ranks a mighty horde of Infidels;
Their flags flap high on Aspremont this minute;
Your fight is near, the truth cannot be hidden."
"Praise God," says Charles, "and pray God we shall
    win it!
For they would take what God Himself has given; 4005
Upon my soul we shall avenge this insult;
Good glorious God, I pray You be my witness:
No one but I shall rule in my own kingdom!
Now let the sounds of my big brass horns ring out
The call to arms! Our battle is beginning!" 4010

PART 5

221

Carlon calls all his men to arms at once;

Behold that camp with action all a-buzz,
Four thousand trumpets urging on everyone!
Behold those byrnies, the buttoning up of studs,
And those green helms, their visors snapping shut,   4015
And those good blades laced on by valiant-bloods
And steeds so many all swiftly saddled up
As hastily Carlon's command is done!
The constables form ranks as up they come
And Charlemayn into his saddle jumps;   4020
His battle-flag he gives to a duke's son
And his whole army to his marshal entrusts:
"Behold all these rich ranks!" declares Carlun;
"No King of France ever assembled such;
Safeguard henceforth my Oriflamme, Fagon!"   4025
Charles hands it over and weeps a tear for love;
Fagon replies: "You have honored me much;
I'll guard it well, with the help of Jesus."

222

Carlon rides out, our great and mighty Emperor,
With all the lords of his own land together   4030
With all those of Touraine and all the Bretons,
Counts from Le Maine, the Normans and the Flemish,
Lords from Lorraine and all the German Empire,
One hundred thousand beneath one great green ensign;
So far they ride the steep slopes and the levels   4035
Till they join Salemon and reassemble.

223

Carlon rides out, our Emperor the mighty,
And at his side full many a valiant fighter;
This is the day to fight, he has decided;
With good Ogier his bravest knight beside him,   4040
And good Duke Naimes, his closest friend and wisest,
And four full counts an entourage providing,
Carlon rode out and Aumon's tower he sighted;
Atop its walls, where they are built the highest,
He sees the flag, the Saint Maurice a-flying;   4045
And Girart's men he sees attacking wildly
The Paynim breed both head-on and behind them;
But his heart chills! He does not recognize them!
"My lords," he says, "we cannot change our minds now;
I see the Turks--behold their ranks arriving!"   4050

224

Carlon calls Naimes and Ogier to his side,
And Dukes Flavent and Berenger alike:

"The Turks are here, this cannot be denied;
I knew Aumon would seek me out betimes,
For his lost gods a swift revenge to find; 4055
I see them now, his men, on yonder rise;
Ride out to them, my noble knights and fine,
And ask Aumon how he desires to fight!"
If you had seen the zeal of their reply,
How their stout shields they snatched and lifted high! 4060
Girart it is who first sees them arrive;
To Ernault and Renier, his sons, he cries,
To Beuvon and Claron the sons of Miles:
"My lovely boys," he says, "the time is ripe
For you to keep your faith with God on High! 4065
If you can now unhorse this band of knights,
Your worth will grow in wondrous wise thereby."
All four respond:"We are prepared to try!"

225

Those four ride out with their rich armor on,
Their spears held straight and pennants borne aloft; 4070
Ogier it is who first selects Claron;
One longbow's range each from his friends is gone
Towards the other, both charging now non-stop;
Ogier strikes first and Claron feels the shock;
His shield is split beneath its silver boss 4075
As the lance breaks, the splinters flying off;
Claron in turn strikes his shield near the top,
And splits it clean and cleaves it in his wrath;
The blow stops there for the hauberk is strong;
His lance is stout, his horse quick to respond; 4080
Claron turns round, his stout lance raised aloft;
To say he was unhorsed would be quite wrong,
But in this fight it was brave Ogier's lot
That his horse slipped--the Dane could help it not;
He and his horse hit hard on Aspremont; 4085
Beuvon, meanwhile, strikes noble Count Flavent
And Flavent him in rapid-raged response;
Both men are felled by blows given and got;
Beuvon it is first gains his footing lost;
He grasps his sword and grips his buckler's thongs; 4090
The silver helm he strikes of Count Flavent
And splits it through, so viciously he chops;
So foul a wound his visage took therefrom
That never again could he put helmet on;
What hate henceforth that bitter blow would prompt: 4095
It caused the death, in time, of Duke Beuvon;
How all of France bewailed hence such a loss,
And women wept all of the land across!

226

Naimes drives his steed, and so does Berenger,
One at Ernault, the other at Renier; 4100
These two likewise bear in, their lances raised;
As all collide they're flung down on the plain;
Behold them now, Claron facing Ogier,
Both Berenger and Ernault face to face,
And young Renier opposing good Duke Naimes! 4105
If you could see the blows they strike straightway!
Before they stop a mortal price they'll pay.

227

If you had been down in that field neath Aspremont,
Hard by that tower from haughty Aumon captured,
You would have heard some shout: "Mountjoy,
    Charlemagne!" 4110
And others yell brave Girart's cry of battle,
And Ogier calling: What is your name, strong vassal?"
And him reply: "I'm Duke Milon's son, Claron;
My uncle is Girart d'Eufrate the baron;
To serve Lord God within this land we've travelled; 4115
And what is your name? Tell me, for I would have it."
"I am Ogier from Charlemagne's palace;
He's reared me from a child to be his champion."
Claron hears this and bows in courtly fashion.

228

Duke Naimes speaks next: "What is your name, sir
    knight?" 4120
"I'm Girart's son, young Renier, sir, am I;
We've travelled here to fight for Jesus Christ;
Behold Girart himself on yonder rise!
He waits for Aumon and all his heathen kind,
Horde upon horde, born of the Devil's line; 4125
No man there is who would not fear their size."
Hear Naimon now: "Praise be to God on High!
How much we need the help you can provide!"
See them all run and kiss, once recognized!

229

In that deep dale fell Aspremont beneath, 4130
As those brave knights identify them each,
Carlon himself rides down, spurring his steed,
And old Girart the other side appears;
What mighty joy there was then to be seen

As each to each rode forward and drew near! 4135

230

When Girart sees Carlon, son of Pepin,
In gold spurs shod and clad all in striped silk,
With a blue Eastern cloak down to his hips,
And on his head a hood of sable trim,
He seems to Girart to be a true-born Prince, 4140
And he repents that he once doubted it.

231

Girart rides up to Charlemayn and then
Pepin's son puts his arms round Girart's neck
And they embrace in friendship and respect;
As Charlemayn then lifts his head erect 4145
His sable hood slips down and off his head;
Girart stoops down and picks it up himself,
Then hands it back and bows in deference.

232

Turpin, this day, beside Carlon is standing;
When he recalls his cousin Girart's action 4150
That day he aimed his sharp steel dagger at him
Back in Vienne, high in his marble palace,
When Turpin came with Carlon's plea and mandate
And Girart would have killed good Turpin gladly,
He takes out now his pen and ink from saddle 4155
To write it down upon parchment in Latin
How Lord Girart made his way down a valley
To meet with Charles and greet him as his vassal;
How he picked up his hood and gave it back to him;
How Charles at last got homage from this baron, 4160
Girart at last defering to Charlemagne;
Thus people say: Good neighbors make strong allies,
But ill-willed ones can give you quite a battle!

233

When Girart and Carlon have made their peace,
All of their knights in joy raise a great cheer; 4165
Then Girart says: "My lord, ride with all speed
To my Burgundian troops camped in the field,
Some sixty thousand with good armor and steeds;
Well should your ranks be reinforced with these."
"Girart," says Charles, "you have my thanks indeed!" 4170

234

Girart, whose fiery locks are grayed with age,
Speaks on and says: "My lord, do not delay!
I have already sent Aumon on his way:
I've won his tower, which was his one safe place;
Let us pass there since I have made it safe; 4175
He will return--let us not be too late."
Carlon responds: "First listen to me, pray,
For I must speak my mind and make it plain!
We are all here from many lands and states;
Though you may not be here just for my sake, 4180
You have come here, like us, in Lord God's name;
Take no offence then, Girart, when I say
You must be ruled by me in this campaign,
Until at least sweet Christendom is saved."
Girart replies, who no ill-will betrays: 4185
"I, for my part, agree and will obey;
When you return to France and royal Aix
And I am back in my birthplace again,
Let my deeds here our future terms dictate."
Charles thanks Girart for this compliance made, 4190
Then he dismounts beneath the leafy shade
And with all speed gets ready for the fray;
He dons a hauberk which was King Macabré's,
Whom Charles defeated at Tortolose in Spain;
Its mail is triple-strength, fine steel its chain, 4195
Through which no dart or sword can penetrate;
Pure silver polished is each link of chain-mail,
With ruff and cuffs in gold of purest make;
Now on his head his noble helm is placed,
With precious stones of such strength all inlayed 4200
The strongest blow of strongest arm they'll take;
Who wears this helm when war is waged in hate
Need never fear that death his life awaits;
Then on his left he girds Joyeuse his blade,
Whose golden hilt with pictures is engraved 4205
Of Saint Denis and of Saint Honoré;
Who holds this sword need never be afraid
Of any mortal wound, poison or pain;
Those squires bring next the shield of Charlemayn:
Its straps are rich embroidered silk brocade 4210
And all its boards are banded with gold paint;
About his neck Carlon sets it in place;
Then they lead out that same white destrier
Which Balan gave before to good Duke Naimes;
How richly saddled up it is this day! 4215
Of melted gold all lacquered are the reins
And coated gold reflects from its breast-plate;
The plate is hunt with little shells ornate

Which, when it moves, with every step its takes,
As they resound such lovely music make 4220
That lute or harp could never imitate;
The horse is clad in iron from head to tail;
Protected thus and fitted out this way
They lead it out to mighty Charlemayn;
He mounts the stirrups of nielloed inlay; 4225
Five mighty dukes stoop down to hold them straight;
They bring him then his battle-spear in haste,
Made out of ashwood, steel-tipped and metal-cased,
With pennant proud clipped on by three gold nails;
Behold our King so richly thus arrayed, 4230
Like an avenging Angel from Heaven's gates!
Carlon is big, well-built and sturdy-framed;
He bears his shield with such an easy grace
It seems to all to be his natural state;
Charles is no knight dressed up for mere display! 4235
His lords in awe look on him now and gaze;
Hear Girart call Anseis Fauqueblé,
His son Ernault and his brother Malré
And all the barons that serve him and obey:
"My lords, behold!" Girart d'Eufrate exclaims; 4240
"This man is more than leader of his race;
He is the great Defender of our Faith!"
. Then Carlon calls on old Girart d'Eufrate,
Who turns his mount and spurs to him apace:
"Thanks be to God, Girart, good shall prevail! 4245
King Agolant has entered my domain,
Destroyed my towns and to my land laid waste;
Now I'm on horse I will not hesitate,
My crown of peace for warring helm exchanged!
If his assault my vengeance should escape 4250
I would deserve derision and disgrace."
"This cannot be denied!" Girart maintains.

235

"True Emperor," he says, "give ear to me!
Aumon the fell, who much is to be feared,
With countless Turks comes ever closer here! 4255
They'll fill this land as far as eye can see;
Behold them Charles, descending yonder peak!
We must act now with wisdom and with speed,
Lest we be caught or forced to flee this field;
Command your van to leave immediately 4260
In serried ranks to fight the Paynim breed!
All of our troops will back them up in brief;
Myself, I'll go to fill my men with zeal,
Then through this vale the lot of them I'll lead,
Outflank these felons and strike them from the rear; 4265

If from two sides our war-cries greet their ears
They'll be uncertain and their fear will increase;
Thus we'll improve our chance of victory;
He who can meet this day's demands with zeal
Will hold till death the memory of it dear." 4270
Then the Pope says: "My lords, now let me speak!
The Turks are here to deal our cause defeat:
I have scant time to sermonize or preach;
God came to Earth, you know, to save us each;
And lived with us for thirty years and three, 4275
And was baptized to live eternally;
This is the Law that He would have us heed,
For He has made two worlds for such as we:
The first is Earth, where mortally we breathe,
The second Heaven, which is so pure and clear 4280
No mortal soul may know how it appears,
Nor any man its wondrous form conceive;
And now these Turks have come across the sea
To fling us all out of our lands and fiefs
And torture us as if we were the thieves! 4285
They'll lock us up in such a dungeon deep
The Lord God's Word will never reach our ears;
This will all happen if they defeat us here;
No preacher hence shall Mass or Matins read;
Consider then a while what Lord God means, 4290
Who died for us upon the Cross's beams,
Who in four places let his body be pierced,
Then took a fifth from the centurion's spear;
The Light of God that Roman could not see
Till blood and water had wiped his blindness clean 4295
And his eyes shone with God's New Light revealed;
He begged forgiveness and instantly received,
As God forgives all those who do believe;
If you would share that soldier's soul's reprieve,
Show your good faith by striking blows of steel! 4300
Slay all these Paynims! Slaughter these heathen beasts!"

The Pope continues: "I would say this besides:
I am a man who does not deal in lies;
He who goes now against this foe to fight
And for God's sake should lose his mortal life, 4305
God waits for him already in Paradise
With crowns and laurels for the soldiers of Christ;
He shall sit us at His own right—hand side;
Without confession, all the sins of your lives
On God's behalf I now collect and shrive; 4310
Your penance is to fight with all your might!"
"My lords," says Charles, "we stay too long a time;

Behold the Paynims approaching us meanwhile!"

237

Carlon urges them on: "Make haste, my barons!
The Paynim ranks are here and soon will trap us;   4315
Collect your men and make up each battalion;
Form up each rank in order of attacking!"
His barons move, spurred now into swift action;
Seven thousand men are brought into the vanguard,
Led from the front by valiant King Salemon,   4320
Geoffrey and Huon and Normandy's Duke Anchetin;
Two flags they raise, two billowing silk banners,
Each with a crest which shows three dragons rampant;
The look on these men's faces and their bold manner
Show their intent to take not one step backwards.   4325

238

Seven thousand men make up the next division,
Which Carlon gives to the noble Duke Milon,
Count of Poitiers, a man of highest lineage,
In company with Gondelbuef the Frisian;
Behold, my lords, their gonfalons a-billowing,   4330
Round helms and hauberks in the bright sunshine
    glinting,
Their spears, their shields, red rampant lions
    depicting!
Aumon and Agolant will know right quickly
France is not theirs while men like these are living.

239

The third division is to be prized and praised;   4335
Twenty-five thousand all told this rank contains,
And they are led by Bavaria's Duke Naimes
And, at his side, Ogier the worthy Dane,
Together with the worthy knight Richer;
White hauberks they all wear with double chain,   4340
With helms of gold and cutting swords steel-made;
King Agolant thought he would win straightway,
When he sailed off to challenge France and claim;
Yet ere this haughty plan achieves its aim
Its architect will be laid in his grave.   4345

240

See the next rank as it goes riding forth,
Led by Garnier, a brave and loyal lord,
And Count Antelme, who owns famed Wirval fort!

King Anseis is also with this force,
Whose fighting strength is ten thousand in all; 4350
Behold their mules and many a noble horse,
Their crystal helms and cutting steel-made swords!
King Agolant was badly misinformed
The day he was advised to start this war;
As for this day, he'll wish it never dawned. 4355

241

Men fifteen thousand fall in to form the fifth;
Three counts lead them, one full duke and one king;
Behold their sturdy helms with padding stitched,
Their shields and gear of gold embroidering
And all their flags of white and yellow silk! 4360
Today, my lords, of fighting fierce I'll sing,
Of Agolant, whose folly was to think
He could wage war against King Charles and win;
All he achieved was fifty thousand killed.

242

Shields thirty thousand possess the sixth battalion, 4365
Which brave Droon commands as king and captain
With King Bruno, Hungary's warlike champion,
And three more kings of the most noble background;
See their white hauberks of small-gauge chain-mail
    fashioned!
See worthy swords and pointed helmets flashing 4370
And flowing manes of white and sorrel stallions!
What blows they'll strike with blades of steel
    sharp-slashing!
A long time ere the Emir reaches Paris
So many dead he'll have, so many vanquished,
All of his days he'll feel the pain and anguish. 4375

243

Brave Aleman troops make up the mighty seventh,
Men from Lorraine, Apulia, Romany;
Didier the Lombard carries this day their ensign
With Duke Fagon and Tuscany's duke together;
These ranks are swelled by sixty thousand Frenchmen; 4380
For in this column rides Charlemayn himself too.

244

When Charlemayn has marshalled all his forces
He rides the ranks, encouraging and talking,
Inspiring them, assuring and exhorting:

"Frenchmen, Alemans, so let us now ride forward!   4385
You Englishmen, you Flemish, Frisians, Normans,
You Toulouse braves and you my Lorraine stalwarts,
Men from Manseau, Angevin and Tourangeaux:
God and myself in this fight will support you,
And your own blades, your mighty cutting broadswords;   4390
Behold the army of Agolant and Aumon,
So many men from heathendom's wide borders
No man alive could reckon or record them!
Be not afraid of that or them for all that!
Their cause is false and their intent unlawful;   4395
You are God's knights, know this and thus fight for
    Him!"
Great Carlon turns and tearful spurs his war-horse;
The Pope meanwhile, riding through every quarter,
Displays a relic, Saint Peter's naked forearm,
From its red shroud unwrapped for their good fortune;   4400
Each rank he blesses, holding the arm towards them:
"Good Christian men, advance now, nothing daunted!
The gates of Heaven have opened up this dawning
And God's Angels are singing as they wait for us."
The French at this are filled with fresh rejoicing   4405
And face each other their lifetime's sins deploring;
They do this now to save their souls from torment;
Then with red crosses they cover all their hauberks
To recognize each other amidst the slaughter;
Wasting no time they grip their bucklers staunchly   4410
And lift up their great spears, to Heaven pointing;
The time has come; they watch the Afric hordes now,
Some sixty thousand, approach them evil-awesome;
They charge full-armed, an arrow volley pouring,
With drums and tambours wild and trumpets roaring;   4415
So shrill they shriek, those instruments and voices,
Lord God Himself would not be heard a-calling!
Up front King Balan conducts this hell-hound chorus,
His shield displaying the marks of his importance:
Three golden lions, the largest one a small one;   4420
He rides brown-helmed, his flag rising and falling,
With four more kings, charged each with holy orders:
Two fight for Jove, to serve him and restore him,
One for Tervagant and for Mahom the fourth one;
Both armies close and as the distance shortens   4425
The flash of gold and steel lights up the morning;
Not one man there, erstwhile so hard and haughty,
Did not feel fear at that, the geste records it;
Now hear me tell of that hard day henceforth, lords,
Which widowed wives and changed children to orphans!   4430

245

The shouting's wild, the Paynim cries are deafening;
It is all noise as both sides come together;
Their trumpets roar in hundreds ten and seven,
But our brave van of seven hundred Frenchmen
Are first to move and fly towards the enemy; 4435
Out front behold brave Flavent and Anchetin,
Geoffroy and Huon--may the good Lord protect them!
These men were first to draw blood in that melee:
Behold them spur their good fleet-footed destriers,
Clad in stout hauberks and gold and silver helmets! 4440
Balan's four kings ride out to intercept them;
Behold it, lords, as proud with proud meet head-on!
As our French strike, the ground beneath them trembles;
They unhorse three and kill them without ceremony;
Balan strikes Hugh of Clarvent then in vengeance 4445
And knocks him down, blood pouring from a flesh-wound;
He kills him not, our Lord God does not let him;
The noise explodes as both ranks break unchecked now;
Brave men start fighting whose fate is sealed already;
Look at them fall--good men--and bleed to death there, 4450
And Paynims too lie breathing their last breath there,
By many a lady henceforth to be regretted!
See spears and wiverns* struggle to gain supremacy!
See sword strike sword and skin and sinew sever!
Those who did see it and lived would never forget it. 4455

246

How loud the noise as they begin this struggle,
As everywhere lances thumping and thudding
Hit hard and break on floral-patterned bucklers!
Saddles are spilled and high-priced horses run off
As knights and counts are unhorsed and discomfited; 4460
The Paynims, too, enormous losses suffer;
Our vavasors strike hard, though far outnumbered,
Their swords enforced with strong faith and strong
    muscles;
The Paynim armor cannot withstand such punishment;
Faint-hearted men, cowards until their coming, 4465
On Aspremont took on such strength and courage
That in this fray they outfought all the others.

247

How loud the noise beneath Mount Bitter's peak

    * Large snake-shaped darts: a favorite weapon of
      the Saracens in the *chansons de geste*.

When Carlon's troops met Aumon's in the field
And Christians struck the hated Paynim breed, 4470
Hard helmets crushed and Orbrey breast-plates pierced!
So many fell no man could number these!
All would have died of that foul race, indeed,
Had not their ranks with archers been replete,
Who loosed their shafts in one enormous stream; 4475
Behold those barbs transfix our lovely steeds
And turn our near success to near defeat!
But then one rank, may Jesus bless them each,
Whom Charlemayn within his realm had reared,
Who trust in God and hold Lord Jesus dear, 4480
Sweeps down a pass to the aid of their peers;
They strike so hard, so savagely and fierce,
That one bow's range those Paynims now retreat;
They would, in truth, have forced them all to flee,
But for Balan, who guides them all and leads; 4485
He sounds his horn to rally them and keep.

248

How loud the noise, how great the hue and cry!
Girart d'Eufrate is not one to waste time;
His worthy troops see and identify!
With lance and shield are sixty thousand knights 4490
Dressed in white hauberks, good destriers astride;
See now this force charge down the mountainside
And rush upon those Paynims from the right!
Few heathens now are not struck once or twice!

249

The clash is fierce and wondrous wild the clamor 4495
When Girart swoops so swiftly down the valley;
Those Turks are shocked and knocked down on the
    sand there;
One half a league he drives those felons backwards;
Beuvon and Claron hold high their uncle's standard,
Amidst the fray unceasingly attacking; 4500
Claron slays there the mighty King Angalion,
A haughty wretch and wealthy lord of Africa;
And Beuvon kills the haughty Emir Malcolon;
Their flashing swords leave many an empty saddle
As they cry out: "Strike on, stout-hearted barons! 4505
The right is ours and, God willing, the battle!"

250

Trusting in God see now Girart Eufrates
Spur hard his horse in the thick of this mayhem

To strike a king, one Nabigant his name is,
Lord of Abisme, an eerie faraway place!   4510
Their King has coaxed him thence with the persuasion
That Burgundy would be his if he came here;
See Girart come to challenge this new claimant!
He lifts his lance and charges at the Paynim;
The blow he lands is heavy with his hatred;   4515
It cracks the shield and splits it like a wafer,
Then penetrates and pierces the breast-plating
And then the body, its steel in dark blood bathing;
He flings him dead, then turns towards his patriots
And says to them: "Let not your courage waver!   4520
Though I Girart am old, I am the same man,
And I will lead you with God our Lord and Saviour;
If you die here you've nothing to be afraid of;
And if you live you will be rich and famous."
His men reply: "None of us here will fail you."   4525

251

Neath Aspremont, down in a valley's meadow,
Is where it started, this harsh and hard-fought melee;
From day's first hour, when dawn's first light is
    spreading,
Until the ninth and the singing of vespers,
As the sun's arc has gone from start to setting,   4530
Blows have been struck so many and so telling;
See now the corpses, so many of them headless,
Bestrew the field, whose length one full league
    measures!
In all this land there is no space so empty
That you could graze a mule or give it shelter;   4535
For all the field is littered with men's weapons,
Their owners dead or close to death with head-wounds;
Aumon had thought that France was won already;
But ere all France to his will is subjected,
Before he steals the crown of Carlon's Empire,   4540
Few will remain of all of those he's led here;
Few will return to their own lands--if any;
And many French will die their lands defending;
Few shires there'll be or duchies not lamenting
Their brave counts killed and high dukes lying dead
    here;   4545
Those who fight well and live will hence possess them;
In duel and dole this bloody day progresses
Till daylight fades and evening shadows lengthen;
Both sides withdraw and fighting is suspended;
One crossbow's range away the Paynims settle,   4550
With a huge ditch between them and the Frenchmen;
Immediately those Saracens post sentries

And our men too place pickets for protection;
The night is cloudless, the moon shines down from
    heaven;
Among our ranks the wounded men are many, 4555
And Paynim losses, dying and dead, are heavy.

252

In the French camp that night how great the grief
As wounded men cry out in pain uneased
And the unhurt sigh hard in anguish deep
For fallen friends and mutilated peers-- 4560
As Paynims do likewise beyond the trees!
With shock and woe those Turks all wail and weep,
The hands and arms of some slashed with our steel;
Those wretches talk and say now each to each:
"A curse, Emir, upon your pride and greed! 4565
Curse you for wanting to rob Charles of his fiefs!
There is no fear in these brave Frenchmen here;
Ere France is yours and to your pleasure yields,
It will be you, not they, will sue for peace!
There's wrath for you and nothing else, Emir, 4570
For these French knights are fearsome in the field!"

253

Between both hosts there's but a narrow plain;
No man there is of high or low estate
With strength to eat his meat or bread to break,
Nor horse with strength to chew barley or hay; 4575
Brave men lie prone, exhausted from the day,
Some with one hand holding their horse's reins
And with the other clutching their unsheathed blade.

254

Neath Aspremont, down on the valley floor,
See men lie where they drop who can no more 4580
Save clutch the reins of their weary war-horse
Among the dead about them score on score;
They pass the night in hardship till the dawn;
A cheerless night and comfortless for all.

255

All through this night the Christians lie awake; 4585
Girart sets pickets to keep the army safe;
Not one man there, though he the least afraid,
Feels safe enough his helmet to unlace,
Nor from his neck his buckler to undrape;

The wounded weaken as their life slips away 4590
And weary horses drink not nor eat their hay;
Aumon of Africa has made no gain;
His army's stunned and their losses are great;
One half of them, well nigh, lie on the plain,
Some of them wounded, some of them past all pain; 4595
And the unhurt are struck down with dismay;
They'll never hence set foot into the fray;
Fierce threats alone will force them back again;
Aumon sees this and flies into a rage:
"You sons of whores, you charlatans and knaves! 4600
Your words it was which set me on this trail
Of dole enough to haunt me to the grave."
At this Balan moves to Aumon and says:
"Aumon, my lord, why are you so amazed?
When Agolant sent me to Charlemayn 4605
To speak his mind, his challenge and his claim,
And I returned with what I had to say,
Your father's court, these men, cursed me straightway,
Called me a coward and traitorous renegade,
And would have hanged me had not your will prevailed; 4610
They spoke as if France were already gained;
Yet in the hour when action calls their name
They turn tight-lipped, glad only to escape."
Aumon replies: "I've learnt the truth too late;
Yet should I live I'll make these cowards pay; 4615
They'll all be exiled and lose all their estates."

256

Aumon's heart grieves in wild and wondrous wrath
To see so many Turks slain on the spot:
"The fault lies in ourselves," he tells Balan;
"We lost our gods, Jupiter and Mahom 4620
And all our idols whose power makes us strong;
If we today cannot win back these gods
Our fight is finished and France forever lost."
"The fault lies in these villains!" Balan responds;
"I told the truth to mighty Agolant, 4625
Now I tell you--beware of King Carlon!
We shall not sail again the sea we crossed,
Nor see again our Africa far-off;
The French lie waiting, and you are whom they want."

257

The night endures until the first light grows, 4630
Then the dawn breaks and the sun starts to show;
Aumon's heart grieves as wondrous wild in woe
He rides his ranks and rallies as he goes;

He pledges more than ever he'll bestow;
He groups his host in seven ranks all told,   4635
Some twenty thousand in the smallest of those;
Aumon exhorts them as their brass bugles blow:
"Now ride, you men, and curse him who is slow!
For your gods' sake let vengeance take its toll!"
And Carlon's men in their encampment close   4640
Take up their arms as into rank they go;
Behold Carlon as he spurs through his host,
Rallying his men in God's name and his own!
He tells them all to trust in God and hope;
Should they outlive this day, they swear an oath   4645
To live a life sinless beyond reproach;
Such discourse done Carlon makes his will known:
To charge full-tilt! And they do as they're told;
How fierce it is when real force meets real foe!

258

See our French ride against that race of savages,   4650
And share the shock as both sides lock in battle!
This day shall stain all future days with sadness
Somewhere in France for men lost in this action;
In all our past this fight had none to match it;
So many men left their entrails on Aspremont   4655
The plain ran red with all the blood shed that day;
See Aumon now astride his Spanish stallion,
In hauberk strong, engraved Messina-fashion,
And helmet gold of strong inlay and strapping,
Inset with stones well worth Brittany's ransom!   4660
His ashwood lance he grips with its great banner,
On vengeance bent--naught else for him now matters;
See him ride out before his Paynim vassals
To strike a duke, the brave German Duke Antelme!
The blow is fierce, his armor can't withstand it;   4665
Right through his bowels the lance-head drills a
    passage;
He flings him dead, uncaring in his anger.

259

King Triamodes charges down the crest;
Well-armed is he, his horse Castillian-bred;
Behold him charge Geoffrey Grise Gonelle!   4670
He splits his shield and rips his shirt to shreds;
His steel-tipped lance he bathes in Geoffrey's breast;
Aumon, once more with buckler fitted fresh,
Swings Durendal, of all the blades the best,
And slays Garnier and Rainault d'Orbendele: 4675

"God, says Ogier,"this Paynim fares too well!"

260

Ogier is strong and nothing if not brave;
He draws Cortain, his sharp-edged fighting-blade,
And strikes Aumon with all the might he may;
Aumon is awesome, but Ogier's not afraid; 4680
He trusts in God: "Almighty King," he says,
"It hurts my heart that this one is still hale."
He swings Cortain and strikes him from close range;
High on the helm his sword a-flashing flails
And strikes his coif, slicing it clean away; 4685
Leather and blood together hit the plain;
The blow deflects away from Aumon's face
Right through his saddle and strikes his destrier;
Through thigh and shoulder its deep thrust penetrates;
The stallion falls and Aumon's in dire straits; 4690
He sees his plight and struggles up again,
Saying the while: "All hell curse you, you knave!
What devil made your sword, what prince of pain?
If its foul blade were longer, well might I rate
My Durendal and your dagger the same; 4695
I fear you for it, I'm not afraid to say."

261

"Sir knight," says Aumon, "you're brave, I grant
    that much,
With a good sword in which to place your trust;
I've seen none better in any warrior's glove;
You might survive if it were long enough! 4700
You can be happy; you have had wondrous luck,
To have unhorsed the King of Africa
And harassed me harder than any's done;
But, by Mahom, who judges all of us,
See now my steel! Regard sharp Durendal, 4705
Which blazes more that brightest brazier does!"
He draws it now, my lords, as he moves up
To aim a blow high on the helmet swung;
So sleek's the blade it slips instead of cuts;
It shaves Ogier, but with diverted thrust 4710
It strikes his shield and cleaves one quarter thus;
That eager blade cuts through the saddle-front
And stallion's neck before it's had enough;
Will he or not our brave Dane bites the dust;
Ogier's no coward and to his feet he jumps 4715
To gain revenge or die there if he must;
Anchetin saw him fall, now see him come
And strike Boidant, whom Aumon much does love!

He lands his axe on his crown with a crunch
That halves his helm and cracks apart his skull. 4720

262

Anchetin is a Norman noble and valiant;
When he sees Ogier down and Aumon standing
He goes to help him and strikes Boidant savagely;
He splits his face down to his Paynim palate;
Taking his horse he calls the Danish champion: 4725
"Sir Dane, mount now, this is no time to tarry!"
Ogier moves forward and swings astride the stallion
Just as Aumon bears in on him, attacking;
This duel's not done, both would continue gladly,
But they are swamped by onrushing compatriots 4730
And lose each other in the thick of the battle;
Aumon in rage looks round and strikes an Aleman
So viciously his armor's of no value;
He splits his face from forehead down to palate,
Then turns and sees Boidant his friend and vassal: 4735
And his heart heaves to see his dead companion;
He swears to Mahom, using his native language,
That never again will he be fooled by flatterers
Or any man whose words outweigh his actions.

263

Neath Aspremont the losses are immense; 4740
King Charles has lost so many of his best,
God's servants all, His will be done with them!
Their loss leaves Christendom sorely bereft;
And Aumon too has lost so many men;
For each one living who can fight for him hence, 4745
Three or four others are out there lying dead;
Across one league their corpses lie outstretched;
Not half an acre of empty ground is left
That is untouched by French or Paynim death:
Bodies and blades, ownerless shields or helms, 4750
Or horses waiting to see their lords again;
Aumon sees this and anger fills his breast;
He grips Durendal and swings it overhead;
The man he strikes knows that his life is spent;
It's up with him on whom that blade descends; 4755
It has to be, Aumon has too much strength
And Durendal has too evil an edge;
If King Aumon lives on for any length
He will have France, unless Lord God prevents.

264

Such a fierce fight, my lords, you never saw one; 4760
I have told you about fierce-visaged Aumon,
Who stalked the fields and wrought such awful slaughter;
Now hear a while of Girart's deeds, my lordships,
Who fought upon the crest with all his stalwarts;
Claron, Beuvon, young Renier too he brought there; 4765
What wondrous strokes Burgundian knights employed
    there!
But Mahom's men were there in great proportion!
Girart sees this as there he sits on horseback,
His heavy lance in tight-clenched fist supporting;
With his warm tears his white moustaches moisten, 4770
As do both sides of his white beard long-forking;
He says: "In Your most holy name, O Lord God,
I came here, Sire, for You and for Your glory;
Fine men so many, whom I had raised since boyhood,
Were sacrificed for You yesterday morning; 4775
And so be it, for thus our faith has taught us:
You died for us and we should die for Your sake;
Therefore, brave men, renew your strength
    henceforward
And give to God the service that we ought to!"
His men respond: "With glad heart, now and always! 4780
Let us commend ourselves to Him therefore, men,
Who by baptism made all our souls immortal;
May He spare us from slavery or slaughter."

265

Down in the field Girart's brown war-horse thunders,
Hot on its heels its sixty thousand brothers; 4785
Wherever they charge, the Paynims shake and shudder;
And yet, like it or not, they bring cold comfort
To Charlemayn, whose heart is sorely troubled;
So many nobles he sees with their heads cut off:
Two kings are dead of seven who had come there, 4790
And dukes and counts more than fourteen in number;
Now from all sides their men, bereft, run up to him
And ask alike: "My lord, what's to be done now?
If in this hour sweet Jesus does not something,
Then France is lost and your Empire is nothing." 4795
Great Charlemayn that day would have been humbled,
Without Girart close by and God above him.

266

Widespread the fight and brutal-fierce the fray;
Those Christian men begin to feel dismayed

As they behold their best whittled away; 4800
Their war-cries drop as each strong challenge fades;
Across the field see those stray mounts escape,
Here ten, here twenty, with none to hold their reins!
Now Duke Gaifier rides up to Charlemayn,
With strong Garnier, the brave duke of Lorraine, 4805
And Duke Antelme and Sanson and Renier;
Not one of these, whose war-skills all are great,
Does not a shattered quartered-shield display,
A battered helm and spear-shaft torn away;
No jesting sport their jousting was this day; 4810
They have fought hard for Lord Jesus' sake;
Charles see them come, in blood of battle stained,
And his mind reels in saddened shock and rage;
His heart o'erflows and tears stream down his face;
He summons God and loudly supplicates: 4815
"Glorious Lord," fierce-faced Carlon proclaims,
"Who in my care so many men have placed:
Must I behold them all cut to shreds and maimed
By Paynim tribes who vilify Your name,
Who loathe Your laws and shun Baptism's grace? 4820
Who have no will to pray to You or praise?
Can I lose men whom I am sworn to save,
And You, our heavenly liege, not feel the pain?"
As Carlon speaks, Ogier rides up in haste;
Five shafts of iron hang from his destrier; 4825
Of his brave shield so little now remains
That never hence could it be used again;
His helmet's rear has been rammed out of shape,
And on the left his hauberk's ripped in twain;
Dark blood drips down from the wound he's sustained, 4830
Which flows unstaunched and his bright stirrups stains;
His right arm still holds high his blade Cortain;
The French, the Germans and the Bavarians say:
"In Ogier rides our knighthood's noblest brave!"
Ogier speaks firmly, his passion unrestrained: 4835
"Carlon, your Majesty, do not delay!
My men have taken a Paynim renegade,
Who came to us fell Aumon to betray;
Aumon will never request his father's aid!
He'd rather lose his head, this man maintains; 4840
His men are losing hope, this fellow states;
Send word, my lord, back to our camp straightway!
Let no grown man that's able stop or stay;
Let all of them seek vengeance for our slain!
When Aumon sees our ranks fill up again 4845
His men will panic and all try to escape."
"Your plan is good, Ogier," Carlon acclaims;
"We'll do it now; we have no time to waste."

267

On the advice of Ogier, son of Gaufroi,
Carlon sends off worthy Droon and Audfroi: 4850
"Ride hard to camp astride your swiftest horses!
Tell them I want them all to come and join me!
If they lack steeds tell them to saddle palfreys,
Or, failing that, command them all to walk here!"
Both men reply: "Right willingly, as always!" 4855
They hurry off to do as Carlon orders;
Our Emperor now moves his phalanx forward,
Some twenty thousand stout-hearted men and loyal,
Strong in their faith and eager to enforce it;
Hid by some trees Aumon observes these forces; 4860
He sees the Oriflamme coming towards him,
The King himself and all of his supporters;
He says out loud: "In truth Mahom, my lord god,
What I see now bears out Balan's stern warning;
I'd be a fool in future to ignore him." 4865

268

Our Emperor is filled with a deep sadness
To see his men all fight and fall in battle;
With twenty thousand Franks he joins the action
And strikes at once a heathen, Moridant he;
He splits his shield and shiny breast-plate smashes, 4870
Ramming his spear right through the stinking savage;
Then Carlon turns, one Morant next to challenge:
An Emir he and cousin of King Agolant;
His spear spikes through, but as it strikes it
    shatters;
He draws Joyeuse--no better blade was fashioned, 4875
Save Durendal, whose blade I'd say would match it;
He slays the Afric and sends his soul to Africa:
"Mountjoy!" he shouts, his war-cry and his rally:
"Strike hard with me, you valiant-fierce chevaliers!
Defend your faith against this faithless rabble, 4880
Who have come here to take your land in capture."
Duke Naimes sees this as does Normandy's Anchetin;
He points Charles out to both Ogier and Fagon:
"Behold our King! He openly attacks them!
I am afraid of his unselfish valor; 4885
If he should fall, we and our cause collapse too!
These haughty Persians will kill every last man here."
Ogier and Naimes approach Charles at a gallop:
"For God our Saviour's sake, Carlon Your Majesty,
We beg of you, henceforth hold yourself back, Sire! 4890
If you should fall we and our cause are vanquished;

All of us would be killed--this is a fact, Sire;
All of us fight for you stoutly and gladly
Because we know you live, whatever happens."
Carlon responds: "Your words are wind, my captains! 4895
I will not live through the death of my vassals;
If you all die then I am surely captured;
May God the King of Bethlehem and Nazareth
Never let me flee should death claim my companions."
Naimes weeps at this as does Normandy's Anchetin 4900
And all the others around great Carlon gathered;
They wait no longer, they charge those malefactors;
Those twenty thousand with naught to hold them back
   now
Kill seven thousand, their outrage running rampant
Against the breed of Mahom and Tervagant; 4905
Some seven hundred make haste to Aumon's standard,
Most hurt to death, with their intestines dragging:
"Ah Aumon, lord, all we can give we have done!
We ask you now to save us if you can do!"
Aumon hears this and almost bursts with anger; 4910
He lifts Durendal to its attacking angle,
Which drips and sticks with blood on blade and handle;
Before too long Carlon will curse this dagger!
Aumon strikes Anchetin, a prince so valiant
That Charles has none more brave among his barons; 4915
Aumon strikes Anchetin a blow so massive
No helmet made could have withstood its challenge,
Nor chain-mail hood could have held back its passage;
It cleaves his head and neck down to his backbone;
But lords, hear this! A wondrous thing then happened! 4920
His body dropped, his corpse cartwheeling backwards,
And came to rest in normal sitting fashion,
His face to East, to Heaven both his hands clasped!
God's choir of Angels take his soul back to Paradise;
Carlon looks on, whose faith in God is absolute; 4925
But God! How he laments the loss of that one!

269

Charles burns with grief as never in his time
As he beholds Anchetin fall and die;
Loud he laments: "Dear friend, ill-starred your life!
You would have stood like a rock at my side 4930
Though all the rest had fled with turning tide;
In Rome it was you who welcomed me erstwhile,
Gave me your land to add to my Empire;
If ever God gave ear to plea of mine,
Let it be this one--have mercy on this knight!" 4935
This said, Charles spurs a Saracen to smite;
From top to teeth for Anchetin he's sliced; 4936[b]

"Mountjoy!" cries Charles, "Men, draw your swords
 and strike!"
When they hear this they willingly comply;
They draw their swords and cast their spears aside;
With blades of steel they hit those Paynim lines; 4940
If they but hold this force for a short while,
Help's on its way to put these dogs to flight.

270

The clash is great and no place for the timid;
Now would I tell of that message delivered
Back to the camp by swift envoys sent thither; 4945
They reach the camp and shout to those within it:
"Good men, make haste! Charles needs your help this
 minute;
He's in great trouble fighting beneath Mount Bitter,
And all his friends are in great danger with him;
They'll all be dead if you don't come this instant; 4950
He who holds back for fear of being injured,
Carlon himself, should he survive, will kill him!"
Those in the camp, to hear this, are indignant;
Servants and squires all snatch up weapons swiftly;
See cooks and butlers and chamberlains all grip them, 4955
And valets, porters and bearers seek equipment!
Even the wounded bind up their wounds new-willing;
Who has no horse mounts any palfrey's stirrups;
Who has no sword takes up a rod or picket;
Cudgels they clutch and great knives from the
 kitchens; 4960
They run and snatch large staves of oak and trim them,
Then cut up strips of towel and table linen
And make up flags to shock the Paynim spirits;
Young Roland watches and a great anger fills him;
He calls to Haton, to Berenger and Guion: 4965
"My lords," he says, "my uncle needs help quickly;
Now I would know, in truth, he who is with me,
And who will come to my uncle's assistance."
Young Roland mounts in haste, this challenge given,
And rides the ranks exhorting all his kindred 4970
And waving for a spear a wooden picket:
"My lords, make haste! Of bravery be thinking!
Our Emperor will honor you in victory,
And I shall lead you and show the flag unflinching."
And they all say: "What a man this boy will be! 4975
He has the heart to start a fight and finish!"
Some forty thousand to Roland's words have listened;
They leave their tents, youths callow, keen and nimble,
Who will stand fast though lives and limbs go missing,
For Roland leads them on and thus has bidden; 4980

Behold those boys! Roland rides in the middle
Of Berenger and Haton--God, what ambition!
Aumon the Afric thought it would be so simple
To make the French renounce their faith as Christians
In favor of Mahom and all his minions, 4985
Who are not worth one sou of true religion!
Young Roland hastes, and I must hurry with him
Back to the battle, fresh news of it to bring you,
Its din to tell and its deadly decisions,
And Girart's part within it to continue. 4990

PART 6

271

Peace my lords, pray, for God our Maker's sake,
As to Girart once more I turn my tale!
What a great fighter was that lord of Eufrate!
He formed his ranks away from Charlemayn
And rode them straight at Aumon's oriflamme; 4995
Where it was worst Girart was first that day,
Leading his barons, his fifty thousand brave,
To fight against one hundred thousand knaves;
That day Girart paid back the Paynim race;
God, Lord of Life, grant him eternal grace! 5000
And now, my lords, give ear as I relate
How Aumon's flag by that brave duke was claimed!

272

Girart heads straight for Aumon's own position,
His fifty thousand Burgundian fighters with him;
Hot on their heels his Gevaudan division 5005
And Cosence men, on each flank, all move swiftly
To make it hard for those heathens to kill him;
In a loud voice Girart speaks and they listen:
"Now hear me well, my nephews, sons of Milon,
And my own sons and barons of my kingdom! 5010
We're far from home and everything is different;
If back at home I'm challenged by some brigand,
Who burns my land and sets alight my cities,
Then I'll burn his and turn his crops to cinders;
If he steals keeps of mine then I'll steal his ones 5015
And so it goes till we resolve the issue
Or I put him or he puts me in prison;
Even then I'd flee, and though he chased me quickly
That very night I'd be back home in Vienne;
But here on distant soil against the Infidel, 5020

If we are routed where would we run to, kinsmen?
This way or that, they'd catch up with us quickly;
Our choice stops here; to God's hands I commit us,
Who shapes our fates from the first to the finish."
Girart speaks thus and straight these words
    delivered   5025
The grand old man spurs his horse called Killvillain,
Then lifts his lance and sets his flag a-billow;
He strikes and makes one Macabré his victim,
Splitting his shield and his sleek hauberk's stitches
And ripping out both his lungs and his liver;   5030
Among the foe from saddle-bows he flings him:
"Strike hard, brave men, and cry 'Vienne' for
    victory!
The right is ours and the fight too, God willing!"

273

Girart d'Eufrate lifts his voice louder still:
"Strike hard non-stop! Give God your everything!   5035
And as for me, I ask you for this gift:
Aumon's own flag--do not deny me it!
I want his flag--such is my will and wish;
You'll lose your lands if you should fail in this!"
His barons say: "Has Girart lost his wits?   5040
Can he not count how many guard that ridge?
There's sixty thousand, and all armed to the hilt!"

274

Girart says on: "Claron, up and away,
And you, my children, Beuvon, Ernault, Renier,
And all of you who own lands by my grace!   5045
His flag I want and will you to obtain!
I tell you now, if you in this should fail
And I return to Burgundy again,
I'll disinherit you from your estates;
You and your sons will lose all former claim."   5050
His men all say: "Old Girart's lost his brains,
But nonetheless we must do as he says."
They sound their horns and hit those ranks again;
Now left now right they strike with spears and blades
Till they're so close to Aumon's battle-gage   5055
That one glove tossed would land right at its base;
Now when they see our Frenchman come their way,
Two Paynim kings who guard it make complaint,
Kings Amargon and Esperrant their names:
"How right was Balan the messenger we blamed,   5060
When he described the Christian knights as brave
And bold in battle and fearsome in the fray;

And how wrong Aumon in his conceited haste
To take them on without his father's aid;
No son was ever the cause of so much pain! 5065
If Agolant with all our troops now came
We'd halt them here and conquer Charlemayn
And have all France beneath our rule and sway;
Instead, before the sun sets on this day,
Aumon will see the price his pride will pay; 5070
And should he not, to others it will be plain;
Are we not fooled and fools then all the same,
That we so long by this lost standard stay?
What are we doing that we do not escape?"

275

About their flag the Paynims press in panic; 5075
Now when they see old Girart coming at them
And all his men advancing on their standard
Each says to each: "Too long a time we tarry!
Ere long at all Aumon's flag will be captured."
Still Girart shouts: "Claron, what are you at, boy? 5080
Beuvon! Renier! Ernault! What is the matter?
And you my barons, are you not my companions?
If Aumon's flag is not here in my hands soon,
All my goodwill and love for you will vanish."
His Burgundians respond by running rampant: 5085
With their steel blades so many helms they hammer
They hack their way one lance-length from the banner.

276

The roar of war resounds across the heights
As Girart's men broadcast their battle-cries
And their intent to take Aumon's ensign; 5090
For they well know if they can wrest this prize,
Aumon's support will last but a short time;
His men, unsure, would lose the will to fight,
Think of themselves and quickly take to flight;
If you could see Girart's troops storm their lines, 5095
Send Paynims sprawling and falling on all sides,
Behold yourselves the measure of their might!
So far they thrust, the flag is theirs well-nigh;
And those Turks know that if they stay they die;
Behold, my lords, their heathen hauberks sliced 5100
And rods run through their rotten heathen hides!
"Welcome the wounds, brave men!" old Girart cries;
"You will be martyrs if you should lose your lives,
Served with the Saints who dwell in Paradise,
All garlanded with the blest crowns of Christ, 5105
There to enjoy whatever you desire."

Hear now Esperrant and Amargon of Tyr:
Our flag is lost--we cannot stop these knights!
"This is the end--this foe won't be denied!
Our lord Aumon left us here to decide 5110
To stay as long as love for him required;
We should leave now--we think it would be wise!"
These words once said, they waste no further time;
They turn their reins and quickly take to flight.

277

More fierce this fray than any one of yore: 5115
"Onward, my brave Burgundians!" old Girart roars;
"My Gevaudans, why do you stop and stall?
You Cosence men, what are you stopping for?
You Auvergnats, hell take you if you halt!
I want his flag--seize it and bring it forth!" 5120
His men reply: "Right soon it will be yours!"
They hurl themselves at those heathens once more;
See now Esperrant and Amargon, those lords
With whom Aumon his battle-flag installed:
Each turns his rein and makes off on his horse, 5125
Abandoning that flag without a thought,
And at its base their olifant and horn!
See Girart's men lift up that flag with joy!
His nephews then take Girart's shield and sword;
They take his hands and lead him at a walk 5130
And sit him down upon the flag spread forth:
"My lord," they say, "now you have your reward!"
Girart replies: "Great thanks, my lovely boys;
My years of care for you were not for naught;
My worthy knights, I thank you each and all; 5135
I have been harsh, but you can rest assured,
For your deeds here, if we survive this war,
I shall unlock my deepest treasure vaults
And give good wives to the unmarried poor."
Girart is tired to death, so hard he's fought; 5140
He has been hit and from his nose blood pours;
His men look on and weep to see their lord;
But Girart says: "I charge you, weep no more!
We all must bleed betimes for our great cause;
Now let us mount and fight with greater force! 5145
Seek out Aumon--for now I want his corpse!"

278

The flag is his, of that there's no disputing;
How loud the cries of Paynims in confusion
And Christian cheers as bravely they pursue them!
Carlon hears this and watches their brave doing; 5150

He calls Ogier and summons Naimon to him:
"Give ear, my lords, to yonder battle's tumult;
The shouts of winners and the laments of losers!
Girart d'Eufrate is fighting like a fury;
If he should die all of my days I'll rue it." 5155
Girart meanwhile is in no way slow-moving;
From his command one hundred men he chooses:
"Ride like the wind with this great flag, our booty,
To Charlemayn, of all the Franks the ruler;
On my behalf present it to him duly; 5160
Tell him from me to be of happy humor:
The Paynims weaken, with many dead and wounded."
His men reply: "Your orders are our duty."

279

In haste they turn those brave one hundred men
Girart has picked to act at his behest; 5165
They gallop hard and reaching Charles say then:
"God bless Carlon, great King of all the French!
In Girart's name this token we present:
It it the flag of King Aumon himself;
Great King rejoice, so Girart recommends: 5170
The Paynims weaken and soon all will be well."
"Sweet Lord," says Charles, "with Your redeeming
    strength
Guard brave Girart from capture or from death!
Tell him I thank him from my soul's very depths;
And should God grant, Who all our fates directs, 5175
That I return to France and Laon hence,
Girart shall have his rightful recompense."
Girart's men leave once these words have been said;
Lo now, my lords, Aumon amidst the press,
Quite unaware of his lost flag as yet! 5180
Durendal flies as Aumon deals distress,
Striking down Frenchmen like a demon from Hell;
Full many are killed or filled with wondrous dread.

280

Aumon's well-armed with a right wondrous weapon;
He wields Durendal and deals out many a death-stroke; 5185
Hear Triamodes, though, upbraid his nephew:
"In truth, Aumon, how terrible your error
To take on Charles alone without the Emir;
You'll bear the blame of this mistake for ever;
There is no fear in the hearts of these Frenchmen; 5190
How hard they fight for their homeland and heritage;
We'll not survive the damage done already;
You've lost the best of all the men you led here;

Prince, sound your horn, before we all regret it!
It will be heard by the Emir in Reggio; 5195
You have no choice, King Agolant must help now;
If you do not then all of us will perish."
Aumon hears this and looks at him with menace,
Then answers thus, his fierce contempt expressing:
"By Mahom, uncle, how truthful, how prophetic 5200
Good Balan was with all he tried to tell me;
Back home at court your bragging boasts were endless:
"Get me a boat and sail me there!" you said then;
"I'll give you France, without the help of any";
But now you show that all your boasts were empty; 5205
You beg me now to blow my horn for rescue;
You've played me false, both you and all the rest
      here;
Your tongues attack but your weak hearts surrender;
If I return to my African Empire
Then all of you will lose the lands you cherish; 5210
For I long since have sworn Mahom and pledged him
That I'll not sound my horn for any enemy;
No friend of mine shall ever suffer censure
For fault of mine not worthy of his friendship."
See then a Paynim, his face a mask of terror, 5215
His shield half-sliced, the other side all dented,
His hauberk's rings on both sides ripped and severed,
His body bleeding where many a blow has entered,
Reins cut to ribbons, his shaft shorn at the centre!
It is quite clear he has faced mortal peril; 5220
See him ride up, seeking Aumon his general;
His shield he grips and says amidst the press there:
"Africa's King, your honor is all ended!
A band of Christians, of their knights but a section,
But none I've seen with arms or armor better, 5225
In hauberks white, pure silver-like, protected,
With spears of steel well-sharpened and well-tempered,
In burnished helms of the finest forged metal,
Attacked the flag which you left us defending;
What can I say? We were routed and fled, sire; 5230
They took your flag, then some rode off together
Bearing the flag to give Charles as a present."
Aumon hears this and looks at him with menace;
His whole face flushes then blushes wild with frenzy:
"Silence, you coward, you inbred cur!" he bellows: 5235
"It is all lies! Do you really expect me
To think that so few French could beat so many?
If they themselves were made of steel thrice-
      strengthened,
They'd be no match for those fine men I left there;
I left my flag with men of peerless mettle." 5240
The wretch replies: "It is true, none the less, sire;

127

Your flag is lost--it lies in Carlon's tent now;
King Amargon rode off when they o'erwhelmed us,
And Esperrant rode after him directly."
Aumon hears this and sorrow fills his senses; 5245
Clutching Durendal, his blade so richly lettered,
He sallies forth, his whole soul set on vengeance
Both swift and strong, so to Mahom he pledges;
He strikes a knight, a strong man called Engerran,
A household knight of Salemon white-headed; 5250
So huge a blow he brings down on his helmet
All in its path it splits right down the centre;
Down to the saddle the big man is bisected;
And if his horse had not turned as it felt this
It would have been cut clean in half itself too; 5255
He strikes another, in his rage unrelenting;
Right through his belt he rips, right through his
    belly
And flips one third of him across the leathers;
He cut a swathe so deep through all our men there
That brave ones run when his wild eyes select them; 5260
The shout goes up: "Carlon, where are you Emperor?
If you let live at length this fiendish felon
We'll all be killed; with no one to prevent it
France will be lost for many a long year henceforth."
Mark now Ogier as he sees Aumon's frenzy! 5265
A valiant knight, this nobleman of Denmark,
A champion proven in many a previous melee;
Until this time the world had seen none better;
Behold him now, his steel-tipped spear held steady
As he speaks out: "For pity, God in Heaven! 5270
What hurt today we've suffered from this hell-hound;
One duel already I've fought against this devil;
God curse me now should I shrink from a second!"
He spurs his mount, speeding in his direction,
And strikes Aumon off-guard and unsuspecting; 5275
On Aumon's shield he lands a blow so heavy,
Flat on his back he fells him on the meadow;
His hauberk's strong, still stitched the damask
    threading,
But through the mail the spear-point finds an entry;
It knifes the knave and on his haunches sets him; 5280
See from his fist fly forth the fierce Durendal!
Ogier jumps down from his fleet-footed destrier
To seize the prize--but Aumon intercepts him;
He grasps his sword and turns to Ogier, yelling:
"Fool to dismount! As I live, you're a dead man!" 5285

281

How wild was Aumon, how fierce his anger burned

To see himself knocked down upon the dirt!
He grasps his sword and jumps up all alert:
"You dog!" he cries, "You rabid reckless cur,
To come at me with such selfless concern! 5290
It's only right you get what you deserve!"
On his round helm a crushing stroke he curls;
But Ogier sways and the sword strikes the earth;
It leaves our duke with never a scratch or hurt;
But his shield's edge it slices as it curves 5295
And carves his leggings to shreds down to his spurs.

282

Ogier is brave; he draws Cortain his sword,
Whose blade was wrought with Durendal's and forged;
Once it was shaped, well-sharpened and adorned,
They struck it on an anvil to test its force; 5300
It split that anvil down to its base and boards,
But snapped itself that was so newly-formed;
Had it not been so brutally employed,
So swore the smithy whose job it was and joy,
It would have beaten even fierce Durendal, 5305
Which was its match in no respect at all;
Its blade, still good, he sharpened all the more;
Now Ogier draws it, his sword of many a war,
Whose blade shines brighter when from the scabbard
    drawn,
Than candle's glow lights up the gloomy vault, 5310
And aims a blow so fatal as it falls
On Aumon's helm with golden band well-wrought,
That had the Turk not turned his head, my lords,
He would have lived to fight Carlon no more;
But turn he does and on his shield it bores; 5315
All that it meets that mighty blow destroys;
Great bands of iron from Aumon's shield are shorn
And rings one hundred from his hauberk fly forth
As down to his gold boot his byrnie's torn;
The blow ploughs on until it strikes the soil; 5320
It would have stuck had not the blade been short;
Aumon sees this, observing it with awe:
"Vassal, well struck!" Aumon to Ogier calls;
"I know you, knight, your short sword makes me sure
That we have met in this pitched fight before; 5325
You are most brave, this much I can't ignore!
Shall we still fight or come to some accord?
If you renounce your Christian creed and law,
All Femenie will straightaway be yours;
You'll be its king, I'll crown you in my court 5330
When France is mine from the south to the north!"
Ogier replies: "Paynim, perish the thought!

We've parted once but now we shall not pause
Till one of us lies here a headless corpse;
And should I die my day were well employed, 5335
With my soul saved, in Paradise reborn;
But should you die your soul is damned withal,
For your faith's fake and all your gods are false!"
"So die the death you crave!" fell Aumon taunts.

283

Thus Aumon boasts, while all the time he stalks him, 5340
And Ogier too steps fearlessly towards him;
See now Duke Naimes and Salemon on horseback,
Richer the German and Fagon, duke of Touraine,
With King Droon and King Didier the stalwart,
Together with one thousand reinforcements! 5345
They save Ogier, the worthy count and war-lord;
About Aumon on every side and quarter
They question him with loud-uplifted voices:
"Who are you, Turk? What do the heathens call you?
Give us your name, and by God not a false one!" 5350
"By Tervagant you'll know the truth!" he roars back;
"I'll never hide it nor ever have I sought to;
Though you had hundreds more here to support you
I'll tell you my intent--and let me warn you
I never lie nor ever have my forebears; 5355
All Africa, across the sea, I'm lord of!
I am the son of Agolant, called Aumon;
I rule Alfagny and all Befany's borders;
The Persian shahs all rule by my appointment,
And I own Syria up to the river Jordan; 5360
I rule alike the mighty land of Moriane,
And Babylon to my command is loyal;
All Alexandria obeys my orders
And Greater Indies in all its far-flung corners;
And Prester John patrols that lone land for me 5365
Where no man lives or even has explored it;
What's more to say? Why waste more time with talking?
All Africa to the Split Tree I'm lord of;
All of the East to the turn of the waters
My Empire is--the limits of the Orient; 5370
If I can win all of the West henceforward,
All earth will be my fief, all mine its fortune;
Carlon's the one who bars me now and baulks me;
Were it not shameful for me and those I've brought
  here
I would have sent to Reggio town this morning, 5375
Where waits my father with all our other forces;
He has more men, of this I can assure you,
Than I brought here with me upon this foray."

The French say then: "God help us, we implore You!
Whoever could catch a king of this importance   5380
And take him back to Charlemayn at sword-point,
No future hour of his would be but joyous!"
They rush Aumon, behind him and before him;
But he is strong, his height and size enormous;
A whole palm's width between the eyes his forehead;   5385
He wields his blade, the razor-edged Durendal;
The man it knives knows well his life has faltered;
And yet, my lord, Aumon would have been caught there
But for his shouts of "Africa!", his war-cry;
Straightway behold King Moysant race towards him,   5390
Salatiel, the rich emir and haughty,
Triamodes, the great king of Valorie,
Strong King Balan, Cador of Egypt also
With seventeen hundred Saracen knaves--nay more so!
See now, my lords, a swift and bloody slaughter,   5395
Our men outmanned who cannot hope to halt them!
They save Aumon and then return his war-horse.

284

To save Aumon, their rich and royal champion,
Two Paynim kings come charging at the gallop;
Triamodes is first to vent his anger;   5400
On Milon's shield so hard a blow he hammers
The spear breaks through the hauberk and the blazon,
The samite coat and ermine-padded jacket;
The pennant rips clean through his ribs and backbone
And all his bowels burst out across the saddle.   5405

285

Triamodes is a fierce knight and king,
And our Milon lies dead because of him;
Hark to him crow and show his joy at this:
"Hey Aumon, sire, avenge yourself at will!
This duke for one will stop you not, I think!   5410
See him fall in with your least wish and whim!"
Berenger spurs across the field therewith
And sees Milon lain in his grave of grit;
He'll hate himself if vengeance is not swift;
He drives his lance with its steel-sharpened tip   5415
At Triamodes and thrusts the spear-point in;
Right through his breast he drives it further still,
Then flings him dead one full lance-length with this:
"Begone! God rot your soul, pernicious prince!
I've paid you back--it was my brother you killed!"   5420

286

Triamodes lies dead down in the field;
Aumon cries out and tenderly he weeps,
Lamenting him in his own native speech;
See now Morant and young Richer appear!
Morant strikes Macre, from past Jerusalem he,   5425
A haughty lord, all Syria is his fief;
Right through the ribs he forces his sharp spear
And flings him dead spread-eagled on the lea;
Richer in turn strikes Moysant eagerly;
A blow so hard with his steel sword he deals   5430
He splits his skull right through from top to teeth;
The Pope looks on and blesses as he weeps.

287

When Aumon sees all his good comrades die
And sees the field fill up with his dead knights,
He feels such woe he thinks he'll lose his mind: 5435
"This is the end for me, Balan," he sighs;
"Behold our dead about us on all sides!
I cannot save them if such is Carlon's might."
"What wondrous words I hear!" Balan replies;
"Does Aumon now for so little take fright,   5440
He who would rule some seven realms entire?
Did I indeed not tell the truth erstwhile,
That Carlon's men were mighty-mettled knights,
Brave-hearted men who would not think of flight?
They will stop here as dead men or alive;   5445
You did not deign to sound your horn in time;
Now it's too late for us to leave this fight."
Aumon hears this and heaves a heavy sigh;
Will he or not he lifts his horn on high;
He gives it breath and blows in wondrous wise;   5450
But Reggio's far and no one hears its whine,
And never again shall this son see his sire;
Some hear it though and rallied by its cry
These runaways turn back new-fortified;
The noise of war once more begins to rise   5455
As men return to battle and to strive;
Without God's help our men will not survive.

288

Aumon despairs and his heart aches in anguish;
He blows his horn so strongly in his sadness
The cry resounds across the heights and valleys;   5460
But far too far is Reggio town to catch it;
His father hears it not, though there he tarries

With host on host of Paynims round him gathered;
Some hear it though and runaways are rallied;
Once more they bleed as both sides lock in battle; 5465
No man before or since ever saw such passion;
So many men on both sides fall in action!
Hark to those horns, those trumpets and those tambors
And the Pope's voice as it calls through the clamor:
"Hold ground, you Franks! Be brave, my noble barons! 5470
You are all held in your Creator's hand now,
Who draws you forth from your own soul's great
    blackness!
In this dread field be steadfast in your valor
And all you sins, both great and small, I'll balance
Upon my back as heaven-bound we travel!" 5475

                289

The sound of war, its angry roar, is great;
As they return, those Paynim runaways,
The French and Limousins are sore afraid,
So too the Normans, Poitevins and Lorrains;
Carlon himself with woe casts down his gaze; 5480
To God, as if He stood there, Charles makes complaint:
"Ah Lord," he says, "Who wine from water made,
Made Saint Paul see and gave Saint Firmin faith,
Will you allow the world to fall from grace?
Shall Paynims rule and Christendom give way? 5485
If Pagandom wins in the field this day
There'll be no morning mass in France again;
I'd rather kill myself with my own blade."
These words bring tears to many a noble's face;
They groan full hard; but while such moan they make 5490
Behold Audfroi spur up to them and say:
"Son of Pepin, no longer be dismayed!
Forget your fear of fell Apollo's race!
Help is at hand, and no mean help I'd say;
Full forty thousand youths are on their way! 5495
There is not one, though lowly his estate,
Bears not of silk or cloth a banner brave;
Your nephew Roland leads on this cavalcade,
With young Haton, young Guy and Berenger;
When they arrive these Bedouins will pay!" 5500

                290

When Carlon hears Audfroi stand there and tell him
That all these youths are on their way to help him,
Some forty thousand young men-at-arms together,
Armed and equipped with sticks and sundry weapons,
And that they're moving as fast as wind to get there, 5505

Then he thanks God the mighty King of Heaven;
He marvels much at Roland his young nephew
And Gui and Haton and Berenger his friends too:
"Redeeming Saviour," says Charlemayn the Emperor,
"I thought those colts in Laon town were tethered! 5510
What lucky hour drove them in my direction!"
Carlon looks up and sees them in that second
As they appear across a valley's entrance;
Such noise they make with calling out and yelling
The ridges ring and valley slopes all echo; 5515
Charles lifts his hands and gives them Lord God's
    blessing.

291

So hard they ride, those eager squires and valets,
Those lovely lads, young nobles and young lackeys
Whom Charlemayn had left back at his campsite,
They start to climb the steep-backed slope of
    Aspremont; 5520
Their flags fly proud, though far from rich their
    fashion:
Most are made up of linen strips and napkins,
Of pillow-slips and sheets and even blankets!
If you, my lords, saw such a host come at you,
Would you not sign the cross like Charlemagne? 5525
Some swing great stakes, while some thick rods do
    carry;
Some brandish cudgels, snatched from the cook's own
    pantry,
And others staves cut from the strong sorb-apple,
With both ends trimmed to tips as sharp as arrows;
Some clutch steel knives and others heavy hatchets; 5530
Like a dense wood they move along in phalanx;
Young Roland now is sat astride a pack-horse
Which has no breast-plate, no stirrups and no saddle;
No matter how he strikes his beast or slaps it,
He cannot make that pack-horse more than amble; 5535
This drives the lad to madness and distraction,
So much he yearns to aid Carlon in action--
And on this day his aid is needed badly!
Droon d'Estampes, who bears this day their banner,
Leads them across the ridges and the valleys 5540
Until they come to that dread field of battle;
Roland looks round and sees a war-horse standing:
He leaves his hack and jumps upon the back of it;
He sees the hauberk on a dead Paynim vassal:
He strips the corpse and dons himself the jacket; 5545
A helm of gold he finds tossed in the track there:
He picks it up and on his head he straps it;

He sees dropped swords: but these he will not handle,
For he as yet has not been dubbed chevalier;
But see him seize a rod of wood right gladly   5550
That a strong peasant would have found hard to manage;
Though Roland's young, he's strong as lion rampant!
Armed like their leader are Berenger and Haton
And all the rest of matching rank and value;
Wherever they look fine weapons are not lacking,   5555
Left there by lords lain lifeless on the paddock;
When all are armed hear Roland now harangue them:
"Let your aggression loose henceforth, my barons!
Let each lay claim to knighthood by his valor!
Seek out your sires amidst this mighty challenge   5560
And stand by them as strongly as you can do!
Now for God's honor, into whose care I hand us,
Let my strength strike where it can do most damage!"
He charges in and starts to vent his anger;
With both ends of his rod hard helms he hammers,   5565
Staves in the steel, those shiny helmets shattering,
And pounds their skulls, the blows their backbones
      battering;
Before his blows the Paynim ranks all scatter:
"Hell curse this captain's craft!" say all the
      Saracens:
"None's more to fear than this one is, by Mahom!"   5570
Young Roland turns, his comrades all to rally;
He cries: "Mountjoy! Lay on, lusty companions,
And Charles will give each man a girl to marry!"
Now see them leap to follow their fine captain
Into the fray, full fearless in their manhood!   5575
Chain-mail they rip and hauberks tear to tatters
As they slay Paynims and spin them from their
      stallions;
Ten thousand Turks are knocked down in this sally,
Who nevermore shall cast on earth their shadow;
The Paynims look and see our army massing,   5580
See Carlon's ranks regrouping and regathering,
And they all say: "False courage makes us tarry!
Carlon has called his rearguard to attack us;
We cannot hope to stay here and withstand them;
A swift escape is surely our best plan now;   5585
Aumon our king was mad when he began this!
How right and true the messenger Balan was,
Who told us Charles was much too proud and valiant!
France will be his, for he will not be banished;
We have no right to lay claim to his lands here."   5590
These words scarce out, the Paynims ranks all scatter;
Those craven curs turn tail and flee in panic;
Aumon looks up and sees at every angle

135

And every side his men all running backwards
And dropping weapons, the battle to abandon,　　　　5595
Now ten, now twenty, and then a whole battalion;
He thinks he'll go quite mad with rage and rancor;
Across the field to vent his spleen he gallops;
He fills his lungs and yells his war-cry "Africa",
His runaways to rally if he can do;　　　　　　　　5560
But Girart's there, still eager for his capture,
With Beuvon, Claron and over five thousand landsmen;
Will he or not, Aumon is driven backwards;
By force of arms he flees the field--he has to.

292

Aumon the Turk is brave and bold indeed;　　　　　5605
A noble lord and fighter fierce and fleet;
When he beholds his ranks run in retreat
He roams the field relentless in his grief
For his dead friends lain lifeless on the field;
He swings his blade, whose beauty has no peer,　　5610
And strikes Anseis, a duke of high esteem;
He halves his head, the flesh and bones he cleaves
And his corpse falls at mighty Aumon's feet;
Small joy it is to him and brief relief,
With Claron and Beuvon hot on his heels　　　　　 5615
And Renier too with troops armed to the teeth
And Charlemayn approaching with all speed!
If Aumon's caught then dark disport we'll see;
He'll lose his head--no less shall be the fee.

293

He leaves the field, his head in horror sunk　　　5620
To see his ranks in all directions run;
With his own blade he would shed his own blood;
But he has a good horse and fast enough;
There is none better this side Jerusalem,
And Aumon flees thereon as fly he must;　　　　　 5625
Hid by a rock he now laments his luck
To but three others--the worthy King Balan,
King Synagon and the strong King Gorhan:
"My lords, he cries,"I thought my worth so much;
But now, alas, I know how wrong I was　　　　　　 5630
To blame those men, my father's counsellors,
When they advised my father Agolant
To not make me a King while he was one;
Mad is the man who listens to his son."
Balan hears this and says in voice full-lunged:　5635
"Hey Aumon lord, why torture yourself thus?
Are you a woman bewailing her lost love?"

294

Aumon rides off, whose heart is filled with rage,
With those three kings whose love for him is great;
How oft he swoons upon his horse and faints, 5640
For all his men left lifeless where they lay;
In his great grief his every thought brings pain;
Charles chases him with Girart and Ogier
And Roland too with all those valets brave:
"My noble knights and lords," Carlon exclaims, 5645
"See that gold shield a-glint! There goes our prey!
There goes Aumon with three kings of his faith;
He could still kill us if we let him escape;
Ride hard, brave men, without one moment's waste,
And I myself will help you as I may." 5650
Behold those hooves and all the dust they raise!
Those Paynim kings alike increase their pace,
Aumon himself keen now to make all haste;
But then, neath Synagon, his horse goes lame:
"What now, Balan?" Aumon cries once again, 5655
"We cannot leave King Synagon this way;
He was my liege, the lord of my young days;
It's but four French who tread upon our tails;
The rest of them are not in arrow-range;
Let us turn round and challenge them, I say! 5660
For if we thus can win a destrier
Good Synagon needs one without delay."
But Balan says: "Aumon, it is too late!
Leave Synagon, my lord! You cannot wait!
If you are caught there will be no debate, 5665
You'll be cut down beneath their steel-edged blades!"
Aumon hears this but he does not obey;
His lance he lifts, his courser's flanks he flays
And moves to strike Bavaria's Duke Naimes
High on his shield, on its first quarter's face; 5670
Right through the boss his spear-point penetrates
But it cannot unhook the hauberk's chains
Or find the flesh beneath to mark and maim;
Naimes is unhurt but unhorsed just the same;
Down on the ground he thinks he'll go insane; 5675
He draws his sword and starts to stand up straight;
The first he meets he strikes with all his hate--
And Synagon's old head flies o'er the plain!

295

When Ogier sees Duke Naimes attacked and fall
He spurs his mount and aims his spear's sharp point; 5680
On Gorhan's shield so savagely he bores

The buckler's split, the close-meshed hauberk's torn;
He threads the shaft right through his ribs and forth;
Down in the field he flings the Paynim corpse;
When Aumon looks and sees what has befallen,   5685
His old lord slain and dead his seneschal,
His spirit churns with rancor and remorse;
He stalks Ogier and swings dread Durendal:
"You wretch," he cries,"so now we meet once more!
How many men I've lost whose deaths you've caused!   5690
Lest I lose honor too, here's your reward!"
At helmet-point Aumon swings his great sword,
But Ogier sways and is not scathed at all;
The blow slams down and through the saddle saws,
Clean through the neck and breast of Ogier's horse;   5695
Ogier joins Naimes down on the ground, my lords;
Had he been struck by that blow's awful force
Then Gorhan's death would have been dearly bought.

296

When Balan now beholds this mortal scene
And sees his son Gorhan slain in the field,   5700
His heart is broken, his sorrow is so deep;
He gores his horse, in woe bereft of speech;
He grips his spear of strong iron from the East
And strikes Carlon with all the hurt he feels;
His shield he splits but not the coat beneath,   5705
Which saves our King from metal and from steel;
Behold Carlon give back what he's received!
Breast-plate nor girth keep Balan in his seat
As he's knocked down by Carlon at his feet,
His crystal helm embedding in the heath;   5710
Charles thunders on who after Aumon speeds
Down a deep dale--ah, why was he so keen?
Dear God in Heaven, do not desert our liege!
Ere he returns he'll have his share of grief.

297

Balan is down, unseated from his stallion;   5715
Now see him rise, his mind a blank with anger,
Save that he knows he must regain his saddle;
But look! Duke Naimes in mighty rage comes at him,
His sword drawn forth, his heart intent on challenge;
But Balan, lords, sheathes his sword in the scabbard   5720
And walks to Naimes as hostage to his captor!
Ogier runs in, Carlon's good Danish champion,
And young Estous and Berenger and Haton
And Roland too, whose mighty rod has fractured--
Yet still he holds a full lance-length unshattered,   5725

Which ere day ends Carlon will be right glad of;
Now Balan knows that they will all attack him;
He calls to Naimes: "Hold hard, worthy chevalier!
To kill me here would be of little value;
If I could find Duke Naimes, Bavaria's landgrave, 5730
To Christian faith I would be raised in baptism;
He holds me dear and I know for a fact, sir,
If he were here that he would stay your hand now."
Duke Naimes replies: "Who are you then, chevalier?
"Sir knight, I am the Emir's envoy Balan, 5735
Who came to France to bring the word of Agolant."
"God," says Duke Naimes, "from my heart's depths I
    thank you!
Ogier, for love of God, harm not this vassal!
No man has helped me more than this Balan has."

298

"Dear Balan, is it you," Duke Naimes exclaims, 5740
"Who rescued me from Agolant's high rage?
His Persian court all sought to have me slain,
But thanks to you my life and limbs were saved;
At my disposal all of your wealth you placed
And told me then that you believed Christ's faith; 5745
Will you, in truth, all Lord God's Laws obey?"
"In truth," says Balan,"from this time on always."
"Then fear no more, Balan," the good Duke says;
At this behold young Roland come apace!
So hard he's run his stallion all this day 5750
It is worn out and weary with the strain;
So keen's the lad to follow Charlemayn
He spies Morel and leaves his horse in haste;
He swings astride the swift horse of Duke Naimes
And flays its flanks to follow Charlemayn, 5755
Who seeks Aumon as swiftly as he may;
Duke Naimes is left to stand there and to rage!

299

Aumon escapes, both angry and remorseful;
How things have changed for him since yestermorning!
When light of day displayed his force at dawning 5760
Aumon could count at his command and order
Seven hundred thousand Turks, all strong and stalwart;
Now not one squire is left there to support him;
They are all dead or prisoners of warfare;
Those left with limbs to run have fled before him; 5765
Charles chases him, but has as yet not caught him;
At every turn he pledges God the lawful
That come what may he'll find this devil Aumon,

Who of our best so many men has slaughtered;
Dear God in Heaven, why is Carlon so dauntless? 5770
Ere this day ends he will endure such torment
He'll not survive it without the help of Lord God;
Hot on his heels see Roland spur his war-horse!
He'll follow him though life and limbs go forfeit;
A worthy kinsman is priceless above all things; 5775
Aumon escapes and down a rock-face forges,
Deep in a dale where grows an olive orchard
On the rich bank of a clear fount of water;
When he sees this how gladly he heads for it,
Sure in his mind that no more Frenchmen stalk him; 5780
For three whole days without a stay he's fought now,
His thoughts so set on the relentless tourney
That's he's drunk nothing nor touched of food a morsel;
So Aumon stops, dismounts, and ties his horse up,
Sets down his shield and drops his spear and
       sword-belt 5785
And then unhooks his helmet and withdraws it;
Now he stoops down before that fount of water
And drinks thereof, deep draughts his thirst
       according;
Yet ere he drinks his fill he will be thwarted
By Charlemayn, who down the slope is drawing; 5790
The Paynim hears him and spins around forlornly;
Although he's quick his speed avails him naught now;
How can he reach his horse or grip his broadshield
Or any weapon when Carlon has him cornered?
Aumon sees this and anger through him courses: 5795
"Paynim, do not despair!" great Carlon calls him;
"Upon my soul it shall not be recorded
I struck a man who was not ready for me!
Go get your arms and get yourself on horseback!
We two must fight, and this my challenge formal: 5800
This fount is mine and I'll defend it staunchly;
How dare you drink it? Right dearly you'll pay for
       it!"
Aumon hears this and how his heart rejoices
At Charlemayn all of his arms restoring!
Now see him move with nothing more to stall him! 5805
From ground to horse he jumps in one leap forward
To grasp his arms and grip his buckler surely;
He looks at Charles and loudly now he taunts him;
"By Mahomet, chevalier!" he chortles,
"You will regret you ever saw or sought me! 5810
It is not often that people ride towards me!
That horse you have must be a wondrous courser,
To have outrun so far your reinforcements!
And you're not dressed like a scout questing
       quarters;

Your back is clad in a good double hauberk   5815
And on your head's a helm of gold the choicest;
You are no child of low-born lackey forebears!
You can't deny that your descent is courtly;
I knew that much as soon as here I saw you;
You had a chance to kill me then, but scorned it   5820
To let me mount and have the arms I bore not;
You've served me well and now I will reward you:
You can return unharmed, this I assure you,
But you must leave the weapons that you brought here;
And if you would forswear your faith as falsehood,   5825
By good Mahom I'd welcome you so warmly
Your children's children would bless me for it
    always!"
"Cursed if I will!" says Charlemayn, retorting;
"How ill-bethought to trick me with such talking!"
Then Aumon says: "What is your name, proud courtier?"   5830
And Charles replies: "I'll not let you ignore it,
Nor will I lie to anyone of your sort;
My name is Charles, lord of fair France's borders,
Prince of the Picards and King of all the Normans
And all the German states southwards and northwards,   5835
The Berrichons, the Manseaux and the Lorrains;
As far as Rome I rule and am held royal;
And I've come here to fight with you for all of it!"
Aumon hears this and how his heart rejoices!
He says to Charles: "At last my luck has altered!   5840
All that I've lost I will account as naught now
As your blood flows, my pain all purged outpouring."

                        300

Aumon says more: "Are you that Charlemayn,
Who men so many of my rich best has slain,
So many a king and prince of my domain?   5845
I challenge you to fight me straightaway
For the Romagna, alike for Calabray,
For Germany, Bavaria and Lorraine,
For all the land to the limits of Spain!"
"Indeed," says Charles, "what a gain to gainsay!   5850
Yet is he King whose words are all his claim?
Your challenge I accept--since it is made;
Let him who lives and leaves makes no complaint!"

                        301

"Sir knight," says on our loyal lord Carlon,
"In my regard and in respect of God,   5855
The claim you lay to my own realm is wrong;
I hold this land from none of mortal stock;

By right of God I rule and others none."
Aumon replies: "Your logic suits me not!
If you've said all you have to say, let's on!"   5860
At this they turn and spur their mounts along;
With such great blows each other's shield they shock
Both bucklers break, each one beneath the boss;
Their horses charge at such a pace non-stop
That those two kings, so valiant each and strong,   5865
Are both unhorsed and from their saddles drop;
Breast-plate nor girths can save them falling off;
So hard they fall, both Carlon and Aumon,
That their two helms strike in the earth and lodge,
Embedded thus up to the nasal-knob;   5870
Aumon's first up and brings forth Durendal;
Then Carlon lifts his great Joyeuse aloft
And both strong kings in deadly combat lock.

302

These kings have both much power and much pride;
They are both fierce and full of enterprise,   5875
And are both rich in money, land and lives;
In all the world beneath the driven skies
You would not find two rules of such might;
One rules the world on all its Eastern side;
The other rules the Western world entire;   5880
Such rivalry the two of them divides
They'll not concede one inch the other's right;
Hear Aumon shout: "Carlon, give ear a while!
Will you greet me as your liege-lord and Sire
And give me France? Tell me your inmost mind!   5885
And will you heed my Tervagant, besides?
"Never!" roars Charles, "In truth, I'd rather die!"
Aumon hears this and leaps at him in ire;
He catches Charles a wondrous blow and wild
On his crown's crest, upon his helmet high;   5890
It would have cost another man his life;
From top to teeth that same blow would have sliced;
But Carlon's helm withstands it in this wise:
It has a stone set in the nasal tight
No blow can break, and thus our King survives;   5895
Now Carlon swings and sparing naught he smites
So hard the shield that Aumon holds upright
That on the field one mighty quarter flies;
Had Carlon's sword deflected not in flight
Aumon's front foot would have been shorn alike;   5900
The sword a-glint through Aumon's leggings glides
And shears the mail ere in the ground it strikes.

303

Aumon is shocked, his face with passion flushed
Almost to madness when he beholds his blood;
Durendal flies, which ever burnished was, 5905
As Aumon aims at the ear of Carlun;
But Carlon's helm bears sacred stones first cut
In Jeremiah's time, whose strengh is such
Aumon's best blow hurts Carlon not a touch;
His helm's unmarked and quite unscathed his skull; 5910
Aumon sees this and his heart sinks at once;
See him draw back and curse his good sword thus:
"Ill-spent the hour that forged you, Durendal!
How long I've worn you and what great deeds we've done!
With you I took my knighthood's vows in trust, 5915
And ever since, whenever a man I've struck
With your great steel, he knew his life was up;
I never needed your strength as now so much,
And now you fail me! Your blade has turned so blunt
You cut no better than an axe gone to rust" 5920

304

Aumon and Charles stand facing in the meadow;
Their swords are drawn, their mighty shields raised ready;
They strike great blows, their strength alike contesting;
The King of France holds up Joyeuse and sends it
Flying at Aumon, two blows in quick succession; 5925
His byrnie's old and Joyeuse rips and rends it,
Drawing blood twice as Aumon's flesh it enters;
In quick response Aumon lifts high Durendal
And strikes and strikes strong blows on Carlon's helmet;
But still in vain! He harms it not a penny, 5930
Because of that same stone therein embedded--
A wondrous jewel touched by God's Hand in blessing,
Whose mighty Love such virtue in it vested,
That while it stays set in good Carlon's helmet
Our King is safe from death or any peril; 5935
Aumon sees this and blood burns his complexion;
He blames his blade and curses it right heavy:
"Ah Durendal, how blunted now your edge is!
From the first day I won you for my weapon,
I never struck a man who lived to tell it; 5940
Now you are beaten and all your fame has ended!"
Aumon looks up at Carlon's gold-ringed helmet;
He sees the stone set in the nasal's centre

And knowing it straightway his whole heart trembles;
Then to himself in soft tones he confesses: 5945
"Ah Durendal, how I blamed you in error!
I wonder not your finest strokes were feckless!"

305

Right full of wrath and mighty rage is Aumon
That he cannot break Carlon's helmet open,
His blade rebounding with every thrust he throws him; 5950
With hate in heart he looks at it right closely;
He sees the stones in their gold circle glowing
And straightaway is certain that he knows them;
He cannot hide his feelings at this moment
And tells Carlon, these words from his lips flowing: 5955
"How much I wish, King of the Christian soldiers,
That I could have that helm of yours and own it!
While those stones sit upon your brow so boldly
No stroke of mine will harm or overthrow you;
But when your head in my two hands I'm holding 5960
Without your helm, you'll die a death right doleful!"
Carlon hears well the words of his opponent;
God, Holy Spirit, guard Carlon and watch over him!
If not he'll never return to France his homeland.

306

Aumon sees well that it avails him not; 5965
The more he strikes that helmet of Carlon
The more his sword rebounds and bounces off;
But if he can he'll have that helm ere long:
"Carlon, I will not lie," he says anon;
"By Mahomet, that man loved you a lot, 5970
Who gave to you those stones your helmet's got!
How much more worth are stones as those beyond
All I possess here in my weapons' stock;
A man might laugh at death with that helm on--
But that man won't be you, by great Mahom!" 5975
Carlon retorts: "You will be wrong, please God!"

307

Hard by that fount beneath the olive broad,
Where for so long both Kings so hard have fought,
See Carlon lift again his naked sword
To rip and wreck Aumon's hauberk once more! 5980
Both left and right the Paynim's sides he gores
And from four wounds his blood bursts out and pours;
Now Aumon knows he has no other choice;
Unless he overcomes Charles with brute force,

And from his head that helmet can be torn, 5985
Then he himself will die here or be caught;
Aumon the wretch runs at Carlon therefore,
Who quick to parry his two strong arms employs;
What lusty blows with bare hands each one scores!
So long they lock and lunge in this wild brawl 5990
Till Aumon grasps that helmet with his claws:
He has great strength, he's tough as teak and tall;
He grips one ring and wrenches back and forth
Till it comes loose and then at last withdraws;
Bareheaded now stands Charles our Emperor, 5995
Uncovered quite save by his hauberk's coif;
When he sees this, great Carlon's heart is stalled:
"Dear God," he cries, "our everlasting Lord,
Look down on me and help me, I implore!
If I die here then all my French will fall: 6000
Fine men so many--dear God, where are they all?"
Aumon hears this and shakes Charles, angered sore;
Our King strives hard to fight off this assault,
But, lords, he would have died, the geste records,
When up rode Roland! He'd ridden like a storm 6005
Astride Morel,that was Duke Naimon's horse!
God willed it not, the Father of our Lord,
That Charles his man should die at this time's point;
Thus Roland comes a-gallop down that gorge:
"What are you doing, my lord uncle?" he calls; 6010
It's me, your nephew Roland, your pride and joy!
Shall you or I be heeded in high court
If two of us can't tame one heathen hawk?"
"Sweet Lord be praised!" says Charles with thankful
     voice;
Aumon sees Roland, but scorns him for a boy; 6015
Yet see this lad dismount his horse of war,
Lift high his pole and strike the Infidel!
High on the helm with awesome power he bores
And knocks the Turk to ground upon all fours;
Shame floods Aumon and he leaps up full-galled 6020
That he was felled by such a youngster raw!

308

How wondrous wild was Aumon as he wrestled!
Full fourty times he turned Charles as he held him;
If Lord or God had not looked down from Heaven
And sent young Roland in wondrous haste to help him, 6025
He'd not have ruled henceforth in France or elsewhere;
See Roland now lift of his rod the remnant--
For he has slain full many a foe already,
And strike Aumon the obdurate a second;
He breaks this time one circle on his helmet; 6030

Harder his skull than bull or bruin's head is;
Not that it matters, for once again he fells him:
Aumon gets up, all fury his expression:
He turns to Charles and loudly thus he tells him:
"You fight alone no more, King of the Westworld; 6035
This boy's a villain, but very brave and reckless!
What fiend gave him that rod, what living devil?
If this lad lives he will be knighthood's best one!
And if today should mark my lifetime's ending
I pray Mahom, my great god, and request it 6040
That this lad have my sword Durendal henceforth;
For it would be too wrong and too offensive
If a weak, wavering man wielded Durendal,
Who lusted not for battle and its perils;
But I am sure and do not doubt one measure 6045
That I in brief shall kill both of you Frenchman;
Your precious liege, lord God, shall not protect you!
I am alone, but though you two were seven
You'll not be saved, nor have you hope of rescue
More than the lamb by four wolves trapped has ever." 6050

309

Aumon is sick at heart and sore dismayed;
Hard-pressed he is by Charles and Roland twain;
He wields his sword, wherein he sets his faith;
But as on high he lifts it up and aims
To strike Carlon on his uncovered face, 6055
See Roland lift his heavy rod again
And bring it down atop his pointed blade!
So hard he hits, Durendal flies out straight
From Aumon's hands and one lance-length away;
Aumon alone, without his sword, remains; 6060
He looks to run, but by Carlon he's claimed;
And now at last all his bravado fails
As Roland moves with all the speed he may
Towards the Turk, his rod already raised;
He strikes his helm up front a blow so great 6065
He splits his skull and out spurt all his brains;
Still Roland strikes, again and then again,
And Aumon drops, who no more steps shall take;
His brains spill out and all beside him lay,
And thus he dies, writhing his life away; 6070
Lords, you could say, and I would grant the same,
That Charles would never in his lifetime one day
Have gone back home to France, his sweet domain,
Nor worn again his bright gold crown of state,
Without God's help and nephew Roland's aid; 6075
Young Roland gained his Olifant this way
And Durendal with which he won such fame,

And his swift horse that was called Wideawake;
The lad comes now to Charles, who has remained
In great distress and sweating with the strain;   6080
From seven wounds his face with blood is stained;
He comes to him and kneeling down in haste
He gently weeps and looks at him and says:
"Uncle, do you still live, for good God's sake?"
"Alive I am, but I am in great pain,   6085
For wondrous strong was that oppressive knave."
Young Roland stoops to bathe his uncle's face;
And now behold Ogier ride up and Naimes
And Salemon and Tiorin apace!
With Duke Fagon and Elinant they came;   6090
How hard they grieve, bemoaning Carlon's fate;
They weep and wail, lamenting loud and grave,
Sure in their hearts that they have come too late,
That Charles is dead, by the Emir's son slain,
Aumon the strong whom none could stand against;   6095
So far they ride this way and that in chase
Till they find Charles down in that grassy dale.

                        310

Ogier and Naimes, down from their saddles leaping,
Find Carlemayn, who's taken such mistreatment
That all his face from seven wounds is bleeding: 6100
"How wrong of you, my lord," thus Naimon greets him,
"So far alone to follow that fell heathen!
He was in truth a living, raging, demon;
Behold his body--his massive limbs and features!
If you had seen how I was floored so fiercely,   6105
And Ogier's horse, how viciously he cleaved it!
He robbed us of our steeds so quick and easy,
And when he thus had felled us both so freely
He did not seem like a man to be beaten!
If you had heard me then and thence had heeded,   6110
You'd not have given chase with heart so eager!"
"My lords," says Charles, "I've paid the price right
        dearly!
But what's done's done and nothing can retrieve it;
If you could know how sorely he aggrieved me!
If Lord our God had answered not my pleading,   6115
And Roland here, who to my side came speeding,
I would have died, you must know this quite clearly."
They turn the Turk face upward at their feet then,
And Duke Naimes says: "Who could not be agreed, Sire,
That if this king has been baptized for Jesus,   6120
No better man would have been born than he was?"
Then Naimon moves and kisses Roland three times:
"Yours be this corpse and all its spoils completely;

                        147

You won this fight--it's only right you keep them."

311

They bring Aumon beneath the olive's bough 6125
And on his back they lay his body out:
"In truth," says Naimes, "he was a prince of power;
Had he been Christ's in his baptism's hour,
No better man in Christendom were found."
These words once said, they help Carlon remount 6130
And then ride back so far round and about
Till they return to the main battle-ground;
There Carlon finds his barons and his counts
Grim-visaged all, their heads with sorrow bowed;
Then when they see that Charles is safe and sound 6135
They weep for joy full many a tear and loud;
To Aumon's tent they gently take Charles now,
Where he dismounts and his armor's unbound.

312

In Aumon's tent the French are all assembled;
Girart the duke has sent troops out already; 6140
So many men of life and limb lie severed,
The fields are filled and overspilled the meadows;
Those left alive have taken so much treasure
That just to see it, lords, would make you jealous;
Men who till then had never been shod in leather 6145
Now had war-steeds of wondrous stock and merit;
Girart commands that Aumon's tower be emptied:
For all are grieved, even the very best ones,
That for two days and one long night together
They have drunk nothing nor touched of food a
    vestige; 6150
How glad they are this vigil now is ended!
How their grief fades as good food fills their
    bellies!
When this is told to Agolant the Emir,
You can be sure he will rage with a vengeance!

END OF BOOK ONE

BOOK 2

PART 7

313

In Reggio town was strong King Agolant 6155
When there arrived the strong King Boidant
And Moadas from past Jerusalem,
With such support I never saw so much;
He goes to meet them, right joyful that they've come,
And rich rewards he vows to them enough; 6160
Now he sits down; my lords, behold him thus
As he plays chess with strong King Abilant!
At day's first hour their game they have begun
And are not finished when the ninth hour is up;
The Emir frets and then his rage erupts 6165
As with some spite he finally gives tongue:
"Why such delay for nothing lost or won?
I'll stake Apulia against this right hand glove!"
Abilant laughs and gently calls his bluff:
"Bet on Messina before Apulia! 6170
Since yestermorn, at dawn, Aumon your son
Has ridden out from his great tower in front
Of men one hundred thousand, all valiant-bloods;
Yet you know not how he has fared or done."
At this see Amargon and Esperrant 6175
Astride their mounts, one black and one gray one,
Ride up before them and from their saddles jump!
These two have news should it be asked of them;
Says Agolant: "You are well come to us!"

314

Both kings in turn hail Agolant and greet; 6180
They ask: "Great King, what are you doing here?
Your son has fought with Carlon in the field;
He took with him your battle-flag, Emir,
And men one hundred thousand placed in our keep;
What can we say? We suffered great defeat; 6185
On our right flank a fearsome host appeared,
Whose leader was a small man white of beard;
We were defeated and put to flight by these;
Of our three hundred thousand not one still breathes
With strength enough to henceforth hold his shield." 6190
The King replies: "Esperrant, what do you mean?
What has become of my son? Where is he?"
"In truth, my lord, your son we have not seen."

When Agolant hears Esperrant's sad speech
He very nearly goes mad with rage and grief; 6195
In his right hand he holds a cutting spear;
Now his arm shakes and strongly sets it free;
Esperrant turns and sees the javelin speed
Right past his body and strike a wooden beam;
The wood sheers off as clean in half it's cleaved: 6200
"You fool!" says the Emir, "I'll not believe
My son could be defeated or forced to flee
By any man of baptism received;
You will be hanged for your words like a thief!"
Says Esperrant: "I hear you well indeed; 6205
But what is stolen cannot now be retrieved."

315

King Agolant, when he hears this reply,
From all his host calls up his chiefest knights;
High in the palace which was King Jeremiah's
Sits Agolant, yet has no cause to smile: 6210
"My lords," he says, "hear now the conduct vile
Of these two kings--may Mahom curse their hides!
They've shamed my house and left my son to die!
I order you, upon your limbs and lives,
To judge them both of this most wretched crime 6215
That they have done--may Mahom curse their hides!
Each one of you shall truthful speak his mind,
As you hold dear your own limbs and your lives."
Without delay all in the council rise.

316

Some twenty kings in council all are sitting 6220
And four emirs and one almanzor with them;
Apart from these no others are admitted;
The Almanzor it is speaks to begin with:
"My lords," he says, "give ear to me and listen,
For I would state my own thoughts and decision! 6225
Though the Emir has made clear what his wish is,
Both of these kings are close to me in kinship;
The two of them are children of my sister;
I do not think that we have here the witness
To prove to us that they should be judged guilty; 6230
They're noble men of high and blameless lineage;
I greatly fear, in truth I tell you this much,
That this dispute may set us all in discord."

317

Antelme the old, up on his feet next standing,

Speaks out his mind like a man who is angry: 6235
"You are too arrogant, my lord Almanzor,
When you declare that we have not the man here
To prove to us the guilt these two kings carry;
Since both of them owe all their power to Agolant,
Who strengthened them and gave them their high
    standing, 6240
Put in their charge his son and one battalion
Of men one hundred thousand, hand-picked and valiant,
And since they held and lost his battle-standard,
Yet are themselves both safe and sound come back here
Without a wound to show for all their valor, 6245
Their shields unstruck and neither lance-head
    shattered,
Their helms unhit and neither breast-plate battered,
They do condemn themselves, these facts established;
Within this army are many worthy barons
Who sent their sons and brothers on this action; 6250
For all of these our hearts are filled with sadness;
And each of us is angry in his anguish;
Like it or not, Almanzor, or your family,
You shall bear witness as we arrest these vassals,
Until at least Aumon returns from battle." 6255

318

Acars of Flors next on his feet stands up;
He speaks out loud, for is troubled much:
"My lords," he says, "let us not quarrel thus!
All of you know how great is Africa,
And great therein have been our ancestors; 6260
There have been many, rich and content enough
Not to desire another man's kingdom,
As the Emir, urged by bad counsel, does--
By young hot-headed knights, their spurs new won;
King Agolant should not be here with us, 6265
But back in Africa where he can hunt
With dogs and trackers in his own forests lush,
And fly his hawks where his own rivers run,
And leave Aumon this land to overcome;
Let him find out the weak vain-glorious ones, 6270
Who call us cowards and scorn us and insult!
The old in life are not helped by the young;
Yet they will age ere this land brings them luck!
In Africa two better are there none
Than King Amargon and red-haired Esperrant, 6275
Whom you would treat as traitors here at once;
There are no knights more true, more chivalrous,
More fierce in battle or more experienced;
It would be wrong and wondrously unjust

To act in haste and judge in ignorance;   6280
So, if you please, both men to me entrust
Until we know what is and has been done,
And glad or sad may be as a result."

319

Up on his feet stands next strong Abilant;
So all can hear he speaks as loud he can: 6285
"You never loved Aumon or Agolant;
Now you stand up and shout out from the back
For all to hear such counsel as you have:
My lord Emir should hold these men in hand!
It is not right that traitors thus may brag   6290
In royal court, in knowledge of the fact
That for their crimes they may escape the rap;
No man should be crowned king who would do that;
Without delay, while we all witness stand,
Both of these men should be run through the ranks,   6295
Stripped to their breeches, defenceless and unclad;
Fifteen strong sargeants should follow either man,
In their gloved hands each one holding a lash;
Whoever's strokes should fail both men to gash,
Shall lose straightway the hand which thus did lapse;   6300
Then, as we watch, let both these traitors hang,
And both their bodies be tossed on flaming brands;
And those who like this not or look askance,
Let them alike be dealt with and be damned!"

320

Of Befany see next the king arise: 6305
"My lords," says he, "give ear to me a while!
Aumon himself much honored these two knights,
Put in their hands his own and his men's lives,
With those one hundred thousand hand-picked to fight;
The French, it seems, have stormed them from all
    sides,   6310
Their troops led by an old man bearded white;
They've beaten us and put Aumon to flight;
We all know Aumon, his conduct and his pride;
Since this defeat he's cast them from his sight;
We cannot blame them for coming back betimes."   6315

321

At this speaks up the ruler of Fenia;
There's no man wiser in all the world of heathens;
A rich king he of many lands and peoples;
He holds and rules the realms of Murgalia,

Halape, Tabarieh, Hamon and Caesarea, 6320
Beirut, Iconium, Sort, Esclaudia;
His head and hair are dark, his face white-bearded,
His look is fierce and bold and strong his features;
In all their host there's none more brave than he is;
He says: "My lords, hear now the conduct evil 6325
Of these two kings--may Mahomet curse each one!
Their sin is great, they know it is, and we do;
Through cowardice they did desert their liege-lord
And all the army of which they were the leaders,
And battle-flag which was in their safe-keeping, 6330
And those one hundred thousand, our knighthood's
    dearest;
These two thought only of their own well-being
And fled the field--as every man can see here;
These kings know nothing of the great dues of fealty;
I judge that they lose life and limb for treason; 6335
If there is any who'd speak against my reasons
I'll have his head with my sword sharp and gleaming
Before the bell tolls out its last this evening."
Not one man there has any word to speak then;
The king of Esclavonia says to the meeting: 6340
"This lord speaks well and makes his point right
    clearly."

322

King Manuel responds to this with anger:
"My lord emir, you speak wrongly and badly;
All of us here know for a fact established
You never loved the strong ties of our family, 6345
Nor any man who honored the Almanzor;
And I will tell why this is so exactly,
The feud between our families and what began it,
And how your clan always frustrates our actions:
Once with brute force we ran you out of Africa; 6350
Nor would your clan have grown again or gathered,
But Agolant his will in this enacted,
Gave back your lands and to your honor added;
In all the East there are no better vassals
Than King Amargon, who over there is standing, 6355
And Esperrant, one of our closest clansmen;
Although you hate them, out of your family's malice,
You should not judge them as cheaply as you have done;
We still know not whose fault is what has happened;
These are high men of much land and much value; 6360
Within these ranks they've kinsmen and companions,
Know this for certain, who'll not let you harass them;
In peace, therefore, and with good grace hold back now
Until we know the whole truth of this matter;

If they've done wrong let vengeance then be
   practised." 6365

323

Up to his feet stands next wise Synagon,*
King of Halape and its surrounding spots,
Lord of the city and tower of Antioche;
Greatly he loves Agolant and Aumon,
Whom in his house he reared in days bygone; 6370
Behold him stand, clutching in hand a rod:
"My lords," he says, "hear now and heed the wrong
Done by these two, who are of Nero's stock
And nephews both of that dissembling dog
Sat yonder on his seat of marble rock, 6375
Dressed in his mantle of rich vermilion cloth;
Treason and tricks with him have never stopped;
When just a boy I saw him scheme and plot,
While with my spurs I served King Agolant;
Our Emir should have banished him straight off! 6380
He and Angart and that base wretch Lanpal,
That wretch Estols and those kings Garahon
And Esoran and wicked Managon
And all their breed--a curse upon the lot!
How badly they've repaid the gains they got! 6385
I had three sons who all were with Aumon,
As was my brother the worthiest Sanson,
Who used to bear the King's gold gonfalon;
I know for certain that we shall see them not;
The Almanzor entreats us loud and long 6390
To put aside revenge or fear his wrath;
Indeed we'll not, nor let our will be crossed!
These two have acted like knaves of lowest stock;
They are both guilty of treason, by Mahom!
They should be hung like thieves caught as they rob, 6395
Their corpses burnt in flames all fiery hot,
So all may see their crime and know its crop;
The Almanzor can shake his head or nod,
Talk of his family, who never did but wrong;
Yet if he still opposes this hereon, 6400
Then let him lift his shield and lance aloft,
Put on his hauberk and lace his helmet on;
If with my sword, which hangs by my belt-knot,
I do not take his head, no less the cost,
Then in the lion's den myself I'll toss." 6405
Not one man there of speech so bold there was
To speak against these words the smallest jot;

* The killing of Synagon by Duke Naimes earlier
  (LL.5677-8) seems to have been overlooked here.

King Uliens confides to Pharaon:
"This lord speaks well his message clear and strong."

324

King Pantalis next to his feet does rise 6410
And speaks out loud so all may hear alike;
He speaks as one who feels great rage and spite
For those kings' sakes who both stand there on trial;
They are his nephews and of his kith and kind;
When he hears them thus cheaply judged to die 6415
He'll not hold back from speaking out his mind:
"By Mahomet, what an almighty pride!
Men of Synagon's rank should not decide
On punishment, it is the Emir's right;
Now will you hear what I have to advise? 6420
None of us knows the full truth at this time;
But, by Mahom, whoever crows or cries,
I'll speak the truth as I know it meanwhile;
Amargon and Esperrant are high-born knights,
Both of them bold and valiant in a fight; 6425
In all our host no braver two you'd find;
To kill them now will lead to bitter strife;
Let strong Agolant wait, this my advice,
Until his son with all his knights arrives;
Through them you'll learn the compass of their crime; 6430
You men of council should act along these lines;
But, by Mahom, whose servant true am I,
There's no one here of such renown or might,
If he judged now that they should lose their lives,
Whom with my cutting blade I'd not defy, 6435
To judge so lowly such men who are so high;
These men aren't cowards, nor guiltily contrite,
Nor yet accused with proof of words or eyes."

325

Godrin the Carruier next takes the floor;
On a knight's shoulder he leans for some support; 6440
He's a rich man and rules by law enforced
All of the land of King Tempier's before,
This being Brugier, a big domain and broad;
Godrin is wise and very skilled in war
And much does know concerning Paynim law; 6445
To Agolant he is chief counsellor;
No better knight there is in all their horde:
"My lords, give ear to me!" Godrin exhorts;
"I'll speak the truth, whomever it may gall;
These traitors two who stand before us all, 6450
Think they can hide the treason they have wrought;

They have deserted their rightful liege and lord,
Who gave them both his battle-flag withal,
Where all his men could rally or withdraw
With those one hundred thousand of our most choice; 6455
These two did flee like feckless craven sorts,
Desert their liege from Africa's far shore,
Who were supposed to give the rest support;
I rightly judge, whomever this annoys,
That both of them like thieves be hung and drawn, 6460
Then in the fire their bodies burned and scorched;
Let traitors have the punishment they ought!
If Pantalis, who yonder makes his noise,
Who's tried so hard to steer us from our course,
Whose family's worth is not one denier coin, 6465
If he persists and with my steel-blade sword
I do not make his head roll for his talk,
Then have me burned and cast my ashes forth
And throw my heirs out of their homes and halls."

326

Hard on these words speaks Hadequin the Sultan; 6470
A wise man he and theologian wondrous;
To those two traitors he is the closest cousin;
He owns the land up to Montmatin's summits;
In his own tongue he hails Godrin of Brugier:
"In truth, my lord, in you I've a poor countryman! 6475
For on this morn you have made a bad judgement
On two high knights from families of substance--
That they be drawn between the tails of sumpters;
By Mahomet, this thing shall not go thus far!
We do not know this battle's true result yet, 6480
Nor of brave Aumon and all those other youngsters
On whose fate turns this trial and all this trouble;
But, by that faith I owe Apollo humbly,
You will not see tomorrow morning's sunrise
Without some word from Aumon and the others; 6485
Guard both these kings, meanwhile, within these turrets,
Then judge them fairly as fits our Paynim custom;
Let no Persian or Arab have cause to utter
That out of fear for ourselves or our brothers
We are prepared to judge a man unjustly." 6490

327

Next to his feet is one King Maladient;
Of Africa he rules the far-east region;
Before his time no other living creature
That we know of had ever even been there;
It was a land of sea and sky and breezes; 6495

What wondrous wealth and power now he wields there:
Not counting towns he owns one hundred keeps there;
His skin is tanned, his features fair and cheerful;
Neath arching brows his eyes are proud and piercing;
He has big shoulders and ample build between them;   6500
His hands are large and are as white-appearing
As is the snow that falls from heaven's ceiling;
His chest is broad, his body fine and pleasing,
His hips low-set, his posture nice and easy,
Even and firm when on his horse he's seated;   6505
He wears a robe with a fresh ermine gleaming;
Of Afric cloth it is and fashion recent,
With a rich silk cut to his trim beneath it;
The cloth alone, down from his shoulders sweeping,
Bears gold and jewels worth one hundred mark pieces;   6510
In voice full-lunged he speaks so all may hear him:
"By Mahomet, sir Almanzor," he greets him,
"How scornfully you and your family treat us!
But I am here to stand by this agreement:
If I don't take these two straight to our liege-lord,   6515
Let him hang me tomorrow--or scorn him freely!"
All know this king and none at first impedes him;
Then forty rise, then five score to their feet there;
Mahom their God invoking, they entreat him:
"Take one more step and this thing will turn evil!"   6520
Then from all sides they seize on Maladient;
One Hogier speaks in a loud voice and fiercely--
Emir he is of land far in the Eastworld,
A man of wealth and holder of great fiefs there;
A high-born man of much wit and experience--   6525
He speaks out loud in front of all those heathens:
"By Mahomet, you speak with words unreasoned,
Such high-born men as these to treat so cheaply,
Condemning them to pain and death for treason!
We still know not where lies the fault of fealty;   6530
That these two held the flag, this is indeed so,
Till in low wise they were both forced to flee it;
But even if they'd stopped there, though defeated,
Aumon their liege was not there to relieve them;
And all their friends would now be fiercely grieving--   6535
For had they stayed they would have died quite clearly;
We must judge here as fits the misdemeanor;
If we rush off to the Emir with these two,
I know for certain he will kill them unheeding;
The gold of all the world would not redeem them."   6540

328

Of Orcany stands up King Calides,

A powerful man of great wealth and estate;
Four lands he holds beneath his rule and sway:
"My lords," he says, "let each man have his say!
When each man's words have all been heard and weighed, 6545
Let us adopt the good and bad forsake!
All Africa was Agolant's terrain,
And rightly his through strong ancestral claim;
No Syrian mule there is in all our train
Of strength enough, though journeying each day, 6550
Which could in seven years cross his domain;
The King was strong and vigorous and sage;
A worthy knight and in all combat brave;
Few men if any in all our baronage
Could split as quickly a mighty lance in twain, 6555
Nor better blow have struck with burnished blade;
But in one thing he made a grave mistake:
He crowned his son as king while he still reigned,
And gave him land though still alive and hale;
And when Aumon this land had thus obtained, 6560
He in his turn gave all of it away
To those who'd lost it once through some foul play;
Ever since then he's shunned us and disdained;
But Agolant misjudged his son again:
From France the sweet a spy with tidings came 6565
Of Christian faith in Holy Mary's Babe;
So sire with son a new agreement made,
Which gave Aumon his Empire if he stayed;
But overseas with all his ships he sailed
Against this pact, much to his father's rage; 6570
To Aumon's cause cling self-indulgent knaves
And callow youths of our knighthood's brigade,
While with their King the barons keep their faith;
This younger group, which to Aumon dictate,
Will split the land just as their fancy takes, 6575
If they can urge him to act in foolish haste
While each of them lies in their love's embrace;
By this fell pact our great land will be shamed;
When in one land two masters are obeyed,
Whatever one does the other will frustrate." 6580

329

Up to his feet old Galindres has risen;
A wise man he and ruler of great riches;
He's king of Batre, that admirable city;
In a great ermine mantle he is outfitted;
Down to his waist flow his white beard and whiskers; 6585
In all their host there's no man more articulate
And none with whom the Emir is more intimate:
He says: "My lords, if now to me you'd listen,

I will tell you the train of my own thinking;
Both these two kings are men of mighty lineage   6590
And both bold knights of most audacious spirit;
If you pursue the plan that's been considered
Then you will set all of our ranks in discord;
It cannot be the whole truth of this issue
That these two men of such great wrong are guilty;   6595
If Aumon comes back here, and his knights with him,
Let us proceed according to his witness;
And if Mahom has willed it in his wisdom
That in the field the lives of these have finished,
Then we may judge these two for their part in it;   6600
This is my counsel, no other shall I give you;
Judgement can be too hastily delivered;
I'll never strive to do another's bidding,
For all the wealth and power of my own kingdom;
I'd fear the shame and wrong it thus might bring me." 6605

330

A mighty fierce emir next takes the floor;
A fighting prince, Floriades he's called;
He is most wise concerning Paynim law,
And as a knight none better holds a sword;
He speaks out loud so all may hear his voice: 6610
"Lord Almanzor, you and Acars of Flors,
And Salatiel, son to your sister born,
And Esperrant and my lord Amargon,
Your clan it was that gave us civil war,
That took away our serfs' service and toil   6615
And our hunt's leisure and pleasure of our hawks,
And of our wives the enjoyment and the joy;
In seven lands no castle and no fort
Of king there was, or prince or vavasor
That you did not attempt to make all yours;   6620
King Agolant, whose empire it is all,
Made Aumon king, who came to their support,
Returned their lands and gave them even more;
A land and realm will only fail and fall
When a wise man makes of a fool his lord."   6625

331

Caliph Gorant next to his feet does rise;
A young man he yet powerful and wise;
He rules the land of Garilant entire;
His beard is white, his hair hoary and white;
He has broad shoulders and is a handsome sight;   6630
His stance is solid and long his legs and thighs,
With strong, long arms about his slender sides;

In white African silk he is attired;
So all may hear in a loud voice he cries:
"By Mahomet, in whom my faith I plight, 6635
I am no child nor any stripling squire!
So I shall speak somewhat my thoughts and mind,
And you may wish to act on my advice;
Amargon and Esperrant are men most high,
Courageous lords and two most worthy knights; 6640
To kill them now will lead to bitter strife!
Let our strong King detain them here a while,
Until we know by proof of words or eyes
How they resigned the field and in what wise;
If Aumon comes, the brave, who loves to fight, 6645
Then let him tell the compass of their crime;
All those who left him there and are alive,
Let him judge them as may to him seem right,
And others not from now until that time."

332

King Moadas of Tyr gets to his feet: 6650
"By Mahomet, what wondrous talk I hear,
Yet see the best still loath the truth to speak!
Aumon, we know, placed in these two kings' keep
His battle-flag to serve as guarantee
For all his men to rally there and meet; 6655
Before this flag no fighting man should flee;
The sort of man whose office is to be
Of one who bears the flag and holds the field,
Should not be someone who might turn tail and leave!
What treachery, to so betray one's liege! 6660
And now, quite safe and sound, they've come back here,
Knowing full well they left their lord in need;
That man should not be lord of realm or fief,
Who'd see them leave once more unharmed and free;
Both men should die so foul a death and fierce 6665
That all their line the shame of it shall feel."

333

Acasalon speaks next in manner angry
And like a man who feels great rage and rancor;
The lofty land he rules of Jubilantum;
His eyes are bright, his face open and happy, 6670
His posture firm when he sits in the saddle;
Big arms he has and long and firmly fashioned:
"My lords," he says, "I have of doubt no shadow
That these two kings have done and acted badly;
In churlish wise their liege-lord they abandoned, 6675
Who honored them above all other vassals;

But they are kings and have here many clansmen;
If you judge them to death in this mean manner,
Know for a fact that there will be great anguish;
I do not think, for so I see this matter, 6680
That they'll stand by and let this lightly happen;
They still don't know the tally of the facts here,
If good or bad are to be judged their actions;
So let us wait till we know all exactly,
Then you may judge them as your desires would have it, 6685
To death by fire or with torture to rack them;
For, by Mahom, whose servant I am gladly,
If you do not, this thing may end in tragedy;
A thousand score and more may die in agony
Before they'll take such shame for naught
   established." 6690

334

King Uliens can no more hold his peace:
"My lords," he says, "give ear a while to me!
I've heard you all debate the judgement meet
For these two kings, who wait outside in fear,
Who so much power over lives and lands still wield; 6695
Whose realms alone cannot be told with ease;
When Agolant erstwhile his court convened,
Full fifty kings that day were to be seen;
To crown his son Aumon he was most keen,
And he set out our thoughts in this to seek; 6700
But he found none who was prepared to speak--
If he desired it, who would not but agree?
So all his land was pledged to Aumon's keep
And to his head the crown of gold decreed;
When my liege-lord then thought to take his ease, 6705
To hunt wild boar and stalk the great stag-deer,
Aumon went off to govern all his lease
And by his will to punish all misdeeds;
And thus he caused those traitors to appear,
Those who had tried to cast out the Emir 6710
And planned this plot to make his father leave;
And he made them abandon all their fiefs,
Those they had taken and their own lands indeed;
But then it was he heard of Christians speak,
Of their baptism in Christ and their belief, 6715
And so set sail for Europe overseas,
With many men of his in company;
They disembarked at yonder harbor's quay;
Then from our ranks he led away all these
And never since for counsel came back here; 6720
Now yestermorn he's fought the Christian breed;
To these two kings his standard he bequeathed,

And now he and his peers have met defeat;
But these two kings quite safe and sound we see!
Whoever knows them must doubtlessly believe 6725
That both in truth must deadly traitors be;
I order you to judge them with all speed;
They should be hung by rights, so I entreat,
This very day, as thieves caught as they steal,
And then flung in a pit both foul and deep, 6730
Or racked more meanly as your thoughts may conceive;
For such an end should every traitor meet!
My lord Almanzor, I see you on your feet,
Raising your eyebrows higher and higher at me,
And every time the blood burns in your cheeks; 6735
If you wish now to stop me or appeal,
You or your family, who all have heard my speech,
Then arm yourselves and I shall mount my steed;
If I cannot defeat you in the field,
Cut off your head and take it as my fee, 6740
Then may the King treat me as vile and mean
As is the common thief caught as he thieves."
When he says this the lips of all are sealed;
The boldest man dares not one word to breathe.

335

Kings Uliens and Mandaquin anon 6745
Each clasp the other by his cloak's ermine cloth
And leave the palace room of marble rock;
They find the King heart-sick and full of wrath;
His head hung low, he sighs loudly and oft;
King Uliens swears by his god Mahom: 6750
"Emir, your heart's too womanish and soft!
Both of those traitors, who are of Cain's own stock,
In all respects have acted in the wrong;
Drag them to death between pack-horses strong!
If this is told by morning to Aumon, 6755
He will applaud your council's swift response."

336

The King speaks up so all may hear and listen:
"Are these men, then, come back to me found guilty?"
"Indeed yes, Sire, to do with as you wish it."
"Then I would have their bodies drawn this instant 6760
And meanly dragged through all of our contingents
And through the town for all to see and witness,
Then thrown into a pit both deep and stinking!
First gather here immediately and quickly
Four score or five low wenches and loose women, 6765
Those who for money will do as they are bidden;

One bezant piece let each one straight be given
And all will come right happily and willing;
On those kings' bodies let each commit apt insults;
Let this be known by everyone this minute 6770
And let a pyre with Greek fire straight be kindled!
Who on a traitor exacts a vengeance bitter
Will set a good example to all his kinsmen;
A simple hanging does overhonor villains."

337

They lead them forth, those two who have been judged; 6775
So all may hear the King speaks loudly thus:
"Ah, traitors foul, where is Aumon my son?
Have you no news? Did you not see Aumon?"
"In truth, Sire, no--we weren't there long enough;
A small old man on a gray horse there was, 6780
Whose army came so fiercely against us
No men alive could ever have borne the brunt;
They drove us from our flag which they all rushed;
Of our one hundred thousand there's scarcely one
With strength enough to bear his armor up; 6785
Aumon still fights amidst the Christian crush,
But we know not how he has fared or done."
"By Mahomet," calls out King Agolant,
"I must be mad to let you more give tongue!"
The King demands four pack-horses at once; 6790
To two of them he ties King Esperrant;
And Amargon, he does not laugh too much;
Four sargeants now bestride those rouncies' rumps
And, nothing spared, they make those sumpters jump;
Lords--flesh is tender and stones do roughly cut; 6795
Both kings soon lose all of their skin and blood;
Those following after pick all the pieces up
And throw them then into a pit of muck;
Those harlots all have heard the bargain struck:
Each shall receive of one bezant the sum 6800
When they depart--now with great joy they come,
The last in line jostling to be in front;
In a short time the press of them is such
That there they stay until the setting sun;
Throughout the Afric ranks the murmur runs: 6805
"Aumon, their lord, helped these two liege-men none."
From Aumon's force behold now Africans
Return to camp with wounded arms and trunks!
These men have news but no one asks of them.

338

Just as the King sits down to dine that day 6810

One thousand men dismount before that place,
Defeated men born of the Devil's race;
There is not one so high in self-acclaim
Whose head or trunk or horse is still unscathed;
Of all their shields not one is still in shape;   6815
Up to the hall these men now make their way;
The first one halts before their King and waits;
This man's been struck so hard by a steel blade,
Which his good horse could not help him evade;
Now from his wound they see the blood escape;   6820
See as it stains that floor of marble slate!
His helm is sliced down to its coif's inlay;
About his shoulders the quarters flap and drape;
He speaks out loud, no more can he refrain:
"My lord," he says, "too long do you delay!   6825
When we set off within our tower to stay,
With men three hundred thousand and archers trained,
Aumon's first thought was to go on a raid
For meat and victuals, his own needs to assuage;
We bore our gods to glorify our faith   6830
And to convert the Christians to our ways:
To towns and towers we went on this campaign,
And all those lords who would not then disclaim
Their God Creator, but still to Him did pray,
We slew them all and took their heads straightway   6835
And slit the breasts of every wife and dame;
From all our booty so large a load we made
That just to see it would make a man amazed;
Then, at month's end, on our way back we came
When the front ranks of fierce-faced Charlemayn   6840
Met up with us by a sloping rock-face,
And we set up to fight their ambuscade;
Our darts and arrows were both of no avail;
Hector was killed, our gonfalonier;
Why should I any more spin out this tale?   6845
Those our four gods they forced us to forsake;
I saw so many drown in a water's drain,
The ditch beneath them dried up as thus I gazed;
I saw a Frenchman pursue Aumon in chase
Right to our tower, its first draw-bridge and gate,   6850
Where with a spear he killed his destrier;
Not one man there could raise that horse again;
Of all the booty that in one month we'd gained,
When we that night at last in safety lay,
We had not left one bread-loaf's worth or weight;   6855
This put Aumon into a mortal rage."

339

Says Agolant: "Is this all true, Valdabrun?

Were our four gods thus borne and thus abandoned?"
"Indeed, yes, Sire, all four of them we carried
So we might teach those Christian lords their value;   6860
For two whole days we've fought with Carlon's
    vanguard;
The French are few, but each one is a champion;
Nor are they armed like boys or lowly vassals;
Their horses' crests are clad in coats iron-padded;
Hauberks and byrnies down to their hooves are hanging, 6865
And whiter they than any ermine jacket;
But we had killed or maimed most of their barons
And struck their horses upon their necks and ankles
When from our right another host attacked us;
At thirty thousand we reckoned then their tally;   6870
This force placed ours straightway in such a panic
We never looked as if we would withstand them;
We quit the field, but only left the battle
As we knew not where we could turn and rally,
For we had lost our flag and battle-standard;   6875
Aumon stayed there with three of his companions;
These were Huber, Gorhan and old Synagon."

340

"Valdabrun, brother, are our four gods, then, lost?"
"Yes, Sire, indeed, and our men dead and gone;
Those Christian knights, when they had stolen our
    gods,   6880
Beat them and struck them as we ourselves looked on,
With lengths of lance and with sharp-pointed rocks;
Then from the frames they all were mounted on
They cast them down head-first into a bog;
No miracles they did or magic strong;   6885
All those who trust in them, I think, are lost;
When we left there we all of us were mocked."

341

Says Valdabrun: "My lord Emir, now listen!
The mighty van of Charlemayn we've witnessed!
It has twelve dukes and two crowned kings within it;   6890
We estimate their sum at thousands sixty,
While Charles himself has five score thousand with him;
Our men have killed one quarter of these Christians;
They, for their part, our cause this much have
    hindered:
By force of arms they've scattered our contingents,   6895
Killed and cut off the heads of our best chivalry
And maimed or shamed those whom they have left living;
But they themselves are tired now and afflicted,

And their war-steeds are weary now and injured;
If you desire to make this land your kingdom, 6900
Mount up, my lord, and cast off your sad spirits!
The man who now assembles them for dinner
Does not have men enough to feed or fill us!"
Says Agolant: "Valdabrun, you have killed me,
Who have no news of my son's fate to give me." 6905
"I have none, Sire, except what has been given;
About his flag our beaten troops were driven."

342

With rage and spite the Emir's heart is heavy;
Time after time he calls himself most wretched:
"Ah, Africans, my noble braves!" he says then, 6910
"Do not be cowards now, neither be hesitant!
Sound out those trumpets, those drums and horns of metal,
And move out now in your best ranks assembled!
Take twenty thousand of our boldest and best ones
Neath your command, Mandaquin, gentle nephew, 6915
And thirty thousand to reinforce and help them!
Acars, the king of Flors, shall be their general
With Moadas and Uliens the redhead
And old Galindres and proud Abilant next to him,
And the Almanzor with both his sons together; 6920
This group shall give myself and mine protection;
If my Aumon were here with us, I tell you,
We would soon see which army was the better."
Says Valdabrun: "Be wary nonetheless, Sire;
Be not too keen to meet up with the Frenchmen; 6925
If you had men one thousand and they twice twenty,
Their forty few could still beat all your many."

343

The Emir's heart is filled with rage and spite;
He plucks his beard and tears fall from his eyes;
So many trumpets and horns and bugles cry, 6930
Great drums resound and big brass cornets whine
As two hundred and sixty thousand ride!
To guard their ships a large force stays behind,
And to protect the loveliest queen and bride
Who ever had breasts upon her chest inclined-- 6935
Had she believed and had she been baptized;
In their front rank see twenty thousand knights,
The boldest best they ever there could find!
King Mandaquin exhorts them in this wise:
"I helped you once when all fled from your side; 6940
By Mahomet, if I may stay alive,
The Christian host shall pay the price this time!"

344

Men thirty thousand the second rank contains;
Behold breast-plates so many and destriers,
Gold helms so many and so many steel blades, 6945
So many arrows and bows both small and great!

345

Acars of Flors and his nephew Manuel
Are overlords and leaders of these men;
Then comes the third led by Floriades;
These have no armor with which to cover them; 6950
Byrnies nor hauberks they put on to protect;
They bear great spears with iron tips sharp-edged;
When they pursue they do so without rest,
And run like stags when are pursued themselves;
In joint command is rich King Calides. 6955

346

And the next rank is led by Eliades;
This race of folk adores fine clothes and armor,
And good war-steeds, strong ones, well-fed and fast ones;
The land they come from is famous for its dances;
Their race is noble and nobly they advance now; 6960
All forty thousand are proud and cruel-hearted;
This race of men did us much harm and hardship.

347

In the next rank of strong King Agolant
Are Uliens and mighty Moadas,
And old Galindres and strong King Abilant, 6965
And the Almanzor who sighs both hard and much:
For his two nephews what wild lament he does,
Whom, as he watched, they dragged past everyone,
And followed after picking the pieces up,
Which then they threw into a pit of muck 6970
And with Greek fire burnt down into a dust;
If the Almanzor's will could now be done,
Then mighty woe will strike those Africans;
Shields green and white see now, lords, as they come;
Breast-plates and helmets all shining in the sun, 6975
So many swords, whose blades so sharply cut,
So many arrows and Turkish bows tight-strung,
And destriers so quick and keen to run!

This rank lines up with a great joy and fuss;
They sound their horns, their tambourines and drums   6980
And cornets too, of which there's well enough;
Behind the rest this rearguard leaves at once;
If these ranks fight as by appearance judged,
Then it bodes ill for Carlon's Christians;
May God protect them, who is the Almighty One!   6985

PART 8

348

The Emir left, I have told you the same,
Our Christian force to find as fast he may;
Now would I tell of our King Charlemayn;
In that same tent which Aumon left of late,
Carlon himself is lodged the following day;   6990
The next king there had best beware, I'd say!
If each knight kept what he found in that place
He'd never be poor in all his life again.

349

In Aumon's tent Carlon is lodged in comfort;
And, as for food, they have acquired so much of it   6995
They could have fared no better in any country;
They've gold and silver and wheel-patterned silk
    covercloths,
Vases and vessels new and old in abundance;
And as for weapons, swords, spears and lances cutting;
But all of this has been bought dear with suffering;   7000
The price of this has been their bodies bloody;
They are content with this fact and this other:
That God our Lord has prospered Christian courage;
They have paid back Aumon and all his cut-throats;
How their grief fades as good food fills their
    stomachs!   7005

350

Our Emperor would waste no further time;
He summons an archbishop when he arrives,
The water there to bless and sanctify;
In Aumon's tent our King sits down to dine
And knights one thousand go there and bathe alike,   7010
Who all can fit quite easily inside
And feast and drink and share talk and advice
With those who serve the meal and meat supply;

This tent of Aumon's all telling does defy:
No man on earth, as hard as he might try, 7015
Could tell in full how that tent was designed,
Or all its cloth, its gold and silk describe;
On its pole's pommel four rubies he's aligned
So that the land and earth are lit so bright
As far as one in four whole days might ride 7020
Where they reflect, that even at mid-night
You could sit down at ease to dine and wine
Or play a game of chess or draughts alike
Without the need for any candle's light;
And if an army should come by land or tide 7025
To take a castle or rob the countryside,
They would not know which way to turn their lines,
Nor how to split their ranks or flanks to hide,
So you could not count up the flags they fly
By simply looking into this mirror's shine; 7030
Lords, we should love that worthy Paynim knight
Who came to France to speak the Emir's mind:
Balan, whom Carlon felled in his last fight;
See, now he comes, before Carlon inclined,
And starts to speak in sweet and gentle wise: 7035
"So please you, Sire, let me be now baptized,
And afterwards such news I shall confide,
That which, in truth, it is not good to hide,
Yet hide I shall, should you my plea deny!"
"My friend," says Charles, "do you such haste
    desire?" 7040
"Indeed, I do--great is my longing, Sire."
"In truth, who'd blame you, friend?" Carlon replies;
So that same day, as soon as they have dined,
The French set up a font prepared aright.

351

The Pope comes then to counsel Charlemayn: 7045
"Behold, my lord, the envoy," Carlon says,
"Who came to France the Emir's will to state!
Ogier and Naimes brought him here yesterday;
Now he would be baptized in Christian faith."
The Pope replies: "Let us thank God and praise!" 7050
Then four archbishops and all the clergy's train
Come round the font, which first they consecrate;
The Pope comes too, to help them as he may;
They strip Balan all naked to the waist;
Except his hose none of his clothes they save; 7055
Thrice in the font they plunge him and they bathe
And Charles himself lifts him upright again;
Whoever would buy the unguent on him laid,
Could not, though he one hundred marks might pay;

The Pontiff speaks: "Now let his rank be raised!"   7060
"Indeed," says Charles "it's right to grant the same;
If I, please God, return home sound and safe,
I'll give him much when victory I claim;
He needs serve none save God and me always."
This said, the King gives Balan a new name   7065
And he is newly-dressed and shod straightway;
About his neck a large mantle they drape;
Balan is big, well-built and sturdy-framed;
His arms are strong and he is fierce of face;
In all our host there stands no knight so great,   7070
Nor sits one better astride his destrier.

352

In wondrous wise is he a valiant vassal;
From Pope Milon he has received his baptism;
This done, the King gives a new name to Balan:
It's Witikin, after one of his barons;   7075
He takes the King by the skirts of his jacket,
The Pontiff too, and with no more companions
They leave the tent the range of one drawn arrow;
Witikin says : "Why should I hide this matter,
Now I have turned to God and Charlemagne?"   7080
"In faith," says Charles, "you have done nothing badly;
You can gain nothing but honor from your action."
Says Witikin: "Such is my understanding:
Should I conceal what we shall meet in battle,
It must be termed a treasonable action;   7085
Look now, therefore, at this pavilion's flag-pole,
At yonder pommel beneath the dragon standard!
Look now and see the swift Messina channel
And all those ships, those dromonds and those galleys!
Of Reggio town behold the tower and battlements,   7090
Whence left this morning so many battle-banners,
So many flags, so many pennants flapping!
With all remaining men, five full battalions,
They have set out to find us and attack us;
Take counsel, Charles, to plan how we should act now: 7095
Shall we wait here or draw our forces backwards?"
"Indeed," says Charles, "why lie in such a matter?
I have not come this far to flee from Aspremont."

353

The King, as bidden, looks now into that mirror,
As does the Pope to verify its vision;   7100
Messina's Strait he sees that flows so swiftly,
The ships and galleys and dromonds in flotilla,
And Reggio town, its tower and many pillars;

The Pontiff starts to sigh from deep within him,
And from his eyes the tears he weeps are bitter:　　　7105
"Hey," says the King, "let be this exhibition!
You could dishearten all of the troops here with me;
Your task is now to go to old Duke Girart;
Tell him to come and speak with me this minute;
And take good heed of the advice he gives you."　　　7110
The Pope replies: "I shall do as you bid me."

354

The Pope, acting at Charlemayn's behest,
Rides from the camp without one moment's rest
And takes with him four archbishops as well;
They ride full pelt until their journey's end;　　　7115
Girart is washing when from their steeds they step
And the first food before him placed and set
The Pope himself with his own hand does bless;
He speaks straight on, this blessing having said:
"God save the duke and all those here his men!　　　7120
The Emperor, who me to you has sent,
Calls on you now, this is the truth my friend,
To come straightway and learn of his intent;
He'll heed your counsel as he can and thinks best."
The duke replies: "All this can happen hence;　　　7125
Right now I'm eating, for I have not at length;
When I have eaten I'll do as he requests."
"Now listen well, Girart!" the Pope says then,
"The first command which God gave us Himself
Was through Baptism, whose Law our lives protects;　　　7130
That man is lost who this Law ill respects."
The duke replies: "When it comes to the test,
All shame on him who fails it the least speck."

355

Now just as soon as Duke Girart has supped
And his war-steeds have all been saddled up,　　　7135
He and his nephews into their saddles jump,
And those two sons who with him here have come;
They ride uphill and come to Carlon thus;
Inside his tents they find a wondrous sum
Of denier coins and gold and silver ones,　　　7140
Of fur-trimmed ermines and vairs and minevers;
And of good horses there are more than enough:
He can have much who ere this time had none;
But for all this the French have outlaid much;
They have paid dearly with their own bodies' blood;　　　7145
But something else they owe to God above:
They have been saved from those of Africa.

356

The duke dismounts his palfrey at this spot;
To hold his stirrups are Audfroi and Droon;
Charles takes him by the hand and ring thereon,   7150
His other hand clasping the duke's belt-knot;
In love and faith he's greeted by Carlon:
"Brave man," he says, "in truth, I've wondered oft,
A man like you, so worthy and so strong,
Why were you not a king in days bygone?"   7155
"I had no say in it," the duke responds;
"My worth was never so great, nor was my wand;
I hold in peace what I am holder of.

357

"Rich King, my lord, pray do not be disturbed!
The type of man who seeks a crown on earth,   7160
Should look to God and in his faith be firm;
He should both honor and serve the holy Church;
He should cast out bad laws and break their curse,
And champion good ones, and try to make them work;
He should help orphans and feed them from his purse,   7165
Look after widows and their safety preserve;
The wicked man he should try to convert,
But none the less destroy if he grows worse;
He should keep by his side men of good birth,
For from their counsel he may find out and learn   7170
The way to govern his own soul and self first;
To promise little and give much in return
Will move the heart of everyone he serves;
A wicked man who seeks his fellows' hurt,
He who would try to steal another's serf,   7175
Who would rob churches, then violate and burn,
Oppress the poor and tread them in the dirt,
That sort of man should not for kingship yearn."
The Pontiff speaks: "You merit to be heard;
He who seeks wisdom may find it in your words;   7180
The Emperor sent me to fetch you, sir;
He'll show you something most wondrous to observe."

358

Those barons three, joined by Girart the bold,
Out from the camp off to one side all go
Four times the range that one might draw a bow;   7185
None of the rest one word about this know;
"Now listen well, Girart!" says then the Pope;
"Within that pommel, where those carbuncles glow,

Messina's Strait you may in truth behold,
With ships so many and sundry smaller boats! 7190
From Reggio town departs the Afric host
In four great ranks with flag-bearers foremost!
If God does not look down now from His throne
All other help may henceforth prove too slow!"

359

The Emperor points and shows this to Girart, 7195
And then, aside, he quietly remarks:
"We must not put our soldiers in alarm;
They are exhausted, and this much hurts my heart."
The duke replies: "Fine King, this much I grant;
Is this indeed the Strait of Messina, 7200
With ships so many and sundry smaller craft?"
The Emperor says: "They are King Agolant's.

360

"Witikin, brother, help me to see the more,
So I may know more certainly their force."
"Most willingly I hope to do so, lord; 7205
I have no wish to go back there henceforth,
For I have lost my son and heir withal;
What shall I say? This evening, ere night falls,
You'll see your fill with those two eyes of yours!

361

"Look first, my lord, down by that firtree grove, 7210
For there is camped the front line of your foe
In tents so many of silk and canvas sewn!
Before the biggest a rich silk flag is flown,
A gonfalon adorned with three fir cones;
This is the flag of Mandaquin the bold; 7215
In all of Africa he stands alone;
But he has left no barons of great note,
Nor knights of birth and good worth that he knows.

362

"See now those ships and many tents erected,
With golden eagles set up atop their tent-poles! 7220
This is a race from a land rich in blessings,
Where you can find good bread and wine a-plenty,
Silver and gold, gray furs and ermines splendid,
And good war-horses, fleet-footed Arab destriers,
And lovely ladies of clear and fair complexion; 7225
Their young men too are well brought up in everything,

Handsome and good, alert and energetic;
Their ladies love them and they return the affection;
Eliades and Pantalis his nephew
Are both of them their kings and lords together; 7230
But do not let this race dismay or vex you,
For these and others who on their feet did get up
And go with Aumon have all been killed already."
The Pope speaks up: "Truly, by good Saint Denis,
All must agree we owe this man our friendship." 7235

363

Says Witikin: "Fair King, now hear me, pray!
When your French force outfought our troops that day,
Those men whom Aumon had led out on his raid,
They had with them the four gods of our faith--
Which, as you know, your soldiers took away; 7240
If you would make this land your sure domain
Do not stop here, but ride on in all haste!
You sacrifice this land if you delay;
If you allow it, their loss they will regain."
King Charles holds Witikin in fond embrace 7245
About his neck: "Continue thus," he says,
"And you shall be my man and intimate."

364

Girart the duke is the next one to speak:
"Give ear to me, my worthy lords!" says he;
"Let him who has good counsel for us to hear, 7250
Now speak it out and not his thoughts conceal!
The best advice that I can find in me
I shall now say, if you please to give ear:
Fair King, throughout your ranks announce with speed
That all of those young men who wish to volunteer 7255
Among those youths whom we as squires do treat,
Who saddle up and tend our battle-steeds,
That all of those who can good weapons wield,
Don hauberks now and take the battle's grief
And willingly go with you to the field! 7260
If we return, God willing, to France the sweet,
You will ensure that each receives rich fiefs,
And thus indeed a landed squire will be!
Now I shall go to fill my men with zeal
And call on them with this selfsame appeal." 7265
Says Charles: "These words are wise and well received."
He has four heralds mount horse immediately,
Who ride the ranks and broadcast this decree.

365

They ride the ranks and this decree they publish:
"Come forward now, you lithe and sporty youngsters,   7270
Cooks from the kitchen and seneschals and butlers,
Boys of good birth and you harpists and jugglers,
And all of you able to handle trouble
With helms of steel and stout hauberks to cover you,
Swords at your side and sat astride good
    thoroughbreds!   7275
You'll all be knights," says Carlon,"in this struggle;
And if once more we see sweet France our country,
You'll all receive rich fiefs to rule and govern;
Your families' weal shall be restored because of it."

366

Right through the ranks this message is relayed   7280
By heralds four who in all haste proclaim:
"Those who will come with Charles into the fray,
With hauberks on and visors o'er their face,
If we return, God willing, to France the famed,
Then so much wealth shall Charles to them donate   7285
Their families' weal shall be forever saved."
Ah God! What joy those youths who heard this made!
Full four leagues down the valley's slope they raced;
So many weapons they found there on the plain!
So many hauberks, good lances and good blades,   7290
And shields wheel-patterned and so many breast-plates
They found to use and brought back when they came!
How many saddles on horses' backs they placed,
Not to be changed henceforth for four good days!
They took whatever each man wanted to take,   7295
And in the evening their food rations they claimed;
The message, next, to Roland makes its way,
Who tells in turn Estous and Berenger.

367

Haton, Estous and Berenger together
Ask Roland then: "What shall we do, pray tell us?   7300
Carlon too long has held us in detention;
Within these ranks we're simply boy-attendants,
Yet now it seems no footsoldier or fellow,
Be he a valet or boy of birth and gentry,
If he wants arms, the King will not give plenty!   7305
Let us find out if he will give us weapons!
If he will not, then we ourselves will get them."
Roland replies: "With God Almighty's blessing!"

368

Roland mounts horse and angrily rides off
With only those his close companions; 7310
They find the King of his entourage robbed,
Except Duke Naimes, Ogier and Floevent;
Carlon sighs hard and in deep anguish sobs;
His heart o'erflows and floods his eyes full oft
With tears that fall down both his cheeks and drop; 7315
Naimes talks to him with tender words and soft:
"Let be this grief of self-reproach, Carlon!
Your task is now to arm fresh vassals strong,
Who'll seek revenge right speedily and prompt!"
Carlon replies: "You speak ill words, Naimon; 7320
In our first fight against the Paynim throng
Men seven hundred and thirty three we lost,
Kings, dukes and counts--all men of highest stock,
Of high estate and rulers of great rod,
With whom was done the will of our Lord God; 7325
Now I must fight once more against these dogs
And lose my best, once more, to Agolant;
When I think this, my heart nigh breaks therefrom."
More words than these our Emperor says not;
For the Pope's sake and Girart's Carlon stops; 7330
Roland the lad dismounts now at this spot;
He sees Duke Naimes and grasps his mantle's cloth,
Then grabs at Ogier's buttons of silver shone;
He asks of both in a voice filled with wrath:
"What says the King? What is he thinking of? 7335
Will he still keep us lads in captives' bonds?
When we came here how poor our progress was!
The horse I rode so rough and slow did plod
That in my head one tooth I've scarcely got
That hurts me not right viciously and throbs; 7340
Within these ranks there's none so woebegone
Who in the wind can hold his frame aloft,
Should he want any weapon, Charles in response
And glad of heart, does not now give him one;
If he does not treat us the same hereon 7345
Then we shall not be here at all ere long!"
At this Ogier takes Roland's cheeks flushed hot
And kisses him upon them fair and fond:
"You shall have weapons and quickly too, Roland."

369

Both Naimes the Duke and Ogier, Denmark's liege, 7350
Before the King in supplication kneel;
Naimon, Bavaria's Duke, is first to speak:
"My lord, we have a message for you to hear!

176

Your nephew Roland would be a knight, says he;
His heart is high and loyal and sincere."   7355
The King replies: "This thought is best let be!
The lad is still too young for this and green;
The long hours spent in hot pursuit afield,
The hungry days and long nights without sleep
Would overstrain a young man of his years."   7360
"So help me God," says Roland stepping clear,
"If you would arm me now and dub me here,
Soon shall the man who scorns me hold me dear!
My lord, I've been your cup-bearer at meals,
And my comrade Estous has cut your meat;   7365
If you will not make knights of him and me,
Then you will need new servants next time you eat!"
"Roland," says Charles, "I do not doubt your zeal;
I still recall right well those olive trees:
I saw you leave your horse in one great leap   7370
And flourish high your length of broken spear;
Fast as a grayhound you came to my relief;
As Aumon raised his arm aloft and free
To cleave my body from top to toe, thought he,
You aimed at him a mighty blow and fierce,   7375
Which from his grasp made fly his sword of steel;
At shoulder-height you broke his arm indeed;
So many times you struck him ere you ceased
That when you did Aumon had ceased to breathe;
If Ogier, though, and Naimes press your appeal,   7380
Then you shall be dubbed knight by my decree,
As will all those who first bathe themselves clean;
Twenty or thirty, five score or fifty even
Shall benefit from your strong claim and plea;
Each one of them shall have hauberk and steed   7385
And worthy dress as fits a knight enfeoffed."
When Roland hears the King this much concede,
He rushes forward and kisses his right heel;
Charles takes his hand and lifts him to his feet:
"Roland," says Charles, "right well should I love
    thee!"   7390

370

Throughout his ranks the Emperor proclaims
That in the morning, without one moment's waste,
Each bachelor should be well dressed and bathed;
If you had seen the rush that then took place
To Carlon's treasures--those leather bags unlaced   7395
And chests unlocked, their wealth to give away!
Each man had more than his two hands could take.

371

From Carlon's camp Girart, Beuvon's son, rides
With young Beuvon and Claron by his side;
Before his tent down from his horse he climbs; 7400
His counts rush to him, his barons and his knights,
All asking him what Charles does at this time;
The duke replies: "Nothing but what is right;
In all his ranks no boy of birth or line,
No foot-soldier nor youth sporty and lithe 7405
Who would bear arms, does Charles not now supply;
I say that we should act in similar wise."
"With the blessing of God," they all reply.

372

Give ear, my lords, to what Duke Girart does!
He summons his two nephews and calls his son, 7410
And all the barons who with him there have come,
And says: "My lords, who now will counsel us?
Let him who can, tell us what should be done!
We do not know the mind of Agolant,
If he will wait for us or turn and run; 7415
Thus he who would be knight shall so be dubbed,
Each one of you prepared to take arms up;
And every knight shall gain good land enough,
If Lord God leads me home to where I was!"
When his men hear that land is to be won 7420
Each says to each: "God, what a lord this one!
All shame on him who ever fails his trust."
Girart the old so many new knights dubs!
Three thousand men that day he honors thus.

373

When this is done Girart his two sons summons, 7425
Miles and Ernault, who are the eldest brothers;
To Duke Antelme he hands them and entrusts them;
"Go now to Charles and greet him with these youngsters;
Ask him to arm them, then bring them back abruptly!"
Antelme replies: "This task I shall accomplish." 7430
They mount their steeds and ride off in a hurry;
In Carlon's tent they find a wealth most wondrous,
And wealthy men, dukes summoned from their duchies,
Who by their sons and brothers are accompanied,
And other folk who are their closest cousins; 7435
They stand about, each saying to the other:
"Carlon fills us with fear, but all for nothing!"
Yet ere four days their course of time have run there,
King Agolant his armies will have mustered;

And all of those who now round Carlon cluster 7440
Are not enough to feed or fill their stomachs.

374

In Aumon's tent are Charles and all his barons
As he this day dubs so many new bachelors;
As long as they are brave and versed in valor
Carlon heeds not their family's birth or background; 7445
Those who were serfs he frees henceforth from vasselage,
Both they themselves and each man's future family;
In perpetuity their debts are cancelled,
Their terms all lapsed, according to his sanction;
Nor shall their lands owe service or pay taxes; 7450
To God and to Saint Peter he plights their actions:
"Assemble now before that race of savages!
If you look on, they will create such havoc
That nevermore shall be repaired the damage."

375

No further time would waste Carlon the Emperor; 7455
Three hundred youths he sends and thirty-seven,
Sons all of dukes, of counts and peers these many;
As long as these shall live and last together,
The Christian Faith and their own selves defending,
They will help Charles to rule his realm and Empire; 7460
When Carlon now his own young days remembers,
And how these lads towards a place are destined
Whence he himself thinks now to come home never,
His heart is burdened by weight of woe as heavy
As if he, Charles himself, was each beheading; 7465
His own two feet can no more hold him steady
And he withdraws to rest upon his bedding.

376

Both King Droon and Brittany's King Salemon,
With Naimes the Duke, Ogier the Dane and Fagon,
Bring Roland now before King Charlemagne; 7470
Three hundred swords are brought before this
    gathering,
Of which there's one that no mere boy may brandish;
By Enisent the Breton see it carried:
Sharp Durendal, whose hilt of gold is fashioned,
Which Roland now, who takes the sword, examines; 7475
There is no blade of such fine manufacture;
Brave Ogier says: "Lord, let us test its valor
Outside, before your tent, on that stone platform!"
The King replies: "Upon my faith, we shall do!"

377

Sharp Durendal the King touches and takes; 7480
He draws it from its scabbard and wipes the blade,
Then buckles it about his nephew's waist;
This done, the Pontiff blesses him straightway;
Then Carlon says, with gentle, laughing face:
"I gird this sword about you with this prayer: 7485
God grant you strength and make your courage great!
God give you valor and bold zeal all your days,
And mighty victory against the heathen race!"
Roland replies, whose heart with joy is gay:
"God grant it so, in His most worthy Name!" 7490

378

As soon as Charles has girt the blade of steel,
Duke Naimes steps up and next to Roland kneels
To place the spur upon the lad's right heel;
Ogier the Dane fits on the left spur-wheel;
Roland himself cannot so much achieve 7495
As to undo the mantle at his sleeve,
Nor from his sword the tassels to release;
Three hundred swords are dressed for knightly deeds
And thirty-seven, with all haste and all speed;
Estous de Lengres is first to be received; 7500
The King straightway girds on his sword of steel
And then invests Haton and Berenger,
Gui and Yvoire and Gascon Angelier;
Thirty and seven are knighted and hundreds three:
"Roland," says Charles, "esteem yourself most dear! 7505
To you and no one else I give all these."
He makes them all take Roland for their liege:
"Uphold the Faith!" fierce-faced Carlon entreats:
"If I return, God willing, to France the sweet,
It's my intent to rest and hunt in peace, 7510
While you and they rule over all my fiefs."

379

Inside his tent sits mighty King Carlon
With young Roland, whose face with valor shone;
He and his friends in Ogier's care will stop:
"Ogier", says Charles, "I give you young Roland; 7515
Safeguard him well in your strict charge hereon!"
"Sire," says Ogier, "with the blessing of God!"
Now Carlon stands and lifts himself aloft;
By the right hand he moves to take Milon:
"Good young my lord, to lie now would be wrong; 7520

You are the son of Girart, are you not?
No better duke in spurs was ever shod;
No cowards ever shall spring from his brave stock;
I give to you the land that was Milon's*;
He has no heir except his daughter one; 7525
If she is truly as I have heard extolled,
She is more lovely than any we know of;
You could not find companionship more fond!
You and Duke Naimes and Ogier and Fagon
Shall of her house be guardians from now on!" 7530
Then Carlon asks the Breton Enisent:
"Where is the sword adorned with a gold cross?"
He hands it over, with bow both low and long.

380

As Charlemayn holds in his hand the sword,
He tests its edge, from scabbard rich drawn forth; 7535
Then to Ogier and Naimes the Duke he calls:
"I took this off, as you saw, yestermorn,
When on Aumon a mighty blow I'd scored;
Then from his head I had the helm withdrawn,
And from his back the hauberk stripped and torn; 7540
Beneath the trees I had his body brought:
How many wounds that mighty body bore!
As for that girl, had I not feared your taunts
And your reproach, I would have paid her court--
Provided that she gave me her accord 7545
To be mine only and totally by choice--
And devil take all thoughts of seeking more!
Esteem yourself most dear Milon, fine boy!
I give to you both blade and bride henceforth;
Fagon, Ogier, Naimes and yourself all four 7550
Shall be from now my closest counsellors;
Serve me tomorrow when we shall dine and talk!"

381

Inside his tent is our great King this day;
By his right wrist he takes young Girardet:
His hair is fair and he is fresh of face, 7555
With long, strong arms and hands as flowers pale;
Handsome his shoulders, more handsome still his frame,
With well-formed legs and feet well-turned and shaped;
In tender tones the King now to him says:
"You are the son of brave Girart d'Eufrate; 7560
In any land we know of none more brave;

* i.e. Count Milon of Poitiers, the father of Claron,
        killed earlier by King Triamodes (laisse 284).

Enisent, brother," calls out Carlon again,
"Of those four swords bring me the longest made!"
In his lord's hands by Enisent it's placed:
"Thanks be to God, my lords," Carlon proclaims, 7565
"This is the sword that vavasor's son raised,
Who in one day won back Gandia's faith,
Its tower and power and golden eagle gained;
In any land I know no better blade."
Then, as all watch, he girds the young boy's waist. 7570

382

As Charlemayn girds on Girardet's sword
He says: "I've given you a good one, boy!
No better blade from steel was ever forged;
With this was won Gandia's land and Law:
The Christian Faith had been downtrod and scorned 7575
When by this blade it was in full restored;
God grant long life to you and it henceforth."
A saddle then is placed upon a horse;
Charles hands it over by its reins' golden cord.

383

The Emperor asks that a horse be saddled, 7580
Which is as white as the flower of the apple;
The saddle's rich and is much to be valued:
He who would buy its harness parts and panels
Would find one hundred marks too few to have them;
Charles hands it over by its reins' golden strapping; 7585
Now it's the Pope who would no longer tarry;
No church there is or monastery standing,
And so they bless a portion of the campsite
And there erect and sanctify a chapel
Where Pope Milon prepares for his next action: 7590
He robes himself to say the Mass for battle;
Not one he's said, since first this office having,
With so many new knights before him gathered.

384

Milon the Pope now says the Mass and sings it;
No other clerk there is for the Epistle, 7595
Except a bishop the name of whom is Girart:
Droon's own brother, the Poitevin, is this one;
The Gospel's read by Sanson the archbishop;
Carlon the King makes offering to Milon,
As does his nephew Roland and all those with him; 7600
Archbishops seven, of rate the most religious,
Dress in their robes to help with this thanksgiving;

The counts and barons to them make their submissions,
As do Droon and Salemon of Brittany;
Four mighty mules, of Aragon the biggest,　　　　　7605
Could not have borne the weight of what was given;
The Pontiff says: "My lords, to me now listen!
What should I say? It is well to consider
Whence we all come and where we all must finish;
We turn to dust, who were dust to begin with."　　7610

385

The Pontiff says: "My lords, heed what I tell you!
When our Lord God thrust Satan out of Heaven,
It was no wonder that his sorrow was heavy;
For nevermore could he regain possession;
But then God said He would restore and rescue　　 7615
All Satan's fold cast out from Grace together;
Thus He made Earth and Sky above erected,
Worked for six days and rested on the seventh;
All things on Earth He ordered to His pleasure,
Yet with His hand itself He touched them never,　 7620
Except one clod of clay which He found left there;
With this He fashioned Adam and then beheld him
As in His like He shaped him and developed;
Then with one rib from Adam's side selected
He fashioned Eve and her to him presented;　　　　7625
Then Paradise He made and thereto led them,
And bade them have all that He had invented,
Except one fruit which He forbade them ever;
But Eve tricked Adam, through devlish intervention,
And he was mad who to that food was tempted,　　　7630
And thus against the Lord's commandment trespassed;
This was the Devil's work, in his great envy,
Who knows full well that all of us are destined
To that same place whence for his sin God sent him;
Mankind was lost, when God beheld its wretchedness;　7635
How God so loves the world you may now reckon:
To save our souls upon Earth He descended;
In human form the Virgin's womb He entered,
Who carried Him, indeed, to her term's ending,　　7640
As any woman who is of child expectant;
She brought Him up till He could spread His message;
Thirty-three years He made with us His dwelling;
He took Saint John, for whom He had great friendship,
Down to the river Jordan Lord Jesus led him;
Upon a rock He sat and called out gently　　　　　7645
And Jordan river obeyed His will's expression;
Then Our Lord God baptized Saint John and blessed him
And gave him unguent so he could baptize many;
And John the Baptist baptized Him and confessed Him,

Exactly as our Lord God had intended; 7650
He who is not baptized as I have mentioned,
Nor heeds these truths as I to you have said them,
Should he want Mercy, then he will never get it;
Should he seek Grace, he will not find one vestige;
Neither shall Mary for him seek intercession 7655
With God; you know she'd not attempt it;
The Jews took God, to Whom Judas had led them;
Evil the hour he earned those thirty pennies!
As God for us endured death and accepted
And let Himself be killed for our protection, 7660
Let us, likewise, to die for Him be ready!
Whoever dies for God shall reap much benefit;
That man's reward I can tell you directly:
He will dwell nobly with all God's Saints in Heaven!
And he who lives shall in this world be wealthy! 7665
The Emir comes, know for a fact unquestioned!
He seeks you out with all his host of Gentiles!
He will be here before tomorrow's vespers,
And he who fights not well will be a dead man!"
The Pope falls silent, who thus his speech has ended; 7670
They take a Cross to him when he requests it;
This Cross contains of that Blest Beam a section
Where Christ was nailed when Longinus did vex Him;
When they see this they fall on their knees bended,
And with their mouths and hearts do humble reverence; 7675
The Pontiff then gives each his tender blessing
And all seek leave, each man his own way wending;
Those who have arms already go now to fetch them;
And those without depart in search of any;
For him who looks there is to be found plenty; 7680
And if he keeps what he may now collect there,
He never will be poor in his life henceforth.

386

My lords, you know of Roland's knightly feats;
He and his friends did so many brave deeds
No man alive could tell the tale complete; 7685
Now I'll leave Charles and tell of the Emir;
He calls his kings and all of them appear:
"My lords, I wonder mightily," says he,
"At my fine son and what he would achieve;
Three times already he has fought in the field, 7690
Yet calls me not nor sends a message here;
By Mahomet," says Pagandom's Emir,
"He's acting like a child, it seems to me;
Mahom and Tervagant he's lost, I fear,
Likewise Apollo and Jupiter the fierce; 7695
Charles has destroyed so many of our breed,

All of our lives the hurt shall not be healed."

387

Says Mandaquin: "Much wonder fills my mind;
There is no night I do not wake thereby;
In counsel cruel your son Aumon abides, 7700
He who has placed our race in such foul strife,
And your four gods has lost in his great pride;
The Christian force are now too well supplied;
From top to toe they are armed with our iron;
They'll not grow tired or weary of the fight, 7705
For they have robbed our gold, both red and white."

388

King Maladient is next to speak and says:
"Lord Agolant, you do wrong to delay;
Since so few knights are come with Charlemayn,
Send him this summons without one moment's waste! 7710
He must return your gods in the first place;
If he'll deny Lord God and take our faith,
You'll spare his life--if ransom thus be paid:
Seventeen hundred sumpters he is to lay
With silver and pure gold to their full weight, 7715
And the same sum of maidens of young age
He is to send, who must be virgins chaste;
These you can give to whom your fancy takes;
And every year Carlon must pay the same;
Make him come here and yield his crown of state, 7720
Unshod, unclad save in a wool-shirt plain!
Should he refuse, you'll kill him straightaway!"

389

Says Uliens: "We still may be too slow!
Choose now one more to mount with me and go,
The wisest man who well to speak does know!" 7725
The King calls up Galindres wise and old;
Cordovan shoes he wears and a silk hose;
Upon his feet they fix two spurs of gold
And on his ears two rings they clip and close;
An Afric mule they bring, as they are told, 7730
And he mounts up while they the stirrups hold;
An olive branch they bring for him to show;
His beard is white and bright his face and bold;
No finer man you'd find, search high or low.

390

Uliens mounts upon his fiery destrier; 7735
In all their ranks there ride no two men better;
They have good breast-plates and floral-painted helmets
And bear round shields with painted bands of metal;
Both men are big, both strong and proud and resolute;
These two shall bring to Charles the Emir's message. 7740

391

Hear now what fierce-faced Carlon does meanwhile!
In five brave ranks his army he divides;
His nephew Roland he puts in the front line
With Duke Ogier as flag-bearer beside;
And yet, my lords, they are but thousands five, 7745
And callow all, young men sporty and lithe.

392

Another rank is led by good King Salemon,
With Breton troops and Manseaux men and Angevins;
And in the third rides good Droon the Poitevin
With Hugh of Mans and Maurienne's Erquenbaut; 7750
They ride close-ranked, without a fuss or clamor;
There are five thousand beneath the Breton banner.

393

Didier the Lombard in the fourth rank is found,
With Jeremy and Hugh, both worthy counts;
Richard the brave with this group rides his mount; 7755
A harsh foe, he, of all the Paynim crowd.

394

In the fifth rank Bavaria's Duke Naimes
And Richer ride, who did much to be praised;
Nor does the Pope in any way delay,
With all those men who in his trust are placed: 7760
No cook or butler in Carlon's camp remains,
No seneschal, no porter nor chamberlain,
No clerk nor canon nor any priest ordained
Who is prepared to bear arms and to aid,
Whom Pope Milon does not dub straightaway; 7765
If he can fight, he never will be blamed
For joining in the great defence this day.

395

Amidst this rank Girart and his sons ride
And Gondelbuef with many of his knights;
English and Normans in this rank have combined   7770
With those of Saxony who have survived
The mighty battle in which their liege-lord died;
These men are filled with dole and darkest spite;
The King of France, our brave and noble Sire,
Grasps now his staff and holds it up on high;   7775
Then he prepares his ranks and battle-lines.

396

Carlon our King prepares his troops for battle
As one by one he lines up his battalions;
Behold Uliens the first envoy of Agolant!
An olive branch clenched in his glove he carries,   7780
Which signifies that he is an ambassador;
They see this waving as he comes down from Aspremont;
Behold him come! His hair is finely plaited--
Down to his saddle it flows behind the back of him;
About his shoulders he has tied up and gathered it;   7785
He sits astride a fiery steed gray-dappled;
Its weight in gold would never match its value;
His green helm is of steel, his breast-plate dazzling,
And his great sword is polished keen for action;
His lance is sharp with a wood-shaft of apple;   7790
His mighty flag he lifts and the wind flaps it;
He's tall and strong, a well-built man and valiant;
In all their host there is no knight more handsome
Or better-looking when sitting in the saddle;
No girl on earth, so high in her own fancy,   7795
Who did somewhat with love delight to dally,
Would ever fail to fall for his attractions;
Thus these two ride to bring Agolant's mandate;
The one has fists, the other threats to back it;
What envoys, lords! How praised and prized both
    vassals!   7800

397

The King rides round to give encouragement
And one by one to line his forces up;
He does not stop till he reaches the front;
He calls Ogier and says in voice full-lunged:
"Ogier, alas! Protect my boy Roland   7805
As you have pledged, for he is still too young,
And I love nothing in this whole world as much!"
Ogier replies: "He has said this, Carlun:

If you grant not to him the first blow struck,
All his life hence your benefit he'll shun!"   7810
"Indeed," says Charles, "I give and grant him such;
To you and God his safety I entrust."
Charles blesses them, then turns and weeps for love;
See now, my lords, those envoys as they come
And one by one move past each rank drawn up;   7815
They do not stop until the biggest one;
In a loud voice speaks first old Galindres:
"Chevalier, brother, on that gray stallion,
Who drag these others behind you in your dust,
Show me Carlon the mighty Emperor!   7820
I know him not, and so must ask you thus."
Charles in response says in a voice full-lunged:
"Behold me here! Your search for Charles is done."
The Paynim says: "Your looks confirm your tongue;
I greet you not, for I do love you none: 7825
We two are sent from strong King Agolant;
You must return Mahom and Tervagant,
Likewise Apollo and mighty Jupiter!
I am to take them now, so he instructs."
"Friend," says Carlon, "his will is fierce enough!"   7830

                    398

"Envoys we are," says in response Galindres,
"Who have come here this message to deliver:
Without delay our four gods you must give us!
You will regret the evil hour you glimpsed them:
Seventeen hundred pack-horses you must fill up   7835
With silver and pure gold to their full limit;
And the same sum of virgins must come with them,
Whom he will take to satisfy his kingdom;
Unshod, unclad save in a wool-shirt simple
You must assist in loading up this tribute,   7840
And, not without your crown, you must then bring it
Before the Emir and kneel down in submission;
If you will then deny Lord God's existence,
Forsake your faith and take up our religion,
Both of us here shall plead for your forgiveness,   7845
And you shall have your crown back on the instant."
"Ah God," says Charles, "this is a tricky business!
I am unused to walking, to begin with;
Nor must you press this talk of gold and silver:
Though well I might, I would not touch one shilling; 7850
Let us leave wealth to those who've dared to win it;
As for those girls, they are such a great hindrance
No man on earth should seek such a commitment!
As for your gods, you may alike dismiss them:
We gave them to our whores a few days since, sirs;   7855

                    188

No head or shoulder still to be smashed exists now."
If you had seen Galindres' back bristle,
And that branch shake between his tight-clenched
    fingers,
And Uliens' eyebrows fiercely sinking!
Behold him, now, upon his stirrups stiffen! 7860
He strains the leather beyond its normal distance
And nearly breaks the iron of both stirrups.

399

Uliens speaks: "Sir King, give ear to me!
I was sent here to you by the Emir
Of Africa, which lies across the sea; 7865
When he arrived in Europe and came here,
He sent out first his vanguard troops afield,
Led by his son of mighty heart and fierce;
Aumon took with him the four gods of his creed;
He went out raiding for one whole month with these, 7870
Which then, your men, as he returned, did steal;
Return them now, our mighty King decrees,
And pay him tribute at the appointed fee!
You know your fate if you should disagree;
Find your best man, for I stand here most keen 7875
To prove to any who dares now disagree,
That your religion must bow to ours and yield!
Our King pursues you, Charles, and will not cease
Till straight to Rome he drags you off in leash;
Aumon his son he'll crown there and enfeoff; 7880
That crown of yours on his son's head he'll seat;
And all shall die who still would Christian be;
My King will kill all those who still believe!"
"He'll not," says Charles "so help me God, indeed!
The silver and pure gold will stop right here 7885
For those to have who've won it with their zeal!
As for those girls, envoy, give ear to me:
Those you can have are yet to be conceived!"
"Hear me, fine sir!" thus Galindres replies;
"Apart from these I see, where are your knights? 7890
There are but few in this your foremost line,
And all their weapons belonged to us erstwhile!
King Mandaquin, the nephew of our Sire,
With twenty thousand men towards you rides!
Our hand-picked best are all those at his side; 7895
By Mahomet, my faith and my delight,
You're trapped as surely as is the bird in lime!"

401

Says Uliens: "Sir King, let me say more!

You should tread softly and curb your angry talk;
Towards you ride men thirteen thousand score, 7900
While on the coast remains a further force,
Who guard our wealth and all our ships of war;
These troops of ours have come to kill all yours;
Before your eyes you'll see your ranks destroyed!
If you were meat to be cut up and hauled 7905
Into the kitchen, we have such hungry hordes
Not one of you would ever be cured or stored!
That you have lived so long is our King's choice;
With his own hands he'll put you to the sword;
You'll curse the hour you met Mahom our lord!" 7910

402

Our Emperor no longer would delay;
He calls the Pope and summons good Duke Naimes,
Ogier the duke and Salemon the brave,
His nephews also and sons with him this day;
Off to one side he bids them move away: 7915
"My lords," he says, "now listen to me, pray!
Of Agolant behold these envoys twain,
Come to demand their four gods in his name!
Seventeen hundred sumpters I am to lay
With silver and pure gold to their full weight, 7920
And send with them the same sum of young maids,
Daughters of dukes, of counts and peers of state,
Who must be found to be all virgins chaste,
Yet ripe to love the knights he nominates;
And my own self to Africa he'd take, 7925
Unshod, unclad save in a wool-shirt plain,
My crown in hand as I walk all the way
To set it down before his feet again;
I must renounce my faith and take his faith,
Proclaim him King and God and you forsake." 7930
Not one man there, at this, knows what to say;
They heed his words and a long silence reigns;
Most of them then begin to weep and wail
And others sigh from their heart's depth for pain.

403

No longer would delay old Duke Girart: 7935
"Do not dismay yourselves, my lords!" he starts;
"Since February full four score years have passed,
That I first laced on helm for Christian task;
If I speak first it should not hurt your hearts;
Send men straightway up to that olive branched 7940
Where Aumon lies, his son, at your command;
Cut off his head and then cut off his arm;

Do not so much his helm as to unclasp,
Nor from his hand lift off the emblem large;
And then prepare his green shield for its charge; 7945
Place both his head and arm upon it, Charles,
And send him this, who for rich gifts has asked!
No man on earth, so high in self-regard,
Would not at this consider long and hard;
With their great woe they'll learn respect at last; 7950
Each one of us seeks vengeance for what's past."
All there reply: "This would be well to grant."
Thus they send off both Richer and Bernart;
Those envoys twain repeat their fierce demand:
"Have you packed up your gift for Agolant?" 7955
"My friends," says Charles, "I'm seeing to it fast!"

404

They climb the hill, those two Carlon has sent there,
And find Aumon beneath the olive spreading;
The heavy shield they move, on which they'd left him,
Then first of all they cut the Paynim's head off, 7960
Without so much as unclasping his helmet;
Beside the head they lay his right arm severed,
But from his hand lift not the large ring-emblem;
They do not change his shield or seek a fresh one,
But take it up and lay it on a destrier, 7965
The arm, the head and jewelled helm together;
And then they mount and both make off directly.

405

Those vassals two down from the hill have ridden
To Carlon's camp and stopped right in the middle;
Galindres sees them and his woe drives him witless; 7970
He is struck dumb who once was so articulate;
Uliens sees the helm and the head in it
And knows full well the great ring on the finger;
In such wild wise had Roland erstwhile hit him
That both the eyes out of his head were driven; 7975
Uliens says: "Mahom, what are you thinking,
That you do not some marvel now or miracle?"
"My friend," says Charles, "in faith, Mahom is
    missing;
We gave him to our whores and our loose women
Just yestermorn, who, with their sharpened pickets 7980
And iron mallets, smashed Mahom into splinters!
Whoever got most, in truth, received but little!
You threatened me and I heard you distinctly;
What should I say? Behold, you have your tribute!
The head of Aumon, his shield and arm I give you; 7985

He who in pride came here to rob and kill me!
I never shall send tribute saving this one;
When you return to your great King, Uliens,
And from your hands he has received this gift here,
Then ask of him if now he does consider 7990
That he was mad to ever leave his kingdom!"

PART 9

406

"Uliens, brother," says one worthy Carlun,
"You and Galindres have threatened me enough!
Now go and tell the mad King Agolant
That such a tribute as he has asked of us: 7995
Those his four gods, for whom he has such love,
And those young girls to whom such hurt was done,
Whom he for life would have made whores each one,
And my own crown of gold all luminous--
While I'm alive not one day shall he touch, 8000
When with my blade good blows may still be struck!
Those his four gods, whom he desires so much,
Tell him in full that I inform him thus:
We gave them to our harlots here at once,
Who broke their flanks and shanks did flay and crush 8005
And through the ranks went round beating them up;
He who got most of what was left had luck
If it was worth of three halfpence the sum;
As for the plunder, I kept not one bezant;
And may it never please our Lord God above 8010
For King of France to have such booty won
And share it not with knights of worth and trust;
In all my realm I know of none so rough
Towards his daughter or his cohabitant,
Who'd hand them over to any Infidel; 8015
But for my tribute, I do now send him such
As France does owe a King of Africa:
The shield and helm and head of his own son,
And the right arm and bright gold ring-emblem!
Neither shall he behold the setting sun, 8020
For I shall do the same with him, I trust!"
On his fierce horse of gray sits Uliens
And on his sturdy mule old Galindres;
They look and look at the head of Aumon;
Out of his mouth has flowed much of his blood; 8025
His eyes are hanging from their sockets in front;
Out of his ears his brains have burst and run;
One Paynim weeps, the other one sighs much;

From his right hand Uliens draws his glove
And in the ground his cutting lance-head thrusts; 8030
Direct to Charles he makes his way at once;
So all may hear he speaks in voice full-lunged:
"Accept my gage to fight on foot at once
Against your best and Christian champion
In single fight, the one against the one; 8035
If in the field your man I overcome
You must believe Mahom and Tervagant;
And if I die, from this day forth at once
All Pagandom in God the Lord shall trust."
"Friend," says Carlon, "control your battle-lust! 8040
I can well see that you are of brave stuff;
Go now and tell the strong King Agolant
That Aumon found what he set out to hunt!
I have his horse, his sword and Olifant,
Which I have given to my nephew Roland; 8045
Tell your King now that I inform him thus:
That I send him the head of his own son,
And his strong arm, from his right shoulder struck;
And that, please God, the King Omnipotent,
Who gives me all I ask for through Jesus, 8050
Before the sun goes down and evening comes
It will be clear to either one of us,
Who of this land henceforth has government."

407

Uliens looks and sees the mighty shield
Which Aumon bore with him into the field; 8055
Next to the arm there placed the head he sees
And Aumon's face of all its blood drained free;
He sighs three times and shakes his head in grief:
"Alas, Aumon, what a day's woe is here!
Tell me, Carlon, wherefore this haughty deed? 8060
You have not brought with you nor do you lead
Sufficient men our appetites to feed;
Your Christian faith is doomed to tragedy;
We shall pursue you up to the Iceland Sea."
"Friend," says Carlon, "such is my destiny; 8065
Now let this head be borne to the Emir
And tell him well how I see things to be:
This head shall not be crowned in Rome this year!
Your King was wrong to sail here with his fleet,
Lay waste my lands and devastate my fiefs; 8070
He shall not see the setting sun this eve
Ere he must fight in melee fierce with me
And learn his fate, whatever that may be!"
Those envoys twain at this take hasty leave,
With tribute such as does them much displease; 8075

Then Carlon's ranks form up in order each,
The one battalion from the next one set clear;
Then sixty trumpets ring out in one great peal
And Carlon's vanguard moves slowly up the steep;
And when they reach the vale beyond they see   8080
The land about on every side replete
With Saracens, that cursèd godless breed;
There were so many, established proof agrees,
That our men there could not their sum conceive;
No Frenchman there, though happy-hearted he,   8085
With joy of life in his heart planted deep,
Had not his joy uprooted all by fear.

408

Those envoys twain at this take leave in haste,
Who can their task no more achieve or gain;
Mandaquin now sets all his troops in place,   8090
Line after line in fighting rank arranged;
He is the first to see those envoys twain
And, seeking news, approaches them straightway:
"You are well come to us, sir knights!" he hails;
"How does Carlon the emperor fierce-faced?   8095
And our four gods, has he returned them safe?
He would not dare to damage them one grain!
Has he yet packed the tribute he must pay?"
When Uliens hears this his anger flames;
Galindres says: "Your words set me to rage!   8100
Those our four gods to their harlots they gave,
Who with iron mallets their bodies then did break;
No head or shoulder still to be smashed remains;
Aumon is dead whom nothing now can aid;
When he came here it was all for your sake;   8105
Whatever you wanted he did for you always."
"Leave off this talk!" King Mandaquin exclaims;
"Do not bring here such news as you relate!
No man on earth so high in self-acclaim
There is, who'd dare to cause my liege-lord pain." 8110
"Let us leave this dispute," says Galindres;
"His body lies beneath an olive's shade;
His arm they have cut off and head the same;
In this steel helm behold again his face!
They did not care his helmet to unlace,   8115
Nor from his finger the ring-emblem to take,
So he who crowned him King may know his name."
"What evil this!" King Mandaquin exclaims;
If you had seen what sorrow then took place,
Hands wrung for woe and hair torn in dismay!   8120
All in that rank such hopeless grief displayed
Even their best despaired then of their fate.

409

Those envoys leave, returning over the desert;
Acars of Flors has heard the rumor spreading
Of the alarm the vanguard troops besetting; 8125
All his own ranks he has lined up already,
His rod held high to give them their directions;
Now he makes out the silk Almerian ensign
Of King Uliens and his Nubian helmet;
He turns his reins and heads towards the envoys; 8130
When he sees both in a loud voice he bellows:
"You band of two, I bid you hearty welcome!
Have Christian hearts our Paynim faith accepted?"
"They would be mad to do so," says Uliens;
"When Aumon seized Calabria and held it 8135
Beneath his sway and bent it to his pleasure,
One hundred thousand men he had to help him;
Then he engaged ten thousand of our enemy;
But when their few met up with those our many
He lost our gods through cowardice and treachery; 8140
When Carlon's men took of our gods possession,
All of their whores had of each one some section;
Aumon is dead and his brave deeds are ended."
Acars hears this and quits his manner merry;
His look turns bleak and blacker his expression; 8145
Throughout that rank wild grief is so o'erwhelming
Each man hears nothing of what the next man tells him.

410

Those envoys ride both angry and distraught;
King Calides, when he sees them on horse,
Rides out to meet them, right through a patch of
    gorse; 8150
He greets them now with a good will unforced:
"May Mahom bless you both!" Calides calls;
"Have Christian hearts accepted our gods' Law?"
Says Uliens: "Our gods have played us false;
All of their ruse and prophesies are naught; 8155
When Aumon seized Calabria by force
And to his sway and pleasure bent it all,
He had of our best men five thousand score;
Ten thousand French engaged them, strong and sure,
And when their few met up with those our hordes 8160
Ours fled the fields those ten thousand before;
When Carlon's men seized then our godheads four,
They handed them to their harlots and whores;
With iron mallets and picks with sharpened points
They broke their bodies, their arms and legs withal; 8165

Aumon is dead and our prowess destroyed."

411

King Acars says: "What do you mean, Uliens?
Has Carlon then kept those our four gods with him,
And is he not come back with you a prisoner?"
"No, he is not; Charles is still with his Christians; 8170
To Agolant he has sent such a tribute
The like of which eyes never again shall witness:
The head of Aumon, his arm and shield we bring him;
From Aumon's side the right arm they have smitten,
But have not taken the great ring from his finger, 8175
Which Agolant, when he was crowned, did give him;
By this cruel proof our King shall know it is him."
King Calides near goes mad as he listens;
As now he speaks, hear, lords, his malediction:
"Mahomet, lord, I curse you for your wickedness, 8180
That you allowed and that you thus were willing
For Charlemayn to beat Aumon or kill him!"
Throughout that rank such hopeless grief afflicts them
They'll not be made to keep their field positions;
Those envoys turn and leave them in the distance. 8185

412

They ride on down, those envoys twain of Agolant;
Eliadas and his nephew Pantalis
To meet them both spur hard their two war-stallions;
They greet the pair right tenderly and gladly:
"You are well come to us, worthy ambassadors! 8190
Is tribute sent from fierce-faced Charlemagne,
Seventeen hundred sumpters with gold all saddled
And the same sum of virgin girls unmarried?"
Says Uliens: "My lords, you are too arrogant;
The French are not at all so lightly vanquished; 8195
Aumon rode out to guard his raiding vassals
And took with him one hundred thousand cavalry;
But the front rank of fierce-faced Charlemagne,
Ten thousand knights, engaged them and attacked them;
They lost our gods like cowards in this battle; 8200
Of all they gained in one full month of gathering
They have naught left of fourpence worth in value."

413

Galindres says: "Pantalis, noble cousin,
Aumon has dared for absolutely nothing
In his desire to conquer all this country; 8205
The Christian folk in God find every comfort

And in His son who dwells in Heaven above us;
This one it was Who on the Cross was hung up,
Who pardoned Longinus the death He suffered;
He is their help and right sufficient succor;   8210
Aumon went out with five score thousand others
And our four gods alike, pledged to accomplish
A change of faith in their poor hearts and luckless;
All that they gained in thirty days of hunting,
Of gold and silver and gray and ermine covers,   8215
Ten thousand French from the land of Saint Denis,
In the front rank of fierce-faced Carlon coming,
Left them with naught worth the least Paris money;
In just two days they have killed of our number
And Paynim faith full seven thousand hundred;   8220
All of our lives right craven gods we've clung to,
Who have failed us completely when we're in trouble;
Now we have lost our kinsmen and our brothers."

414

Those envoys leave, spurring their mounts along,
While those behind bewail their heavy loss;   8225
Throughout their ranks, in threes, they ask non-stop:
"Ah, wretched us, what waits for us hereon?
For we have lost Mahom and Tervagant,
Great Jupiter and great Apollyon
And our protector the valiant Aumon;   8230
There's naught but shame awaiting us hereon."
Those messengers meanwhile go spurring on
Right of those ranks one hundred thousand strong;
To Agolant's redoubt they come ere long,
Where the Emir this moment is ensconced   8235
Together with the strong King Abilant;
And there as well are strong King Boidant,
Maladient and the young Moadas--
And the irate and evil Almanzor;
They recognize the envoys from far off.   8240

415

Those envoys ride, in haste now to arrive;
To tell their news they anxiously desire;
To see them come, the Emir's heart leaps high--
It soon shall sink with the darkest despite!
One on his mule and one his steed astride   8245
To that redoubt they come where they alight;
Young Moadas is first to speak his mind:
"Our tribute, lords, do we have it entire?"
Galindres says: "You are too greedy, child!"
Evil the hour you met those haughty knights   8250

197

Of whom Aumon made counsellors betimes,
And then from whom took most of his advice!
A good five leagues we've covered in one ride
And on their backs five thousand wretches lie,
All our own men, their heads hacked from their hides;   8255
Carlon the great is not so turned to fright
That he has yet dispersed his battle-lines;
What can I say? Carlon in swift reply
Has turned your taunts and threats against you, Sire;
He sends to you a tribute dark and dire;   8260
Never was one more dreadful in this life:
Your own son's head its floral helm inside!
Nor have they kept his painted shield behind,
So that in this they are not seen to lie;
Lo, by his ring he is identified!"   8265

416

The Emir looks and sees Aumon's own visage;
In such wild wise had Roland erstwhile hit him
That both the eyes out of his head were driven
Upon his cheeks, where now they rest quite rigid;
From his right side the strong arm has been smitten;   8270
When Agolant observes upon his finger
The emblem-ring which for so long was his one,
Which he in turn, with Aumon's crown, had given,
Then his heart stalls and all his man-strength quits
    him;
The Emir swoons and on his shield falls limply;   8275
Those heathens rush to hold him and assist him;
When from his swoon the Emir is delivered
He starts to speak--to his reply now listen:
"Those our four gods, is their strength so diminished
That they permit, and thus allow so willing,   8280
Of my own son the conquest or the killing?"
"You have loved them too long," replies Galindres;
"When Carlon's men took all four of them with them,
They gave them to their whores and their loose women,
Who with iron mallets and sharply-pointed pickets   8285
Broke up their bodies and smashed their shanks to
    splinters;
Whoever got most, in truth, received but little;
Those who still love them are fools in my opinion;
I cannot think that gold has virtue in it
If it's not sold, used as a gage or given."   8290

417

The King hears this and nearly bursts with rage;

At Aumon's head he looks and looks again;
The eyes are dimmed and black as ink the face,
Which used to be so glowing, bright and gay:
"Son," says the father, "my heart with sorrow breaks;   8295
For you it was I came on this great raid,
Forsaking my good sense for your own sake;
I made you King, fine son, with rich display;
But you rebelled in a most haughty way;
I made you King, but not once since that day   8300
Did you at all accept advice I gave;
You were led on by the advice of knaves,
Who never loved me or ever sought my gain;
If they have killed you, then they shall die the same!
Their clan shall last but a short span and space,   8305
And never come close to me and mine again!
Galindres, brother, give ear to me now, pray!
What sort of man is haughty Charlemayn?"
Galindres says: "To lie is to betray;
There is no man on earth, however brave,   8310
Who would not lose, incurring Carlon's hate,
His head for it--unless his heart were great;
The Christian race adore a God and praise,
Who came to Earth all of their souls to save,
And Who in Mary was rendered incarnate,   8315
The Holy Virgin who bore Him with high grace;
In Bethlehem this God was born a Babe;
With oil and cream His Baptism was made,
With elements four and salt and water twain;
Who serves this God and His Baptism takes   8320
Shall be made rich on the great Judgment Day."

418

Our Christian force, when they farewelled those envoys
Who with their talk of tribute had so threatened
To make them serfs and servants of the Emir,
Our Christian force dismissed them with a vengeance!   8325
For Carlon sent the Emir such a present
Which so struck down his men when they beheld it,
That terror filled even their very best ones;
If now, indeed, our Christian force were ready
To strike these Turks with all the might and mettle   8330
Of worthy folk with no faint-hearted fellows,
They would succeed and drive them from their Empire.

419

In Agolant there's naught but anger left:

"Son," says the father, "I am sorely perplexed
That you made me start out upon this quest   8335
And follow you against my better sense;
The two of us at first to Mecca went,
To praise our gods and humbly to request
That we might spread their worship with their help;
My Afric gold, the dearest and the best,   8340
For love of you I lavished upon them;
The richest jewels I could acquire with wealth
I did so many on this devotion spend,
The worth of which could have bought cities seven;
You gave our gods to your vanguard's best men   8345
And made of Hector your gonfalonier--
He who would drive me from my own land and realm!
Through you he thought to strike at me myself,
To gain my land and share with no one else;
It happened well that he first met his death;   8350
He has no need to seek an Empire hence."
This said, he lifts the head from its steel helm;
The face is gray, in ghastly grimace set,
Which used to be so glowing, gay and fresh;
If you had seen the King then kiss that head   8355
And clutch it tight and clasp it to his breast!
All of his mouth with blood begins to wet;
Those Africans all say among themselves:
"The one who was to help us--he is now dead!"
If you had seen the grief which swept them then!   8360
Despair took over even their boldest men;
But now once more to Charles we must attend,
Who has drawn up his ranks in regiments
And armed himself to fight with all the rest;
Upon a hill his first in line is set;   8365
When they behold those hordes of Infidels
Approaching them, not one so proud is there
Who does not now turn humble in his dread;
Then, suddenly, three knights appear ahead!
Down from a mount the French see them descend;   8370
Their arms are white and white their destriers;
They do not stop till with the front rank met,
Whose flag-bearer in chief is brave Ogier;
Roland is with him, by whom this rank is led.

420

Now has Carlon his race in ranks established   8375
And set apart battalion from battalion;
Next Pope Milon calls out to one Erengi
And says to him: "Come forward, good companion!
Of that blest Beam I have a goodly fragment,
Where Jesus hung when Longinus did stab Him;   8380

I want you now to carry this in battle;
With this in hand be brave and bold and active!
If from the field the Lord our God seems absent,
You shall uphold us when other help is lacking."
The man replies: "I'm much taken aback, sire; 8385
Why have I then put on this hauberk padded,
Donned this good helm and burnished as I have done,
And with this shield my body steeled for action?
Why am I, then, astride this Arab stallion
If I am never to spur him to a gallop, 8390
Nor raise my lance some heavy shield to shatter
And use my arms to vanquish heathen vassals?
My loyal faith to you I pledge right gladly,
But curse the hour I ever will do that, sire!
You called me and I came--but let me back now, 8395
To take in hand my weapons as I had them;
Then I shall serve both you and God with valor."
The Pope replies: "You have let me down badly."
"Yes, sire, indeed--but I must in this matter."

421

Then Pope Milon calls out to one Ysoré: 8400
"You are a son of rich and noble forebears;
A better clerk than you I could not call on;
Of that blest Beam I have a goodly portion,
Where Christ was hung when Longinus did gall Him;
Of this blest wood shall you henceforth be warden." 8405
"You are too hasty," says Ysoré, retorting:
"Why have I then placed on my back this hauberk?
Why have I placed on my left hip a sword then,
And on my head a green helm jewel-adornèd?
Why is my chest a heavy shield supporting 8410
And why am I set up astride a war-horse
If I am not allowed to spur it forward?
With a glad heart I pledge to you my loyalty,
But let me bear the arms that I have brought here,
For sweet charity's sake, I do implore you, 8415
So I may give God's duty its performance."
An archbishop, there is, observing all this
And who this day is mounted on a war-horse
Both strong and fast, a keen and willing courser:
Its legs are straight and its hooves
    well-proportioned; 8420
This horse, indeed, is made to be spurred warmly;
Its thighs are flat with big square knees and forelegs;
Its flanks are straight and long and white its
    haunches;
Its neck is long and straight, its shoulders broadened;

In all our host there is no beast so faultless; 8425
Towards the Pope one pace its rider draws it:
"Good my lord Pope, well have I heard you calling;
Each of these men is keen to serve our Lord God,
But will not hear of serving as a porter;
You are much vexed, I see, but all for naught, sire; 8430
If you had offered me this holy ornament,
Which these two men have both refused before me,
I'd not have felt the weight of it at all, sire."
The Pope replies: "My friend, where were you born, sir?"
"Beyond the heights, within fair France's borders; 8435
For a long time I served in holy orders
As monk and priest below Rouen in Normandy
At Jumièges, a place of happy fortune;
I was a monk for ten good years and more there
And very nearly as abbot was appointed; 8440
Then I was chosen and so departed forthwith
To be ordained and blessed at Reims high altar;
Lord, you yourself invested and installed me;
Let me now give my duty its performance,
Which shall be clear to all ere this night's falling." 8445
The Pope replies: "You have captured my thoughts, sir!
In wondrous wise you've served me and my cause here;
What is your name? Conceal it not, I caution!"
"Upon my faith, my lord, Turpin they call me,
Ordained and blessed I was at Reims high altar." 8450
"With the blessing of God!" the Pope rejoices.

422

The Pope says on: "Would you aspire so high
As to become flag-bearer of our line?"
"Indeed I would and willingly comply,
If you agree to follow my advice; 8455
For I have brought one thousand to your side,
Who are not sons of low-born lackey types,
But men who serve me when I sit down to dine;
As I watched yesterday three hundred died;
If you leave me the rest then we shall ride 8460
With Duke Ogier and young Roland the child;
With these two lords I would combine our might;
I'll bear the flag if you grant me this right:
If from the field we put this foe to flight,
And with God's will I manage to survive 8465
And come back home again to France alive,
Should any then against my liege conspire,
Grant I may go myself to help Charles fight,
With hauberk girt and helmet laced on tight;

Yet on the morrow, come back to church and shrine, 8470
I may resume my offices divine."
The Pontiff says: "You are strong to advise
That an archbishop should also be a knight."
"I dare not argue with you," Turpin replies;
"If you will not grant this request of mine 8475
Then you must seek another man than I."
Milon the Pope needs not to be asked twice:
He hears the Afric troops as they draw nigh,
Hears their horns blow and hears their trumpets whine
And cornets blare the noise to amplify; 8480
Milon the Pope would waste no further time;
He takes the Cross and to Turpin he cries:
"Let it be yours--but high shall be the price!
I see nothing ahead but lances sliced!"
Turpin dismounts with no further respite 8485
To kiss the foot of the worthy Pope Miles;
If you had seen him then his horse bestride!
Milon the Pope hands him the Cross of Christ;
With his right hand he blesses him and signs.

423

Turpin of Reims delays him not one jot; 8490
He bows down low before the Pope Milon;
In loyal faith this day he bears the Cross;
Now he departs with seven hundred strong;
Throughout the ranks they ride their stallions
And climb straightway the slopes of Aspremont; 8495
Ogier sees them and from his horse gets off,
As do the others in that battalion;
In simple faith they worship then the Cross
And straightaway down to their knees they drop;
The hardest men bewail both loud and long; 8500
Their hearts o'erflow and flood their eyes full oft;
Then Ogier says: "Give ear to me, Roland!
My loyal faith I pledge to you hereon,
That Agolant is dead if here he stops."

424

Ogier mounts up, the brave and worthy one, 8505
As do the others behind him all lined up;
See then, astride their stallions, three knights come
Down from the ridge of lofty Aspremont
And one by one pass each battalion;
They do not speak and are addressed by none; 8510
They ride in haste until they reach the front;
Ogier speaks out in a loud voice full-lunged:
"Who are you, vassal, on that white stallion?

Stay where you are, come no closer to us!
I do not know you, so I must ask you thus." 8515
The first replies: "Restrain your zeal, my son!
I am called George by those I live amongst,
And always have the right of first blow struck;
But this I give today to young Roland;
I give him this and also pledge this much: 8520
That in this fight he shall not shed his blood;
God shall this day show to His Christians
That they are His forever in His love."
As Ogier looks he knows this messenger
And in reply says this to him at once: 8525
"Saint George, my lord, I gladly grant this much;
To God and you his life I do entrust."
Across the field come now those Africans;
They sound their horns, their tambourines and drums
And cornets too of which there's well enough; 8530
Mandaquin sits on a horse swift to run;
His sword is girt, whose blade so sharply cuts;
His shield is round and ivory-colored,
In quiver-leather bound and therewith hung;
His lance is strong and his sharp spear is tough; 8535
His giant flag flaps in the breeze above;
Saint George takes by one hand Roland the young
And says to him in a firm voice full-lunged:
"Do not fear him that he is big, my son;
From this day on call out 'Saint George' for luck." 8540
The lad replies: "My lord, your will be done."

425

Count Roland now beholds in wondrous joy
The messenger sent down from heaven's vault
To help him save God's faith and to exalt;
Saint George it is, who so much loves the boy 8545
That he will lead and teach him in this war
And deign so much as to bestow withal
The right of the first blow in this assault;
If Roland's zeal does not confirm the choice
And he strikes not before the others join, 8550
The lad will rate himself as ripe for scorn
And worthless ever of kinship kissed or sworn;
Those Africans he sees as nigh they draw,
Hears their horns blow and hears their trumpets roar
And cornets blare, resounding back and forth, 8555
And tabors struck to amplify the noise;
King Mandaquin he sees before them all;
See Roland now snatch up his buckler, lords,
And tilt the lance upon the felt-cloth borne!
Now each for each spurs forward his war-horse 8560

As far and fast as each may run the course;
Mandaquin's blow is the first one to fall;
On the top edge of Roland's shield it bores
And buckles it and breaks it with its force;
The hauberk's strong, the chain-mail is not torn;   8565
Mandaquin breaks the shaft below its point;
Now Roland strikes, who spares the heathen naught;
All of his armor is not worth the least coin;
The mighty lance into his body gores;
The shaft is strong and cannot be snapped short;   8570
I do not know if it was ash or sorb,
And Roland too was young at this and raw;
Will he or not, he has to leave it all
And turn for help to his sword Durendal;
To strike the heathen's helm he lifts the sword;   8575
That heathen demon's big and he is small
And cannot thus a level blow employ;
What he can reach is sliced clean off and shorn:
Half of the helm, one ear and half the coif;
His arm is strong and lithe, his shoulder broad,   8580
And that blow splits the double hauberk's coils;
Why should I make this matter any more?
Down to the belt that blow unhindered falls,
Embedding in the saddle-bow before;
His hips are all that stop atop his horse!   8585
Both Saint Domin and Ogier with Saint George
And their flag-bearer, who was called Saint Mercure,
Behold Roland thus fiercely fight God's Cause;
With sword held high he stalks those heathen hordes
And strikes stout blows which none there can endure;   8590
They are not loath to lend him their support;
If you had seen them race towards him, lords,
And rain stout blows upon those wretched Moors!
I do not know nor seek to say for sure
If all those died whom there they did unhorse;   8595
But no one saw them rise again or walk.

426

They join the fight, those three brave barons bold,
Who rode that day down Aspremont's steep slope;
Saint George and Saint Domin his comrade close,
And Saint Mercure in valiant trio go   8600
To Roland's aid, who has struck the first blows;
Although Saint George had promised them and told
That they would not be vanquished or laid low
By Saracens, nor would they be o'erthrown,
Ogier and Naimes for Roland worry both;   8605
To lend him their support they are not loath;
They gallop hard towards the Paynim foe;

But they all flee, those ill-born, ill-bred folk;
May God confound them and His great strength be shown!
Not one of them shall hence be seen, I hope! 8610

427

The Paynim troops, those ill-bred ruffians, flee,
Downcast and dismal as all miscreants be;
They make great moan and loudly wail and weep:
"Who was that stinking dwarf?" each says to each;
"Curse him Mahom and Tervagant in league 8615
With great Apollo and Jupiter the fierce!
Mandaquin, lord, great king of high degree,
No land e'er had so valiant a liege!
No knight was better or braver in the field!
You could not do a conscious wrongful deed! 8620
It was the Devil who brought that villain here;
Against his strength your arms could not compete;
He hacked you down in his uncaring speed
As one hacks down an errant patch of weeds;
Lord Agolant, how heavy now your grief! 8625
This peasant strikes our great lord in the teeth
And splits him down to his front saddle-piece!
Not one glove's worth is left of him to keep;
Mahomet, lord, you were too fast asleep,
Who helped no more than this your man in need." 8630

428

The Paynim troops are hidden in a valley;
They wear no hauberks nor bear great shields wheel-
    patterned,
Nor have they helms with gold of the least lacquer;
They are encased in breast-plates or cuirasses,
With coifs of iron set on their heads and strapped
    there; 8635
Strung bows they wield with feather-flighted arrows,
And close beside their saddle-bows hang axes;
No more than these in this terrain they carry;
But now behold a well-prepared battalion!
You could not find one of its size to match it; 8640
Girart d'Eufrate has picked these men and gathered
From all the lands which God to him has handed;
And so well served was he by these his vassals
That his name never was sung of in base ballads;
He leads them now in serried ranks so narrow, 8645
If you had tossed into the air an apple
At helmet height amidst this well-armed phalanx,
It would have gone full half a league ere landing,
While you yourself one baton's length had travelled;

See Claron now in haste spur forth his stallion, 8650
His mighty flag against the wind unravelled!
More than one cross-bow range out front he gallops;
King Uliens points this out to King Jafer:
"This rank of men, fate meant for us to have them!
They bring with them such arms and such apparel 8655
Which well may serve all Africa once captured!"
Now Jafer asks for first joust in this battle
And Uliens gives it and grants it gladly;
Between both ranks at the base of a valley
This opening joust is watched by foe and ally; 8660
Each man confirms with formal oath his challenge
Then spurs his horse as swiftly as he can do;
Upon his shield embossed Jafer strikes Claron
So hard a blow he pierces it and shatters;
The hauberk's strong and no link fails or fractures; 8665
Below the tip the lance-shaft is extracted;
Claron strikes hard on Jafer's studded saddle,
Worth to him now as much as a peeled apple;
Nor is his breast-plate now worth padded mantle;
Claron's great lance into his body smashes; 8670
It breaks the bones and rends the flesh attaching;
One fathom full of wood right through him travels;
Before Duke Claron can draw the spear-shaft backwards
The Paynim soul from Jafer's corpse has vanished!
The shouting starts, the hue, the cry and clamor; 8675
When one proud race against another's standing,
It is not long before a melee happens.

429

Those Africans attack our Christian host,
Who, well prepared, give welcome to the foe:
In byrnies bound and hauberks' mail meshed close 8680
And burnished helms, their mighty spears they show
And their good bucklers and curving shields of gold;
Those Africans are not in hauberks clothed
And Carlon's men of them take mighty toll;
They slice their heads, their necks and shoulders
    both; 8685
The Afric ranks look on in wondrous woe,
Who hear and see the force of our men's blows;
Their dead and dying fill up the plains and slopes;
Without delay they all would turn and go,
When Uliens in a loud voice explodes: 8690
"You sons of whores, how great your shame and gross!
King Agolant has raised you all at home
And shared among you the lands of other folk!
Now you fail him when he needs you the most!"

430

Those Afric ranks, when they behold our Christians   8695
And to the force of our men's blows bear witness,
Then their most brave lose all their fighting spirit
And their most wise consider themselves witless;
So many men of theirs lie dead or injured,
With shoulders sliced and trunks and heads gone
    missing,   8700
The fields are full and meadows overspilling;
The French are armed but naked are those Infidels,
So when the ranks of Girart charge and hit them
They burst right through and break them very quickly.

431

Those Afric folk no longer can abide;   8705
They see their men hacked from their mounts and die
And their dead bodies fill up the countryside;
All of the field they are forced to resign;
Uliens sees he cannot halt their flight;
He curses fate: "What destiny is mine?   8710
It was my plan to capture France entire,
Then share it out among my bravest knights,
To shame the Christians and to destroy their pride,
To serve our faith and thus to raise it high;
Well might I say, for I cannot deny,   8715
That the proud man may not o'erjoy in life;
It cannot fail that there will come a time
When he is forced to leave his pride behind;
Now it is I who must flee coward-like."
If you had seen him turn and take to flight!   8720
Not one man there can halt his horse's stride;
The man he strikes no longer joys in life;
Gautier of Saint Omer he moves to strike;
He splits his shield and slits his hauberk wide;
Deep in his heart he makes him feel the iron   8725
And Gautier's soul out of his body flies;
Claron sees this and heaves a heavy sigh.

432

Those Africans, when they the field forsake,
Have felled already so many of our faith
No man alive the sum could ever state;   8730
Behold afield their worthy destriers!
Throughout the field they stray, dragging their reins,
With none to own them, to care for them or claim;
Uliens sits on his fierce horse of gray;
No beast alive alongside this one rates,   8735

Nor is there one so powerfully made;
He leaves the press, lamenting loud his fate
And oft regretting the loss he has sustained;
Held in both hands his lance aloft he waves,
Made of an Afric wood which will not break, 8740
Called aloe wood by that miscreant race;
Its shaft is strong, its tip sharp as a blade;
If you had seen him ride and thread his way!
No man there is so high in self-acclaim,
So big in boast, by Uliens engaged, 8745
Whose straps or stirrups now one bit avail;
He leaves fourteen spreadeagled in his wake,
The most of whom of all their blood are drained;
Whoever moves to meet him this man slays;
Why should I any more spin out this tale? 8750
Had Uliens believed in Lord God's name,
Nor Oliver nor Roland were as great;
Duke Beuvon now comes spurring out his way;
In a loud voice he shouts and shouts again:
"Turn back, fell Turk, or die as you escape!" 8755

433

When Uliens beholds our Duke Beuvon,
His flag unfurled, his lance on its felt-cloth,
And sees the rest spurring their mounts along
From that direction, men fifteen hundred strong,
Inflicting on his men such a great loss 8760
That round him now so few of them have stopped,
He sees no end to his unhappy lot;
He leaves the press and like a hawk he's off,
Three times the length of a large arrow's shot;
He climbs a hillock, not stopping till the top; 8765
His lion-shield he grips now by the thongs;
He plies both stirrups with such force and such wrath
His toes touch them but now his heels cannot;
He cries out loud: "Christian, by great Mahom,
If you're alone then you are dead and gone!" 8770
The duke attacks upon his Gascon strong,
Given to him by Poitevin's Droon;
Strong, solid blows both of these barons swap,
Which pierce both shields, their blazon and blue
    gloss;
Though both men's births are heralded aloft, 8775
Down in the dirt both sets of shoulders drop.

434

If you had been down in that field rock-walled,

Hard by a grove of laburnum and sorb,
When those two knights each other did unhorse!
If you had seen them both get up once more, 8780
Pick up their shields and take in hand their swords!
Uliens sees our Christians charging forth
And knows that nothing now will save his cause;
If you had seen him then run for his horse!
Hear how he mounted up, that foe to all! 8785
He leaned upon his lance at its most broad;
Cursed be that stirrup where his foot found support!
That Afric force in thousands up to four
About him come to rally and reform
And start once more to swell their cries and calls; 8790
Some sally forth, but Uliens withdraws:
Duke Beuvon, thus, with all his speed and force,
Can get no closer to Uliens henceforth;
Two messengers to Agolant report;
They start to yell at the top of their voice: 8795
"What evil this, King Agolant our lord!
When light of day appeared just yestermorn,
We had men twenty thousand, our hand-picked choice,
With whom you did King Uliens endorse;
And thus we went to punish that proud taunt 8800
Those Christian men to us had sent and brought;
We went to gain revenge, or so we thought;
But once again our plans have come to naught,
For they are armed with iron and steel, my lord,
So that our arms do grieve them not at all; 8805
We've seen our men all hacked to death and fall
And were not able to help it or to halt;
You'll not see the return of one in four
To help you hence in the course of this war."
The King hears this and he is angered sore; 8810
He marshals men at once one thousand score,
Whose lives he governs and who obey his law;
But now to Roland return we as we ought,
And that most brave of knights, worthy Saint George,
In trio brave when battle-lines are drawn. 8815

435

When Mandaquin their king has been defeated,
His followers cannot fight on between them;
They quit the field and I'll tell you the reason:
They have no hauberks, byrnies nor battle-gear on,
And Roland charges and torments them unceasing; 8820
Acars of Flors by this is made full fearful;
About his flag the blood starts to run freely;
So many die, in faith my lords, believe me,
Acars of Flors fears for his own well-being;

Pointing his finger, to Manuel he speaks now: 8825
"My lord Manuel, look well at what I see here;
Upon my faith, these Christians are stout people;
It wouldn't take much for me to trust in Jesus."

436

Acars of Flors beholds the Christian company
Harass that heathen folk, their forces humbling: 8830
Our men, in strength ten thousand seven hundred,
And thirty thousand seven hundred cutthroats,
Whom Agolant had hand-picked, every one of them,
From his full ranks to the best of his judgement;
He gave them all, quite freely, to Mandaquin, 8835
So that they might obey his orders utterly,
Who was his nephew, his closest kin and cousin;
These were the ones who struck first in the struggle;
For Mandaquin the meeting proved unlucky,
For then it was he met a new-dubbed youngster, 8840
Who cut him down from coif to saddle's front-piece;
At this those Afric troops lost so much courage
That all their plans at this point turned to nothing.

437

In wondrous wise is Acars high and haughty,
In wickedness well-versed, doughty and dauntless, 8845
In battle cruel and very skilled in warfare:
"What are you doing, lords?" he taunts his forces;
"You can have hence both the fiefs and the fortunes
Which were these men's and their families' before them,
The which shall make us all rich and important 8850
When we share out the gains we all have fought for;
For every two of theirs we have five score men;
If one escapes, know this swiftly and surely,
No more in life shall I again be joyful."
At this the fight flares up immense and awful; 8855
Of shafts so many behold the fragments falling!
Great blows they give so many and appalling,
Which leave behind so many headless corpses!
With such great zeal and strength they ply their
    sword-strokes,
No hauberk can, nor florid helm, absorb them; 8860
Our Christian knights know their full share of
    torment;
Those worthy steeds that lose the men they bore there
Stray through the field in larger groups or smaller;
If God helps not our Christians nor supports them,
Carlon the great shall soon be vexed most sorely; 8865

One thousand orphans shall find themselves in
   mourning.

438

Uliens says: "Now I have what I seek;
The Christian folk shall not escape from here!
They're falling back and in great haste they flee;
Take our flag forth and fix it in the field!"   8870
Four arpents full our Christian force retreats;
How evil hence, my lords, it would have been
If Charlemayn with help had not appeared!

439

A mighty joy runs through the Afric race
When they behold our Christian force give way;   8875
Then there begins a most ferocious fray:
Of shafts so many behold the fragments break!
They wield their swords and draw their bows well-made
And our French parry with their burnished steel
      blades
And steel-sharp spears which burnished are the same;   8880
They cut through ribs, through necks and
      shoulder-blades;
Through ribs and breasts the Paynim blood escapes;
Those Turks themselves no longer now would stay,
When Uliens cries out four times and says:
"Ah! Africans, your courage must not fail!   8885
Avenge your fathers, your sons and protégés,
Whom these French here have cut to bits and slain,
And your King Aumon, the valiant, the brave,
Your lord and liege by whom you all were raised;
Defeat this land and all this country claim   8890
And own its riches and rule all its domains!"
When they hear this they willingly obey;
They turn about, attacking once again,
And once again Christ's men retaliate;
Girart the duke, his sons and all his train   8895
And both his nephews a dour defiance make;
Yet if Lord God no mercy on them takes,
Both cowards there and brave shall dearly pay.

440

When Charlemayn into the battle comes,
So many trumpets sound and horns and drums!   8900
The noise is great, you never heard one such;
And great's the loss, to Paynims and to us;

Those lords our best find little rest enough:
Ogier and Naimes and many other ones,
King Salemon who bears the gonfanon, 8905
And all those Bretons who are his followers,
And young Roland on his brave stallion,
Who holds Durendal all discolored in blood;
See there so many a vavasor's brave son
Defend himself, his honor and his skull! 8910
What can I say, save that they would have run
When they are checked by the great Emperor,
Who cries out loud with tenderness and love:
"Stand firm, brave men, high-born and humble ones,
In my defence and for your honor's sum!" 8915
The King himself that day displays such pluck
That his best horse down under him is struck;
He jumps straight up, as fits a champion,
And lifts Joyeuse, with which such fame he won;
The man he strikes no more may turn and run. 8920

441

The Emperor, when to the earth he's felled
And under him is slain his steed the best,
Defends himself like a man of great strength;
About him swarm their high and humble men;
The first of ours to see Carlon's distress, 8925
Who fights close by, is Marquis Berenger;
With sword in hand he comes to Carlon's help
And strikes in haste the white-haired Gaudafle,
A powerful king of much repute and wealth;
Down to his teeth that Paynim's skull is cleft; 8930
He thrusts his sword and flings the villain dead,
Then takes his horse by its fine rein gilt-edged;
To Charles he comes without one moment's rest,
Dismounts his horse which he to Charles presents,
Then mounts the other which was old Gaudafle's; 8935
Both men then turn and ride back to the press;
What blows so heavy and so many fell then,
Which cut through heads, shoulders and trunks as well!
When Charlemayn is spotted by the French,
In all their lives no greater joy they'd felt. 8940

442

The Emperor, when he fell from his destrier,
Was seized upon from each side and from every;
But, following God, that man came to his rescue
And his own horse to Charlemayn presented;
And now beware that foe who'd face our Emperor! 8945
Of twenty thousand men Uliens led there,

Full fifteen thousand have fled the field already,
Who never again in ambush shall assemble;
Back to their host in fright they flee directly,
Watched by Uliens,who almost leaves his senses; 8950
The Afric host deride him and discredit;
At the redoubt of Agolant the Emir
He greets the King and for his mercy begs him:
"My lord, you did with this kingdom invest me;
But now I hate this land and my each breath here; 8955
For now I know I never shall possess it."
The Emir listens; my lords, hear what he said then:
"I hear you very well, Uliens, nephew,
And see the dirt on your green burnished helmet,
And see your shield both pierced and fiercely severed; 8960
I was a fool to ever give you credit!
It was your counsel which made me leave my Empire;
You and Mandaquin have played me false together;
My son is gone and all my honor ended;
In Africa, when my eyes first beheld you, 8965
From the first time you left your nests and ventured
To me, who took you in and raised you gently
Up to the age when you were ripe and ready,
You were good men; but now you are base wretches;
May I be cursed if I trust in you henceforth!" 8970

PART 10

443

"King Uliens, I'll not conceal this thought:
Whoever seeks the counsel or support
Of womenfolk or weak and wavering sorts
Should never rule a mighty realm at all;
A woman marries and weds within the law, 8975
Then undertakes to try to lure some lord;
She tries her best to flirt with him and flaunt
And soften him up for what she has in store;
But if she sees him hesitate or baulk
From doing that about which I'll not talk, 8980
Or should he even abandon her perforce,
She'll find her pleasure with someone else in short;
I say the same of conduct such as yours;
For thus you served a long time at my court:
You drank my wines and drained my treasure's hoard; 8985
You drove from me my best-bred men and loyal
And brought me villains in search of rich rewards;
And you yourself were brave and true withal!
Yet if I come to Africa once more

I'll take revenge on treachery so false!"   8990
Uliens says: "Leave be this hostile taunt!
Now is no time for charges to be brought;
Prepare instead without one moment's pause
Our best and bravest to help you and your cause;
All those who here have held me up to scorn   8995
Were not with me when on the rock I fought
And saw myself so meanly felled and floored;
My helm was buried up to its nasal-point;
No man was there to help me up or hoist;
I did not think I could remount my horse;   9000
My stirrups then were my only support;
We cannot fight with those French knights I saw;
With iron and steel they are well-stocked for war;
Of twenty thousand men I've left but four;
These Frenchmen will not flee or hide, my lord; 9005
I saw them ride in ranks so closely formed,
Between their weapons you could not fly a hawk;
If they surmount the rock and suffer naught
And meet you here, Emir, you can be sure
That many will pay dearly who bear no fault."   9010
Throughout their ranks see now a knight ride forth
With an iron lance-head in his front saddle-fork,
Which has been rammed through his own self before!
Below the iron the spear-shaft has been shorn;
His body's blood has made his hauberk moist;   9015
Behind this knight come men two hundred score;
Not one there is so high in his own choice,
Who has no wound, he or his horse, endured;
On this knight's graven helm a blow has scored
Of such great strength it's split it to the coif; 9020
About his shoulder one quarter of it falls;
The man is wan from flow of blood unstaunched;
Now, weak of speech, he says in a low voice:
"I wonder much indeed, Emir, my lord;
There was a time you held me dear of yore;   9025
But yesterday at the first light of dawn,
Into my hands you placed of your full force
Men fifty thousand; when battle first was joined
Before my eyes half of them were destroyed,
And I stood by and could not help at all;   9030
The rest of us, alike equipped so poor,
Before my eyes were meanly felled and floored;
To pay those left of us will cost you small."

444

"What is your name, my friend?" the King enquires;
"Son of King Fanis, Eliadas am I";   9035
"You are close to my kin," the King replies;

"I and your father were cousins closely tied;
Have you news of Mandaquin, nephew of mine?"
"Indeed yes, lord, for he is dead likewise."

445

King Agolant is filled with rue and rancor 9040
For Eliadas' sake in his great anguish
And Mandaquin and many other Africs;
Loud he laments his wretched state and hapless;
Eliadas replies: "Be not so angered;
This is the fault of all those feckless braggarts; 9045
When back at home in all your Afric palaces
And floral-painted rooms they sweetly dallied
With your young maidens so yielding and attractive,
Who gave them lovers' kisses for all their valor,
Then they were heroes who soon all France would
    vanquish; 9050
Then they were bolder than bear or lion rampant;
The fiefs of France would crumble to their challenge!
But these French fiefs are theirs of ancient family,
Which for my sake or yours they'll never abandon;
Full seven hundred thousand of our combatants 9055
They've killed meanwhile and slaughtered all our
    champions
And your own son, for whom our woe is massive;
These Frenchmen are not cowards or frightened at us,
And Charlemayn himself is fierce and arrogant;
My lord Emir, know for a fact established, 9060
Had you one hundred to each of their two vassals,
They would still come to meet you and do battle."

446

Eliadas speaks on and, sighing, says:
"Of three great ranks the leaders three are slain;
Nor in those left can you now place full faith." 9065
The Paynim throng at first low muttering makes
And then erupts in tumult fierce and great:
With five full ranks Carlon towards them hastes!
So all may hear some sixty bugles bray;
Their gold and steel so glints in the sun's rays 9070
Its brilliant glow transforms the light of day;
Rank next to rank so closely rides its way
You could have tossed a glove o'er any twain;
No Paynim there, so high in self-acclaim,
Did not feel fear at this, the geste maintains. 9075

447

From his redoubt King Agolant has ridden
With thirty kings who are to him submissive
And who to him have pledge and promise given;
Not one of them wears not the crown of kingship;
Their rank and file about them still are milling 9080
In numbers such that none could guess the figure;
Carlon has placed his men in five divisions;
The faultless steel and finest gold and silver
Set in their weapons, their armor and equipment,
Glints in the sun with such a glowing brilliance 9085
The shore-line shines and landscape is transfigured;
The Paynim King displays them to his minions:
"The Christian lines are stocked with men right thinly!
They have not men enough to feed or fill us!
If all of them were lined up for our dinner 9090
Our bellies would be lined right badly with them!
Carlon is mad, this is my own opinion;
If with so few he comes against us Infidels
It is the end of all of them as Christians;
And Charles himself shall be led off a prisoner, 9095
A great iron-collar about his neck close-fitted;
His head shall roll should he attempt to lift it!"
At this the King is called on by Galindres,
Who with a smile and shake of his head says this much:
"My lord Emir, you move somewhat too quickly! 9100
When you have won and conquered all this kingdom
And to your will have bent it and submitted
And are crowned King and wear the crown within it,
Then you can fit the collar on your victim;
Let Uliens be summoned here as witness, 9105
For he and I as envoys have been with them;
All those he can is Charles against us bringing,
Never in such haste in all his life as this time."
The King replies: "Your words are too long-winded!
Though they themselves were made of steel
    hard-finished, 9110
They shall not fight with us and be the victors!"

448

When the Almanzor sees of Africa
One quarter slain from three battalions
And knows he'll never convince the other ones,
In full-lunged voice he summons up his sons: 9115
"You sons of whores!" he calls them when they come;
"You base-born boys, you worse than recreants!
Have you no mind of that dishonor done
To Amargon, likewise to Esperrant?

They were my nephews and my own flesh and blood; 9120
Right through the ranks they dragged them o'er the
    rough,
Then followed after picking the pieces up,
Which then they threw into a pit of muck
And with Greek fire burnt down into a dust;
Your memory's poor for your own worth is such; 9125
But while I live if I avenge them none,
All that I own I do not rate a glove;
I have men here of my own line enough,
And you shall see before the setting sun
That they will do whatever I ask of them; 9130
Why should I hide from you what we've discussed?
Till now they've done as I have said they must;
Now take my horn and leave this field at once,
Then sound it out four times in one full lung,
Whose worth is greater far than Olifant's; 9135
These men of mine will go where best I judge,
And riding hard they will all follow us;
Then you shall sail away for Africa!
If Charlemayn attacks King Agolant,
Let him achieve his purpose and good luck! 9140
If I can gain revenge upon him thus,
I am not old and you indeed are young:
You can all hence rule Africa and run."
They all reply: "This plan delights us much."

449

Those Africs met our Christian forces head-on: 9145
Thirty-five thousand men, some hurt already;
But never were folk so well-armed as our fellows,
With byrnies strong and hauberks burnished-yellow,
And worthy shields and studded bucklers heavy,
And lances sharp and shafts of steel
    full-strengthened, 9150
And worthy steeds both swift to run and ready,
Which have been changed throughout the day for fresh
    ones;
The Africans in battle-gear assemble;
They wear cuirasses and many have on breast-plates
And have great swords girt at their sides and
    tethered, 9155
And carry darts, arrows and bolts with feathers;
Our Christian folk, when they come to contest them,
Straightway strike blows so terrible a-plenty
They rip through ribs and heads and shoulders sever;
There are so many of dying or of dead ones 9160
The fields are filled and overspilled the meadows;
Those left alive tread over fallen fellows;

Those Africans, who earlier had reckoned
That they would drive the French out of their Empire,
And then be paid by Agolant the Emir 9165
The full amount which each one had requested,
When our French knights had somewhat tried their
    mettle,
They now called fools whom once they called most
    clever;
The Almanzor, when he hears of the melee,
Says to the King: "Fine sir, turn back I beg you! 9170
All your front ranks have been beset and bested;
The Christian knights have cut them all to shreds, Sire;
Against our men King Charlemayn has sent in
Thirty-five thousand well-armed and ordered Frenchmen;
Yet I have dubbed and armed knights twice as many 9175
And have as yet not tested out their mettle;
Sire, if you please, grant me leave with your blessing,
So I may lead these men against our enemy,
Whom I have called to go with me together."
Says Agolant: "Brave man, my race you've rescued! 9180
Do this for me and we are friends forever!"
"This I shall do and more than you expect, Sire."
With this he turns and leaves the King directly;
Some twenty others with him make their descent now,
Men of high stock and birth the best connected; 9185
Crowned kings indeed are three out of that twenty;
For Agolant it would have turned out better
If he had killed them all as thus they left him;
But he turned back and rode in one direction
And they made off as you have heard me tell you. 9190

450

The Almanzor, had he not run away,
France would have lost this war--as I'll relate;
They reach those boats in haste as best they may
And smash to bits those ships and skiffs the same;
Still armed for war they board the best and sail; 9195
If Agolant in ignorance remains,
He'll rue the hour his arm for home is raised.

451

While Agolant awaits to see arrive
Those knights who left as he himself desired
So recently, their foe afield to smite, 9200
Girart the duke slips freely past the lines
Of his redoubt and leads his men behind;
Down through a vale they come, hid thus from sight,
A fighting force of seventeen hundred knights;

Girart leads them in ranks closed up so tight, 9205
Between their spears the wind no passage finds;
He will be lucky not to regret this guile;
Uliens looks and almost burst with ire;
To Agolant he speaks in great despite:
"My lord," he says, "a race of men draws nigh, 9210
Who were this day the first I met in fight;
I hoped to do all that your will required,
But these knights killed sixteen thousand of mine."
"This is not the Almanzor?" the King enquires:
"No, not indeed, but something much more dire! 9215
The gold and steel and stones that from these shine
Look not at all like arms of your device;
But of one thing you can be certain, Sire:
He now who fights not well will surely die."
The Emir grieves at this, in wondrous wise; 9220
So all may hear he gives him this reply:
"King Uliens, do as you should this time!"
From Agolant's redoubt Uliens strides;
His fiery gray is brought to him by squires
And he mounts up in such a furious wise 9225
No saddle-bow he grips nor stirrup plies.

452

When Uliens bestrides his dappled stallion
His mood is fierce and foul and cruel and arrogant;
From that redoubt he leads off in battalion
Men twenty thousand our mighty duke to challenge; 9230
And the Almanzor is on Messina's channel:
Those ships and skiffs and boats to bits he smashes,
Then with Greek fire burns their remains to ashes;
If Agolant, in ignorance, is stranded,
He'll rue the hour his arm is raised for Africa. 9235

453

King Uliens now from the Emir goes;
Men twenty thousand he leads off brave and bold,
The hand-picked best and chosen of their host;
This cruel king, when he looks and beholds
Girart's main force, some fifteen thousand souls, 9240
In Claron's care, his favorite, disposed,
And Duke Beuvon's whom he has nurtured close,
He rides at them, o'erwhelming them with blows;
Not one of ours, so daring he or bold,
Does not, at this, in fear and trembling go; 9245
Beuvon and Claron fight hard to help all those;
Yet many men are felled with rapid strokes,
Wounded and wan or slain and stiff laid low;

Will they or not, they flee before their foe
And head towards Girart's task-force below; 9250
Claron and Beuvon a stout defence still show
And bring life's end to all whom they oppose;
Yet the good duke, his nephews to behold,
Of his sound sense well nigh loses control:
"You sons of whores," he shouts, "what lies I spoke! 9255
You are no sons of worthy Count Milon,
When Paynims thus, I see, can vex you so!"

454

Ogier the duke, Roland and Graelent,
Estous de Lengres and Richer and Morant,
Since morn today when the first hour was rung, 9260
Have fought afield four Paynim ranks and won;
Nor can those left replace those killed in front;
They are forced back and killed as our men come.

455

Roland the duke, Ogier and Graelaunt,
Estous de Lengres, Morant and Richer all 9265
From tourney turn, whom all have fled before;
Now as they think to turn about once more
Not one can raise a gallop from his horse,
And they themselves are tired out and worn;
So, in dismay and mightily distraught 9270
All six are forced to turn and to withdraw
To fierce-faced Charles, his vanguard to rejoin:
"Ah God, Judge of all things," Carlon implores,
"Who men so many have placed into my ward;
Must I behold their bodies maimed and torn 9275
By Paynim tribes who treat Your name with scorn,
Who have no will to praise You or adore,
Who shun the Grace of Your Baptismal Law?
Help me avenge the shame of this, O Lord!"
Behold him now lift up his buckler broad 9280
And tilt the lance upon the felt-cloth borne;
Great Carlon never spared himself at all;
He speaks again and says in full-lunged voice:
"This day we'll know the good knight from the poor!"
They follow him, men nigh in thousands four, 9285
Who when he dines attend upon his board;
For Charles and Naimes and Ogier now there's naught
Except a heart filled up with angry thoughts;
They see their men cut down, their bodies torn,
And everywhere their fighting spirits fall: 9290
But then Pope Milon cries: "Enough, my lords!
These trials are sent to you by God our Lord,

Who sent Himself condemned to die for all!
Upon that Cross the pains of death He bore;
Behold it there, it shines and blazes forth 9295
And bars approach by any Infidel!
By hands and feet they nailed Him to its boards
And in His side a great steel lance was forced;
And thus He died for all our sins and faults;
And now God gives to us one more reward; 9300
Accept it well and be no further fraught!
But make quite sure your lives are dearly bought!
And if the souls from you must now be shorn,
Then may God grant I share this with you all;
We shall all dwell with God in Heaven's vault; 9305
You'll find me there, a keeper of His door!"
At this each knight and lord lifts up his voice:
"This preacher makes our future strong and sure!
Not once this day shall our endeavors stall!"
"No more shall mine, my lords," Carlon assures, 9310
"For I think not to fight elsewhere henceforth."
Turpin of Reims, likewise, would not default:
"Milon, my lord, pray do not be annoyed!
I would give back this holy Cross of yours;
For I've a hauberk and a good horse of war, 9315
A bright steel helm and at my side a sword;
I am an archbishop and knight withal;
I would now show the worth of my employ."
The Pope replies: "I thank the Lord God for it;
For as I see I have but little choice!" 9320
They sound the bugles to rally ranks and form;
In their redoubt the Paynims hear them roar;
Carlon the King no longer now would pause;
Inside their lines the length an archer draws
He moves to strike Godrin the Carruier called; 9325
Into his breast he bores his spear's sharp point
And brings it out above the shoulder-joint;
How well from saddle-bows he makes him soar!
Yet ere Carlon can turn his horse once more,
Fifteen sharp spears are thrust into his horse; 9330
How proud and fierce the fight turns then in short!
Of iron and steel how mighty is the noise!
Before our French can rescue that good horse
With which he has struck down that blackamoor,
Two thousand heads are sliced by Paynim swords! 9335
Our Christian knights with fright are held in thrall;
And then at twice the range an archer draws
Behold our men seek shelter from those Moors!

456

The noise is wild, the hue and cry is dreadful;

So many blows are struck so swift and heavy, 9340
Which cut off heads and trunks and shoulders sever,
The fields are filled and overspilled the meadows;
When those alive look down and see the dead men
As prone they lie, across the field outstretched there,
They see their fathers, brothers and sons together, 9345
And our most fierce with fear begin to tremble,
And our most sage begin to lose their senses;
Ogier and Naimes both ride to Charles directly;
They come to him with angered hearts lamenting:
"What woe befalls you now, most worthy Emperor! 9350
Of your twelve Peers we have lost nine already."
Carlon replies: "I understand you well, sirs;
So help me God and His own strength, I tell you
I'd rather die than see our party perish."

457

Within the ranks of Salemon there ride 9355
Men of Manseaux, Bretons and Angevins;
No noise or fuss they make in close-formed lines
One arrow's draw away from the pitched fight;
Then Hugh of Mans says this: "Salemon, sire,
Stay here a while with Driu the Poitevin 9360
While I find out how fare our Christian knights;
Ogier is brave but Roland's still a child;
I am afraid that he will lose his life;
We shall return as soon as you require."
"With the blessing of God," the king replies; 9365
Thus Hugh departs, five hundred at his side,
Who are not armed at all like stripling squires;
Born of his land are all and of his shire,
Their heads held high in helms of Poitevin iron,
With hauberks strong on which they can rely 9370
And sturdy steeds, the best there are world-wide,
The hand-picked choice, selected ere this time;
The good Count Hugh commands them well and guides;
They will strike hard as soon as he desires:
"Mountjoy for Charles," in full-lunged voice he cries, 9375
"The good, the worthy, he with the heart of lion!
In all our host no braver man you'll find!
Now let us charge this heathen folk, brave knights,
And force our way to where their standard flies!
What we owe God let us pay back in kind: 9380
He died for us and we for Him shall die;
I charge you now to strike with all your might!
Let each of us attack in such a wise
That no armor may stay the blows we strike;
From battle joined let us not once retire 9385
If Manseaux men have not won honor's prize!"

One arrow's draw between them now there lies.

458

As now the count begins to ride in haste,
So he can fight together with the Dane,
Good blows are struck by Sanson and Richer: 9390
"Count Hugh, my lord," calls out the brave Ogier,
"Behold the knight on that white destrier!
It is Saint George, the worthy knight and brave!
Saint Domin, Saint Mercure the other twain,
Whom God from Heaven has sent to us this day 9395
To honor and uphold the Christian Faith;
We should love God and cherish Him always,
Who such a one as this sends in His name."
Acars of Flors sees Hugh's men join the Dane's,
He hears the shouts and cries of war they make 9400
And sees within King Salemon's own train
The holy Cross which blazes forth and flames;
Now to his Turks he starts to speak with rage:
"Those our four gods are not worth one denier,
Who let themselves by Christians be waylaid; 9405
No head or shoulder still to be smashed remains;
Christ's men are right to live in self-acclaim
And their great God to worship and to praise,
Who let Himself be hung up for their sakes;
See there the Cross where He Himself was laid 9410
And to its boards by hands and feet was nailed!
My vision and my path it's blocked this day
And blinded all of us who on it gaze;
When I approach, confusion fills my brain;
By Mahomet, I will no longer stay!" 9415
He turns in flight, no further menace made.

459

Acars of Flors the battle-field has fled;
His men have failed and he can do naught else;
He holds his sword, discolored all its edge,
As the French cry: "Mountjoy! God be our help! 9420
Whose burnished sword or lance shall strike them next?"
How can I tell? So many there lay dead,
More than ten thousand in this fight meet their end;
The French drive them across a barren stretch
Towards the ranks of Orcan Calides; 9425
Count Hugh of Mans in full-lunged voice says then:
"Strike hard my lords on this foul race and fell,
Who in the wrong has seized upon our realm."

The Orcans are a desperate race of men;
They do not rate a straw hauberk or helm, 9430
Nor rotten apple rate good destriers;
They would not mount even good thoroughbreds;
This race combat Hugh's men with brutal strength;
If God, Blest Mary's Son, thinks not of them,
And Salemon, he and his ranks the rest, 9435
Then we shall be of Mans' pride bereft;
Of Duke Ogier I know not what to tell.

460

Two fighting ranks mix with this third head-on;
The French attack with all the strength they've got,
And Salemon to help them hastes along 9440
With his own Bretons, five thousand known straight off
By the good byrnies and hauberks they have donned;
What cruel blows they give that Paynim mob!
Brains spill to ground as heads from hides are lopped;
Breast-plates are cleft and trunks and shoulders
    chopped 9445
As Orcan brutes and Bretons strike non-stop!
When they in their bare strength meet Salemon
And his armed men and register the shock,
Then their most brave turn cowards on the spot
And their most sage are held as fools anon; 9450
Along their ranks they raise their cry aloft
As arrows fly and stones and sticks they toss;
Three hundred steeds right gladly now they rob
From Christian knights who to their feet have dropped.

461

This battle is so proud, this fight so fierce, 9455
And so much noise there is of iron and steel,
Well might each man in wonder of it be!
Behold, my lords, so many helmets sheared,
So many shields, so many breast-plates pierced,
And knights so many knocked meanly from their steeds! 9460
Whoever fell leapt late back to his feet;
What heavy hits are made with mighty spears!
See Roland ride across the battle-field
Upon the foe these heavy blows to deal!
And Sanson and Richer strike hard indeed: 9465
"Roland, my lord," calls out the Dane Ogier,
"You know right well your weapons how to wield!
So help me God, most worthy are your feats,
And far beyond what I would have believed!
If God allows your life a lengthy lease, 9470
Well may you aid your comrades and your peers!

I am employed as your flag-bearer here,
For Charlemayn has willed this and decreed;
But do not go too far away from me,
For you are still both young at this and green." 9475
Roland replies: "If I may do brave deeds,
For your employ a rich reward you'll reap."

462

Good blows are struck by both Count Hugh and Richer,
And Duke Ogier and Sanson in addition;
Now Roland calls upon those four friends with him-- 9480
Estous de Lengres, Haton and Berengier,
And a young man called Graelent and christened:
A Breton born and King Salemon's kinsman,
He serves at Carlon's court and is his minstrel;
Brought up by Charles as page-boy since an infant, 9485
He's slept in Carlon's rooms since he was little;
No man on earth makes sweeter sound on instrument,
Nor better tells a line of verse or lyric;
This lad it was wrote the first lay of Brittany;
Now in our need, which mighty has arisen, 9490
And at this time, Carlon with arms equipped him
Among those new-dubbed knights, as I did sing you;
Save his own nephew he knighted no one fitter;
Says Roland now: "I must have your opinion;
Do you see there that banner of vermilion? 9495
That is the flag of the evil Calides;
If we can break his ranks right through the middle,
We may be killed or may kill all his villains."
Graelent says: "We shall attempt it willing!
All of his men are armed like squires and striplings; 9500
They cannot take what we're about to give them!
Yet even if we die we shall be winners:
Our souls shall lodge with all the Saints religious;
And should we live our honor will be bigger."
"In truth," says Roland "you are of noble lineage; 9505
A better one than you ne'er bowed a fiddle!"

463

When they agree to do, those vassals four,
As Roland says and urges that they ought,
Towards the sky their lances high they point;
Roland himself his mighty banner hoists 9510
And sits his shield across his shoulders broad;
They spur their mounts and make a mighty noise
As they shout out their battle-cry "Mountjoy!";
That naked race beholds them sally forth
And straightaway retreats from their assault; 9515

Thus Roland's rank rides through the Orcan force;
Now when he sees how well their plan befalls,
That Calides must bide this pass of war
And yet his ranks have scattered and withdrawn,
Young Graelent has no desire to pause   9520
And let those ranks regroup around their lord;
On his round shield he strikes the Orcan Moor
A mighty blow which smashes through its boards;
His hauberk's mail it totally destroys,
Then breaks his bones and deep within him bores;   9525
From saddle-bow he's helplessly unhorsed
And from his back all of his spine is shorn;
The spear-shaft breaks, so Graelent draws sword;
In that pitched fight full many a blow he scored,
The wounds of which were never healed henceforth.   9530

464

Spurring in haste Roland towards him comes,
His mighty lance in his hand tightly clutched;
Acars of Flors he strikes with force so much
He tears apart his rounded shield in front;
Acars' breast-plate is not worth now a glove   9535
As from his horse one lance-length dead he's flung;
Roland turns rein and sword in hand he thrusts;
Why should I make this matter more long-spun?
More than three score they leave dead in the dust;
One soldier's draw within that Paynim crush   9540
Those vassals five their plan so brave have done
They've killed the kings of both battalions
And have themselves not lost one drop of blood;
What can I say? So many dead they've struck
That all their lives great praise for it they won;   9545
King Floriades next turns tail and runs,
Then Samuel, lamenting his ill-luck;
Ogier turns round and cannot see Roland;
No need to ask if he feared not at once.

465

When Ogier turns and only then sees clearly   9550
That Roland's gone, whom he did not see leaving,
It is no wonder if he at once is fearful;
He calls to Hugh, who is his friend the dearest:
"Count Hugh, my lord, this day is turning evil!
Roland is gone and I know not the reason;   9555
Just yestermorn he was placed in my keeping,
And with my life his life I guaranteed then;
Look, there he is, his pointed helmet gleaming!
Amidst that fierce and mighty crush I see him!

Let's help him, Hugh, I beg you and beseech you!"   9560
Fresh shouting starts and the great din increases;
Straightway is struck full many a blow and mean one,
And many a man is knocked down and defeated;
Ogier, as soon as Roland's side he reaches,
Says to the lad: "I recognized you clearly!   9565
You have not kept your part of our agreement!
In guarding you my own good name I've weakened;
If good Lord God can help me in the meantime,
Till I can give you back to Charles still breathing,
So help me God and His great strength redeeming,   9570
I'll safeguard nothing hence except my shield here!"
Roland at this is so silent and speechless
That in response not one word does he speak there.

466

Those Africans have left behind their lordships,
Who lie afield the three all dead and daunted;   9575
The holy Cross their courage has so altered
That all their ruse and prophesies have fallen;
God loved King Charles for his achievements always,
And all that race he ruled and rallied for Him,
All those brought up within his Empire's borders   9580
And who had been baptized with holy water;
He did not wish that they be set at naught now;
So to His sons those saintly knights He brought there,
So they might see and know those holy horsemen,
Who in the heart of battle would lead them forward; 9585
And this indeed sent Christian spirits soaring;
The weakest man turned into the most warlike;
Those Africans so fiercely were assaulted,
Had you been there you would have seen a slaughter!
They chased those tribes as wolves chase sheep before
       them.   9590

467

Defeated are those first battalions three
And lost the heads of their three lordships liege;
Our Christians chase those Africs like lost sheep
And in their hundreds and thousands kill the beasts;
O'er rocks and flats they drive them with their steel; 9595
Eliadas and Pantalis indeed
Are dressed to fight and have both arms and steeds;
They are not kings whose custom is to flee;
Above the rest they are good fighters each;
They hear the noise, the shouting and the screams   9600
As Christian knights drive theirs across the field;
Eliadas to his advisors speaks:

"These Christian knights are very proud and fierce;
If they find us as feckless as our peers
And news of this should reach Agolant's ears,   9605
No more in life will he regard us dear;
This Frankish pride not two pence do I fear."

468

Our Christians ride in serried ranks right closely,
Two thousand men and seven hundred only;
Now from the rest set off five hundred soldiers,   9610
The hand-picked best as to each one beknown is;
All in this group are armed for war most nobly,
Except for spears which many here have broken,
And, lacking which, their worthy sword are holding;
Right few of them there are, as best I know it,   9615
Whose arms in blood are not bathed to the shoulder,
And horse's tail in similar fashion coated;
As they line up it is not hard to notice;
Ogier is there and Graelent with Roland
And Hugh the count and good Richard of Jovent,   9620
And the twelve peers are there as well, all those
    ones
Whom Charlemayn in recent hour has chosen;
All of them ride in serried ranks so closely,
Between their spears the wind can find no opening;
In front of all ride those three horsemen holy   9625
Whom our Lord God sent Charlemayn in token;
Eliades awaits them all this moment;
He will be lucky not to regret his boasting;
This Saracen is a man of great boldness:
He does not run, it's not his will or wont to;   9630
The Christians cry: "Mountjoy!" and lay on boldly;
If you had seen the fighting fierce that broke then
And sent many to death and set blood flowing
And made the heart of many a woman woeful!
Before it's clear which side has won the moment,   9635
Behold my lords such loss to each opponent
That whosoever wins this land and owns it
And loves his men with tender heart and open
Shall pass no day henceforth and not bemoan it.

469

Good blows are struck by men from Allemayn,   9640
Bavaria, the Ardennes and Lorraine;
Those Africans in wondrous rank are placed
And are well armed in the style of their race;
Their steeds are good and strong and swift and brave;

One hundred of our knights they kill straightway 9645
And of our peers three of the twelve they slay,
Two of them dukes, the third a king most great.

470

If you had been at the start of that struggle!
The Devil's race full fifty thousand numbered
And Christians were two thousand seven hundred; 9650
If you had seen Count Roland lifting upwards
His sword of steel and dealing blows so crushing,
And seen, upon his piebald steed, Graelent
Above the rest assist those knights new-dubbed there,
So that no man could stand before their courage! 9655
Each says to each: "Well may we be called lucky;
For we before were stable boys worth nothing;
How dearly we should hold Carlon and love him,
Who has this way freed us from service humble;
For feudal fee we shall not hence give twopence; 9660
For he has made a knight of each of us here;
And we shall rather let all our limbs be cut off
Before Carlon shall feel the shame or suffer."
Brave Ogier weeps to hear these new-dubbed youngsters;
His heart o'erflows and tears aloft come flooding 9665
And fill his eyes, his visage thence o'errunning;
He speaks aloud, moved now to answer something:
"Well-timed your words! If I so much accomplish
And with God's help return to France the lovely,
Even if Charles in this should prove reluctant, 9670
You shall gain proper thanks each man among you;
For I myself shall see that this is done you;
There's none in France so high in his own judgement
Whom I would not oppose to get you justice;
Now I shall bear the flag for you up front here, 9675
So you may rally all round me in trouble."
"We'll grant this well!" they say to one another.

471

When all those squires once more consider well,
Who at the court were clad in nakedness,
That they forever have left the wretchedness 9680
Wherein till now all of their lives they've spent,
Then they grow strong and bear themselves erect;
And when they find themselves in hauberks dressed,
And their heads laced in good and pointed helms,
And in their hands good spears with sharpened edge, 9685
Then they thank Roland and hail his name and bless;
And rather now would each one lose his head
Ere he'll see Charles defeated here or dead;

Now they attack those Africans full-pelt,
And they in turn right fiercely welcome them,   9690
And straightaway their line is ripped and rent
And they of heads, shoulders and trunks bereft;
Full fifty thousand Infidel troops are set
Against two thousand one hundred Christian men;
If our Lord God does not display His strength,   9695
Then Charles will lose his dearest now and best.

472

The noise is great, the cries are loud and long;
Full many a blow and mean those soldiers swap;
So many fists and feet and heads are lopped,
So many shoulders from bodies are chopped off   9700
That we would never have overcome the loss,
When Salemon arrives, his helmet donned;
In his right hand he holds his blade aloft
And his five thousand men lift up their rods
With pennants fixed, which in the wind do waft;   9705
The lord of Nantes he is, whose fame is long;
He and his house hold privy lease thereof;
His Breton men burst out, their lungs atop,
With "Saint Malo!", their region's cry of wrath;
See now both sides begin a fight so strong   9710
That ere either withdraws and fighting stops
Fine souls so many from bodies will be tossed!

473

The noise is great as fighting starts once more;
Now they show out, those craven boastful sorts,
Who in their fear are the first ones to fall,   9715
While hardy souls fight fiercely to the fore;
Such lusty blows they lay on with their swords,
Which hauberks none can take nor helms adorned;
And those young men such bravery employ,
No Turk there is can hold back their assaults;   9720
And yet they kill full many of those brave boys
And take great toll of our force overall;
Yet lucky he who died in that day's war,
For he dwells now on high with Heaven's Lord;
Young sons came there of lowly vavasors,   9725
They and their fathers to humble service born,
Whom Charlemayn so honored in due course
They left as dukes or counts of Carlon's court;
Great Charlemayn was so rich with reward
That each man's heirs reaped benefit henceforth.   9730

474

In company with Roland, Carlon's nephew,
Two thousand ride along and hundreds seven;
They kill so many the toll I cannot tell you;
Within the ranks of mighty King Salemon
Are Manseaux men and Angevins and Bretons, 9735
Five thousand strong, their tally rightly reckoned,
Which total hence can do nothing but lessen;
Behold alike rich Duke Droon together
With Poitevins and Gascon troops assembled!
A hauberk strong has each of them and pennant 9740
And a bright sword and solid rounded helmet,
A shield or buckler, a gonfalon or ensign;
Their steeds are good, in all the world the best ones;
In all our host no men are mounted better.

475

Those Africs see their warring fortune fade, 9745
Their men so many struck from their destriers,
Who yet do fight but two thousand against;
Our men are armed as fits knighthood's estate
And led up front by those three valiant Saints,
Whom God this day has sent to Charlemayn, 9750
Each one of them in knightly form and shape
And always there when combat is engaged;
Turpin of Reims himself does not delay,
To whom the Pope has given the Cross again;
Those Africs talk and to each other say: 9755
"A curse upon this gonfalonier!
Wherever we look, his flag to heaven waves;
Behold it there up front in pride of place!
Behold it there, it blazes forth and flames
So that the sun gives off a lesser ray! 9760
It blinds us all when we upon it gaze,
And blights our luck against this Christian race;
Against its power we fight to no avail."
Eliades, at this, near goes insane;
He sees his ranks split up and driven away 9765
And all his men hacked to the ground and slain;
Now he himself for safety turns his reins;
If he had thought this battle could be saved
He'd not have left though all his limbs should break;
With grieving heart he lets himself be chased 9770
Behind the rest one bowman's drawing-range;
His mighty spear with rage he starts to shake;
If you had heard him then upbraid his faith
And say its gods did not one penny rate!
Roland meanwhile, Salemon and Ogier 9775

Draw up fresh ranks in close formation placed;
If just once more they could their pluck display,
They could avenge and purge all of their pain!
But none can make his war-horse run again;
To Emperor Charles a messenger relates: 9780
"Rich King and lord, too long may you delay!
Ride off at once your young nephew to aid;
In all the world there is no knight so brave!"
"Ah God, may You be thanked!"Carlon exclaims.

476

Carlon replies: "Is this the truth, my friend?" 9785
The messenger responds: "I swear it, yes;
The first of many whom in the field he met,
Down to the waist he sliced and split him dead."
At this the King is filled with deep content
And he lines up those troops he'll lead himself 9790
Before that rock where Beuvon erstwhile fell
When knocked to ground by haughty Uliens:
He left his army with twenty thousand men,
Hand-picked by Agolant to be the best,
And with the promise of Europe's crown as well; 9795
Before midday he had planned such success
As to exalt all of his family hence.

477

Spurring to battle behold brave King Cahoer,
With thousands four of fighting English souls!
In hauberks good and firm they are well clothed 9800
And in their hands sharp-cutting swords they hold;
Their steeds are strong and anything but slow;
With hate in heart behold these English folk
Towards the flag of that good Afric go,
Who is to the Emir a cousin close; 9805
Full thirty thousands of faithless Turks he owns,
Who are more black than pitch or ink or both;
They wear no helm nor hauberk Eastern-sewn;
They are all archers and from their saddle-bows
Their quivers hang, filled up with sharp-tipped bolts 9810
That they will shoot to lay our Frenchmen low;
Cahoer now joins battle with this foe
And all his Englishmen strike heavy blows;
His sword aloft, around them all he roams
And shouts: "On! On! The Holy Cross invokes! 9815
English lay on! Lay on and be not loath!
Let none of you spare one man's life of those!"
And they perform like knights of mighty mold;
That Paynim force grows weaker till in woe

Those Turks all turn and scurry down a slope; 9820
One English knight there is, both brave and bold,
In Chester born, whose parentage is close
To King Cahoer, who loves the brave man so
For all the pluck and great prowess he shows;
As he rides round he takes a vicious toll 9825
Of all those Turks with his steel-bladed strokes;
Those at his side, whose sum I do not know,
In Paynim breasts bore many a deep hole;
They lose their blood and bowels and liver both;
Of thirty thousand there is not one left o'er 9830
Who'll fight again with willing heart or no;
To Agolant's redoubt one of them goes,
In brutal haste bent o'er his saddle-bows,
Holding his bowels which as he rides o'erflow;
To Agolant he speaks in lowered tones: 9835
"What are you doing, King? Wherefore your sloth?
Charles seeks you out and he is very close;
His Oriflamme is making its approach;
This present morn, before the third hour tolled,
I saw a rank of fearsome English folk 9840
And thought straightway to fell one of this foe;
But he fought back in knightly manner bold;
I and four more could not this one o'erthrow;
Then I was struck by his sharp spear and smote;
Of this, sir King, your eyes may take full note! 9845
I clung to my steed's neck and off I rode,
But did not think I would escape e'en so;
And when I did, King Agolant, in troth
All of my days such joy I'd never known;
Believe me, King, let us all head for home! 9850
Wait here no more for Carlon and his host;
One thousand kitchen boys he has alone
Who better men than you could end of hope."

478

The Emir says, his face with anger flushing:
"Have you come from the fight, Fausarin, brother?" 9855
"Indeed, Sire, yes, you can see from my color
That all my days the woe of it I'll suffer;
Believe me, lord, continue not this struggle!
Each one of them is better than our hundreds,
For they believe in God, who is their succor; 9860
My lord, escape to India your country
And have therein a mighty tower constructed;
If you and yours can there escape from trouble,
Well might you say that you were led there lucky."

479

Give ear, my lords, as I sing a good song　　　　　　　9865
Of Charlemayn, whose face with valor shone,
And Duke Girart, that brave Burgundian,
Who was the son of mighty Duke Beuvon;
No better king in spur was ever shod;
When Girart now beholds the gonfalon,　　　　　　　　　9870
He calls his nephews, lords Beuvon and Claron,
And then his sons Ernault, Renier, Milon:
"My good and worthy knights, let us be strong!
Behold the Turk, his lion-shield aloft,
He who this morn attacked us in such wrath!　　　　　9875
And we did well all that we could, by God!
But now I do forbid you, for the nonce,
Nephews and sons, peers and companions,
To offer fight as we shall ride along;
A curse on him who now obeys me not;　　　　　　　　　9880
He shall not step into my halls hereon!
Let us make straight for that great gonfalon
And get as close as we may ere we're stopped,
Our shields drawn up, each man his helmet donned;
We'll fight them there if they dare take us on;　　　9885
But if we then can slip right through the lot
We'll win this field once we reach Agolant."
"We will not fail you lord," they all respond.

480

Girart rides off, who is most skilled in tactic;
Twelve hundred men he has in his brave vanguard,　　 9890
Led by his nephews twain, Beuvon and Claron;
But now behold King Uliens the arrogant!
Four thousand men he has to start the battle,
With floral-painted helms and good cuirasses;
They cast their darts and many let loose arrows,　　 9895
But do not find Girart's men running backwards;
They find instead courageous knights and valiant;
For never a one you'd find a better vassal;
They do not fight, although the will's not lacking:
They dare not go against fierce Girart's planning.　 9900

481

Uliens sees these Frenchmen will not fight;
Weapon nor word, no matter which they try
To throw at them, to threaten and defy,
Not one moves out to fight them in reply,
Because Girart forbids them at this time;　　　　　　　9905
To Agolant's redoubt they start to ride,

Which the Emir decides to move meanwhile
Four acres full towards the forward lines,
Where, if need be, his troops can reunite;
Yet ere his men can do as he desires   9910
He starts to look towards his right hand side
And sees those Turks all roaming left and right,
Who had set out our brave Girart to strike;
And Uliens, try as hard as he might,
Cannot get them to quicken their slow stride; 9915
From that redoubt which you have heard described,
At twice the range bow sends its bolt in flight,
There Girart halts with all his men and knights.

482

When Girart halts with all his knights and men
He calls his nephews, his sons and closest friends: 9920
"Brave men," he says, "Lord God has watched us well,
For none of us has died in this fight yet;
I've raised you all and cared for you and fed,
Till now you are grown up and in good health;
Carlon's own ranks have struck the Infidels,   9925
For I can hear the noise of battle swell;
Now I ask you to aid them and to help,
And in the field to give me recompense."
And they reply: "Your words we well accept,
For we are armed and they are bare of dress;   9930
If it please God and His redeeming strength,
When we have stopped no one shall know them hence;
For from their trunks we shall cut off their heads."
Three thousand men dismount when this is said,
Of Girart's men the chosen hand-picked best,   9935
And their war-steeds are taken by the rest;
At a slow pace and with strict silence kept,
With lowered shields and lowered heads in helms,
But with sharp picks and cutting lances held,
To Agolant's redoubt they move in stealth;   9940
Then when at last those Africs notice them
They yell out loud: "We have been tricked to death!
For even if we kill these men ahead,
These on our right will surely kill us then!"

483

In his redoubt is Agolant installed   9945
With twelve more kings of the Infidel cause;
On every side are Paynims by the score;
No man alive there is could count them all;
Loud moan he makes about the Almanzor:
"He does delay too long," say more and more;   9950

236

But he has all his fealty forsworn;
Girart attacks with three battalions formed,
His vanguard now made up of thousands four;
No longer slow, they neither stop or stall
But rush and strike without a moment's pause;   9955
Thus brave Girart fights fiercely to the fore,
From Agolant's redoubt one sargeant's draw;
Of act so brave not even Charles shall vaunt,
Nor Naimes the Duke, Ogier, Roland and all
The lords of France to pride and power born;   9960
Had it not been for God on High our Lord,
Who sent three Saints erstwhile to lead their force,
And Duke Girart, his nephews and his boys,
Carlon would have retained as much French soil
As his best man with one glove could have clawed.   9965

484

Beuvon, Claron and Ernault and Renier
Lead on those thousands four who them obey;
In iron and steel so strong are they encased
That Paynim blows shall batter them in vain;
Behold, my lords, the daring now displayed   9970
As men on men they pile and lifeless lay!
When Girart's men add their force to the fray,
From Afric hearts they take all hope away
And force their ranks to quit the field in haste;
To Agolant's redoubt they give them chase   9975
And harry them, who cannot now escape;
No king on earth, so high in his own rate,
To see his men in such a wretched state,
Would not have been perturbed for pity's sake;
King Agolant no further time would waste;   9980
Of his redoubt the end he would delay:
If this delay does not his own end haste,
He'll curse the man on whose advice he came.

485

The Orcan folk now give the French fresh battle;
Before those rocks resolved to make a stand there   9985
They all dismount, their better and their bad ones;
How many blows they give, mortal and massive,
And worthy men and noble-blooded vassals
They strike down dead and hack down from their
    saddles!
Now Charlemayn, the worthy King and Champion,   9990
His nephew Roland, who holds aloft Durendal,
Ogier and Naimes, the worthy Duke and natural,
And all the band of royal France's barons

Attack this folk from the edge of a valley;
The fighting's wild and dreadful is the damage; 9995
The Orcan folk, a faithless race and savage,
Shoot darts and arrows and raise a mighty racket;
What can I say? Those Paynims wreak such havoc
That if Lord God does not think of His vassals,
They'll never have known a day so full of anguish. 10000

486

The Orcan folk dismount to keep the field;
Eliadas and his boy Pantalis
Before those rocks defend their honor dear;
Behold the blows so many struck and mean,
Which cut off heads and trunks and shoulders cleave 10005
And men so many unsaddle from their steeds
And strike down dead and stiff outstretched do leave!
The hue and cry and noise of war increase
And injuries whose like was never seen;
When those of France behold their losses keen, 10010
Fathers and brothers and sons alike perceive,
Each says to each: "What evil this, indeed!
For we have lost too many comrades here;
If we avenge them not our honor's cheap;
May our Lord God deny him strength to breathe 10015
Who moves not now to smite them on their shields."
And they all strike straightway with pointed spears;
Like it or not the Orcan line they breach;
That faithless folk at this are so aggrieved
That all their force and all their valor flee; 10020
No more they'll seize our reins to keep the field!

487

Our Emperor, to see their line split wide,
And all their folk turn round and take to flight
With yaps and yells and dreadful shrieks and wild,
Knows then full well they cannot match his might; 10025
To his own troops he calls: "Now let us strike!
I'll see them all yield up this field of fight!"
His troops obey straightway in strongest wise:
Behold, my lords, so many lances sliced!
In his redoubt the Emir hears the cries; 10030
Three thousand Turks are made to feel French iron,
Of whom no doctor hence shall save the lives;
They fall upon their fallen peers and die;
Like it or not the rest of them retire
And all the field relinquish and resign; 10035
But then they're met by Persians from Montir,
Men thirty thousand loved not by God on High,

Led by a lord himself hard to abide:
King Moadas, son of the King of Tyr,
With Abilant the king of Mount Espir;   10040
Like it or not they drive back all our knights
To Charlemayn's own Oriflamme well nigh;
But Duke Fagon the full retreat denies;
He tells his men: "Let their be no respite
From seeking vengeance and serving Jesus Christ!"   10045

488

The Orcan folk those troops of Persia see,
Who have come down the rocks to their relief,
Men thirty thousand with bows drawn all and each
And with stout rods and sharply-pointed spears
And axes cruel and great picks strong to pierce;   10050
Their leaders twain are both so proud and fierce,
Kings Moadas and Abilant are these,
They rate no other men at a straw's fee;
They charge the French where they find them to be,
Who with great strength their charge so well receive   10055
That all those Persian troops are sore aggrieved;
Behold the blows so many and so mean
And men struck dead, outstretched on fallen peers!
The fallen dead are spread so thick and deep
That fathers fight above dead sons unseen;   10060
Ogier and Naimes are knocked down from their steeds
And Salemon and Richer trapped afield;
When Charles sees this, unwonted woe he feels
And cries: "Great God, what are You doing here?
If I lose these, my strength will disappear;   10065
I shall no more bring shield to battle's need."
He lifts Joyeuse, his sword of unmatched steel,
And makes his stand amidst the battle's heat;
King Abilant he strikes upon his shield
And splits his skull right down from top to teeth;   10070
"Mountjoy!" he cries for all his French to hear;
Seven thousand men come to his side and speed,
His vassals all and his sworn men and liege;
For Paynims bald nor bearded shall they leave;
Roland the young and Hugh of hoary years   10075
And Graelent upon his piebald steed
Break through the press and to their King come near;
When Charlemayn sees these his men appear
He calls to them: "Be sure to hold this field!"
And so they do with shouts so loud and clear   10080
They reach the Oriflamme and Fagon's ears;
He tells his men: "God guard you and God speed!
Charles needs you now to help him and relieve;
With Jesu's help you cannot but succeed!"

489

When Fagon sees the need of his liege-lord, 10085
With tender love his own troops he exhorts:
"My worthy knights and fighters noble-born,
Let us all ride to help our Emperor!
Let blows so hard upon these Paynims fall
That their blood changes the color of our swords!" 10090
With loyal love his troops say one and all:
"Most worthy lord and brave, spur on your horse!
You shall not ride to any pass of war
And we not follow as wild duck does goshawk."

490

The Emperor, when he beholds Duke Fagon, 10095
Whom he had left behind to guard his standard,
Come to his aid with so many fine barons,
To his own troops cries out: "How shall we act now?
If these fine men are led away and captured
I shall not seek to go back to my allods*." 10100
Carlon calls out "Mountjoy!" his cry of battle:
"Let us all ride and strike their biggest banner!"
And so they do and need no prompting added;
They breach their ranks the range of one large arrow;
Will they or not, those Persians take to saddle! 10105

491

Fagon rides forth, the Oriflamme upraised,
Unfurling in the wind that ensign great
Which he has borne for Charles full many a day;
Years thirty-three he's borne this banner brave,
Which God has blessed and honored with such fame 10110
That it has never been moved from fight engaged;
One thousand knights, picked from his own domain
And private house, he leads who him obey;
Not one there is whose helm is not in place,
And is not keen himself to join the fray; 10115
He leads them now in ranks so closely made
That if you tossed an apple o'er their train
It would go half a league ere down it came;
These men of his he calls and gently says:
"Ah, worthy men of honorable race! 10120
I've brought you up and taught from tender age;
I lead you now in foreign parts and strange;

* From allodium, an estate held in absolute ownership,
  as opposed to a fief.

Now you see here a race of wayward knaves,
Who heed not God nor His great strength acclaimed,
Nor love the Laws of our God-given Faith;   10125
May Lord God grant, Who made Galilee's lake,
That in this field my just reward be paid;
Let us so hard these ranks of theirs assail
That we at last take all their hope away!
Hark to the hue and mighty cry they make!   10130
Let them strive hard their heathen heads to save,
For they with mine shall soon come face to face!"
His men reply like folk of noble rate:
"Ride on, my lord, your vizor down, in haste!
These Africans shall not survive our rage;   10135
Three thousand soon shall lie with mouths agape;
Your own renown shall be so well maintained
Your name shall never be sung in ballad base."

PART 11

492

Fagon the duke to battle spurs his horse;
He's seneschal to Charles the Emperor;   10140
Full many a day the Oriflamme he's borne,
Which God has blessed with such fame and reward
That it has never been moved from battle joined;
With men one thousand, good sons of vavasors,
The hand-picked best and bravest of his choice, 10145
He showed more courage than any man before
Who met his foe with entourage so small;
Men thirty thousand the king of Persia's brought;
Fagon calls on Raymond of Moncontour,
A worthy knight and fighter fierce withal;   10150
You'd find none better in all the Christian corps;
Fagon's nephew he is, his sister's boy,
In whom the duke does trust and take great joy;
Carlon's great flag he gives now to this lord
And to his men with tender love he talks: 10155
"Strike hard these heathens and have no fear at all!
"Let their blood change the color of our swords!"
And so they do, straightway, with such great force
That there's no Turk so well equipped for war
Who trembles not and is not troubled sore;   10160
Fell Moadas so fiercely they assault
That from his ranks the battle-flag is torn
And his men flee, both high and humble born.

493

When to the fight they come, those thousand barons
Whom Charlemayn had left to guard his standard,   10165
Before the rest is the seneschal Fagon;
A duke he is and one of Carlon's family,
His counsellor, one of his court's most valued,
And in the field the bearer of his banner;
He sits well-armed astride a Gascon stallion,   10170
With hauberk, helm and shield of lion rampant;
His spear is strong, its tip of iron fashioned;
Before the rest the range of one large arrow
He hurls himself into the raging battle;
He strikes Moadas, the son of King Pharaon,   10175
And nephew too of Agolant the Saracen,
Born to his sister, the beautiful Engelissant;
His armor now does not one button matter;
Fagon splits it like a new silken mantle,
Piercing his body, his lungs and liver smashing;   10180
His kidneys both and his backbone are shattered
As the iron stops in the rear bow of saddle;
The duke thrusts on and throws him on the sand there;
Then, as he turns, his hand drops to his scabbard
And draws his sword, whose knob is gold-enameled;   10185
On Matefelon's head, a king, he lands it
And flings him dead, like it or not the Afric;
Fagon cries out: "Mountjoy for Charlemagne!"
Hot on his heels they hear this, all his vassals,
Who spur their steeds as swiftly as they can do   10190
And one foot-soldier's range outrun their captain;
There is not one who would have worshipped Mahom,
Though he were offered the riches of Besançon.

494

The Africs, when they see those French arrive,
And dead afield see strong Moadas lie,   10195
And Abilant the king of Mount Espir,
Then they know well they cannot long abide;
They turn their reins and take to hasty flight;
To save their lives they flee the mountain-side;
When Charles sees this he calls out with a sigh: 10200
"Well may I serve You, Lord, Who are most High,
Who in my hands have placed such worthy knights!"
He cries "Mountjoy!", their courage to inspire:
"My worthy knights, once more I bid you strike!
This is the last you'll see of them run by!"   10205
And so they do, straightway, with such great might
That thirty thousand Paynims resign the fight,
Of whom the most shall rue it in good time;

If you could hear the noise of lances sliced
And hauberks split so many and ripped wide 10210
And Persians felled upon the land to lie,
Of whom no doctor hence shall save the lives!
To Agolant's redoubt they turn and ride;
Uliens looks and goes berserk well nigh;
When he beholds his men so sorely tried 10215
That he himself cannot maintain their lines,
And sees so many abandoning the fight,
Then he rides out the helm of one to smite;
Down to his teeth he makes him feel the iron.

495

A noble lord indeed is Uliens, 10220
Who is a nephew of strong King Agolant,
And as a knight right brave and valiant;
He sees those Afric troops returning thus
And Persians too lamenting marvellous
For Moadas, who lies dead in the dust, 10225
Together with the strong King Abilant;
So many slain there are of other ones
No man alive could ever tell the sum;
Uliens dies with rage to see them come
And calls on them in a loud voice full-lunged: 10230
"You sons of whores, where is it you would run?
You wicked race and worse than recreant,
What was it that you told the Emir once,
In his great palace back home in Africa,
When you were drinking his wine of Orient? 10235
You did not rate the French or Alemans
And all their force the worth one bezant was;
Yet they are great, this much is clear enough;
Of this their land they'll leave us not one glove;
Come rally all round this white gonfalon, 10240
Which is the flag of your rich Admiral."
But they flee past without a glance so much,
With fathers even not waiting for their sons.

496

When Uliens beholds the French give chase
And sees his troops hacked down by them and slain, 10245
Whose battle-lines he can no more maintain,
Then he, at last, despairs of his own fate;
Against these French his own life now he stakes;
He grips his lance of apple-wood well made
And spurs to strike the shield of brave Richer: 10250
Count Antelme's nephew and son of Duke Renier,
Born to the daughter of Baron Berenger,

Richer became the envoy of Charlemayn,
Who loved him dearly and cherished him always;
In all our ranks he knighted none more brave;   10255
No messenger knew better what to say
Nor was more fit fell Saracens to slay;
Now he is struck a mighty blow and great
'Gainst which his shield is not worth one denier;
His hauberk's strong and unpierced is the mail;   10260
Uliens turns the point, but the shaft breaks
And now Renier strikes back with his steel blade;
High on the helm he strikes the devlish knave
A blow which goes till by the fore-bow stayed;
Why should I any more spin out the tale?   10265
Dead on the ground Richer thrusts him away;
In Afric hearts there's nothing but dismay;
To Agolant's redoubt they come in haste;
The Emir looks and almost goes insane:
"Where are my counsellors," he turns and wails,   10270
"On whose advice this realm I came to take?
It's they should help me now this field to save!"
Not one there is, so high in his own rate,
Who does not now advise he drop all claim;
Round the redoubt right fearsome is the fray;   10275
Behold my lords so many Paynims slain,
Flung one atop the other and lifeless lain!
Among themselves those Africs speak and say:
"How true the words that Balan spoke that day!
This land, in truth, will give us naught but pain! 10280
Carlon is fierce and his Frenchmen the same;
Not one loaf's worth of France we'll ever gain;
Let each man think how best he may escape!
In this redoubt our only hope remains."

497

Round the redoubt the battle they continue;   10285
No more shall woe the like of this be witnessed:
So many men have head and soul relinquished!
Girart the duke of men is much diminished;
Of his own troops one thousand have been killed there,
While on the Emir great loss has been inflicted;   10290
Of his twelve kings nine of them now are missing;
And his own flag likewise has been downsmitten;
When this is known and noticed by those Christians,
When they no longer see that flag a-billow,
Nor any flag that that redoubt flew in it,   10295
Then their hearts soar and they grow strong in spirit;
Acars of Flors to all of this stands witness,
Who has dismounted in this great need arisen;
Full many a blow he deals our men and gives them;

When this is seen by Agolant the Infidel, 10300
That all his men are being felled and finished,
Know this, my lords: he does not wait one minute
For someone else to come and hold his stirrups;
He mounts his horse like any man of wisdom
And rides away in haste for Reggio city; 10305
One thousand French give chase, all very willing
To take his head as soon as they meet with him!
He turns round often, his naked blade a-swinging
And striking dead whichever man he hits there;
No shield or helm can take the blows he gives them; 10310
If he loved God, no better King were living;
One thousand French give chase, with cry uplifted,
And his redoubt is left with no one in it;
Bearded nor bald stop now within its limits;
Should Agolant dare now to ask for tribute, 10315
A fierce response and fell would be delivered!
Our Emperor calls halt now to the killing;
He has not men, nor strength himself, sufficient
To go on fighting, the carnage to continue;
Throughout his host the ranks are so much thinner; 10320
Of men one hundred thousand at the beginning,
Only one fourth are not now dead or injured;
Carlon calls out for his tent to be pitched there;
He'll not depart till he has rested in it;
This signifies that he has won the victory. 10325

498

From his redoubt the Emir has retired,
Thrown out from there by our brave Christian knights;
Against his will he's left his host behind;
Two hundred thousand men of his have died,
And all the rest try now to match his stride; 10330
Beuvon and Claron in hot pursuit both ride,
With Duke Ernaut and Renier called the wise;
Worthy Girart comes too, prepared to fight
With his battalion in serried ranks drawn tight;
Direct for Reggio town the Emir rides, 10335
And yet before he's safe and sound inside
A harsh detour shall he be forced to find!
He's chased towards a ditch both deep and wide
Through which Beuvon has found the ford betimes;
He heads there now to halt the Emir's flight; 10340
Beuvon and Claron are there when he arrives
And there it is that in a crowd they strike
And shaft and shield so many pierce and smite
And men so many unhorse in such mean wise!
To this one spot the fighting is confined 10345
As men so many, dying on dead, are piled!

No man on earth, the full truth to describe,
Would not be thought to be a proven liar.

499

Afield to fight stands Agolant the Emir,
Surrounded by those left of all his generals, 10350
Who in brave wise defend themselves in peril
Against our French who strike them all together;
So many blows they deal so hard and dreadful,
Which of that cruel race do kill so many,
The valley floor is filled and overspread there; 10355
What can I say? The slaughter is so heavy
No mortal man could accurately tell it;
Then brave Antelme, a prince of inborn merit,
And of Girart the highest ranking seneschal,
Brings down the horse of Agolant the Emir; 10360
He'll flee no more down hollows or up headlands.

500

Down in the field King Charlemayn has stopped;
He calls to him his seneschal Fagon,
Ogier and Naimes and Richer and Huon,
And Driu the king and good King Salemon, 10365
And brave Cahoer, king of the Englishmen:
"Without delay spread here my tent aloft
And raise up high my royal gonfalon!
Let those of France make camp around this spot."
Then Carlon summons Estous, son of Uedon, 10370
And that most brave of vassals, Graelent,
And knights of the same shire, one thousand strong;
Beard or moustache the oldest one bears not:
"Mount horse straightway, and spurring hard non-stop
Assist Girart, the brave Burgundian, 10375
The noblest duke who ever put spurs on!"
"We shall not fail you, Sire," they all respond.

501

King Charlemayn, our ruler good and great,
Calls now upon good Naimon and Ogier
And Salemon and Fagon and Richer: 10380
"To bravery once more turn thought!" he says:
"Take of your men those who have destriers
And climb this hill and ride to Girart's aid!"
And so they do, with never a question raised;
Fagon leads them, their gonfalonier, 10385
Together with the marquis Berenger;
They climb the hill and gallop on in haste;

Those Afric troops, to see these come their way,
Know now full well that their defence is vain.

502

The Afric folk watch our French forces come, 10390
Men brave and bold, fourteen hundred in sum;
Astride an Afric horse sits every one,
Which is both strong and swift and keen to run;
Bright helms they have, hauberks and byrnies tough,
And solid spears and swords that sharply cut; 10395
High born or low of arms have well enough;
And as they ride their lines are so closed up
That had you tossed above their helms a glove,
You would yourself a goodly league have done
Ere that same glove upon the ground had struck; 10400
Those Afric troops, when they behold this much,
And can well see and sense their will at once--
That they intend to strike and to spare none--
They do not wait for it to happen thus;
They turn about and spur their stallions; 10405
They take to flight and leave there in a rush,
With fathers even not waiting for their sons.

503

When Agolant beholds his troops' sad end--
Sees his most high all slain and cut to shreds,
And lowliest across the landscape spread-- 10410
When he beholds that so many have fled,
And sees our men still striking blows so dread
That fell his own and slay and cut to shreds,
Then to himself his own thoughts he laments:
"Ah, wretched me, alas, what can I hence? 10415
Those men of mine on whose advice I left,
Well might I now repent of heeding them--
But it's too late!" He sighs with great regret:
"I thought, indeed, to seize all Carlon's realm,
Then share it out among my bravest best; 10420
Now I shall fall far short of my intent;
Let each man think how best to save himself!
By striking hard shall we show best defence;
For I would rather die fighting with my men
Than flee the field alive but honorless." 10425
He draws his sword like a man nobly bred;
The man he strikes has no escape from death.

504

In Agolant there's naught but anguish awful

When under him he sees his war-horse slaughtered
And sees his men all cut to shreds before him;   10430
In hundreds and in thousands the French destroy them;
Twelve kings he had at this fight's start this morning
And now but two still able to support him
And guide his troops with tactic as they ought to;
Of all the rest he sees the headless corpses;   10435
Yet in defence is he himself undaunted
And none on earth our men more terror causes;
Yet his own men cannot so much support him
As to remount him now on a fresh war-horse
Or fit him out with new arms in proportion   10440
To those he breaks upon our knights employing;
At last they make a great axe ready for him,
Whose handle is of apple-wood a portion;
With bands of gold they wrap and tie it tautly
To make it strong and worthy in performance;   10445
With this in hand the King becomes so awesome
That there's no helm or double-strengthened hauberk
That he cannot stave in or break or bore through;
In self-defence this day so fierce he fought them
That none of ours dared more to ride towards him;   10450
Girart the duke to his attack calls halt now;
To Agolant he sends one skilled in talking:
"If you agree to shun Mahom henceforward
And be baptized for Christ in Holy water,
A longer life shall be yours in assurance,   10455
And of great lands shall you still rule the borders."
Thus spoke the man, but Agolant retorted:
"Get out of here, you base-born wretched whore-son!
You are not worth of noble hands the soiling!
Nor should you strive to meet me at close quarters,   10460
For you'd receive straightway full payment for it;
Within my realm it shall not be reported,
Nor shall my line bear the reproof henceforward,
That out of fear to Christian faith I altered;
I'd rather die than bend the knee to your God."   10465
Claron hears this and greatly does it gall him;
A mighty spear he lifts in his annoyance,
Whose handle is of apple-wood a portion;
He leaves the ranks and breaks the press before him;
Towards the Emir he spurs his stallion forward;   10470
He strikes him hard and yet he cannot floor him;
The Emir looks and for a youngster scorns him;
If you had seen that axe-shaft in his claws then,
Towards the neck of worthy Claron falling!
But he, in turn, cannot strike true for all that;   10475
Down to the left the blow deflects and falters,
Striking the shield and shearing off one quarter,
Hitting the saddle and slicing off the fore-bow;

See Claron now! His burnished blade withdrawing,
He aims and lands a wild blow and enormous, 10480
High on the Emir's helm atop the coif-cap;
He takes his head with this steel-bladed sword-stroke!
Among themselves those Africs fret forlornly,
For they have lost their rightful liege and lordship;
They turn in flight through vales and rocky courses; 10485
No path or track they keep in their disorder;
To Duke Girart the Emir's head is brought now;
When this is done, they take off Girart's hauberk
For the heat's sake, and lift his helmet also;
Both Ernault and Renier he calls before him, 10490
The eldest sons that his good wife has borne him:
"To Reggio ride, for I would lodge there shortly!
For me and mine make ready the great hallway!"
And they reply: "Your will be done, as always."
Meanwhile, my lords, young Roland, Naimes and Ogier 10495
To their own camp consider now withdrawing;
For they've great need to rest their bodies also.

505

When the Emir had landed his flotilla,
When he had stormed and captured Reggio city,
He carried there all of his wealth and riches, 10500
Which he locked up in its great tower and hid there,
While other goods he stowed in nearby niches,
Of wagon-loads full thirty-one consisting;
Then when his troops rode off to join their kinsmen
And our Christians did battle with those Infidels, 10505
Lords, it was then that the Almanzor quit him;
He came to Reggio and stole all that was in it!
He never left a thing worth the least shilling;
If he had found the Queen within its citadel
He would straightway have cut her down and killed her; 10510
But there she hides within that mighty building,
With twelve more ladies, the eldest but an infant,
Who each of them have many maidens with them;
When they're adorned and dressed as does befit them,
Their beauty's such as beggars all description; 10515
In time each one shall be baptized a Christian,
And God shall make their future life so blissful
That their most poor shall not be dealt so ill with
As not to have a gold ring on her finger,
To baron, count or duke in marriage given. 10520

506

Girart's two sons arrive at last in Reggio;
They find the palace and all the rooms quite empty;

Stout spears they find and bucklers there full many,
And bows and axes and sharp-tipped darts a-plenty;
The Almanzor has so well used these weapons   10525
That there is not a single soldier left there
Of all of those the Queen retained and kept there;
They have been slain and slaughtered, each and every
To the last man, save four old men white-headed,
Who with the Queen had come and stayed together;   10530
Inside the tower she took them when she went there.

507

Their King is dead and vanquished is our foe;
The Emir's head they give, which off was smote,
To Duke Girart in its bright helm a-glow:
The band thereof is studded with rich stones,   10535
Yet in his need they helped him not a groat;
As if he were asleep his eyes are closed,
But from his veins his blood spurts out and flows;
Through grizzled beard his countenance still
    shows,
But at the back his hair hangs long and low,   10540
Which reached as far as his steed's saddle-bows;
Now Girart rides, who is both brave and bold;
In haste to find the Emir's corpse he goes;
Across his chest that sharp axe he beholds,
And lying there ten brave men of his host,   10545
Whom he had fed from tender years and clothed,
Till kings of rate themselves were each of those;
The duke, when he beholds these men and knows,
So all may hear, laments in tender tones:
"Ill-starred your births, you worthy knights and bold! 10550
If men your like I'd lost through fault my own,
All of my life henceforth would be but woe."
Then he calls out to white-haired Antiaume;
A brave man he, as proven by his pose:
He cannot move, himself so dear he's sold.   10555

508

Barons, my lords, will it please you to hear
Why Duke Girart should always be held dear?
All of those men he summoned as their liege,
Who by his will he took into the field
When he went forth to fight with the Emir,   10560
Whose plan it was to plunder Christian fiefs,
All those whose souls from bodies disappeared,
Can still be seen where now they rest in peace!
Those left alive could never mock or sneer
That to no church Girart brought their dead peers;   10565

For brought they were and buried solemnly;
And then the duke an abbey there decreed,
With wealth enough for monks in hundreds three
To keep the matin's hour in company;
Of his own wealth he gave a goodly piece, 10570
To so provide and care for all of these,
That none of them was ever in such need
As to want boots or shoes upon his feet;
Girart installed an abbot finally,
And asked the Pope to bless him and receive; 10575
With such a one should men a-warring leave!
Then Girart did a further noble deed--
He buried thus Agolant the Emir:
The Paynim's corpse he placed upon a bier
And bore inside the palace for all to see; 10580
Where it was usual for the young folk to meet,
At chess and draughts to play and to compete,
Off to one side and next to a stone pier,
Inside a coffin he buried the Emir;
There he is still for any who would seek; 10585
He left his helmet on his head, indeed
He gave adornment to his face and mien,
So that to all his rich rank would appear;
This done the duke forsook his arms and steed.

509

The duke disarms, who did much to be praised; 10590
Now we once more to Charles must turn our tale;
Our Emperor the battle-field forsakes;
So close to the Emir our Christians came
Ere he from his redoubt was chased away,
That seven of his kings were sliced and slain; 10595
And in less ground than one longbowman's range
The number of dead Christians is so great
That each man left is lost for words to say;
Carlon commands that his tent be upraised
And over it his golden eagle placed; 10600
Then he disarms, this warrior bold and brave;
He is exhausted from all he's done this day,
Striking and riding in the heat of the fray;
Now with good food their strength they must regain;
Carlon sits down, who is filled with dismay, 10605
At his right hand Bavaria's Duke Naimes
And at his left Ogier the worthy Dane;
Of others there I shall not tell the names,
But of all those not one can they persuade
That evening to wait on Carlon's plate; 10610
They can scarce help themselves, so tired are they,
Except those lads Giradet and Richer,

251

Estous of Lengres, Haton and Berenger:
"My lords," says Charles, "I seek not to gainsay;
When we for war came here to Calabray, 10615
Of men eight thousand score our force was made;
Two thirds of these shall never breathe again,
Who three days back were healthy men and hale;
Yet I came not to capture lands or take,
But rode here rather the Lord our God to aid 10620
And to uphold and glorify His Faith;
Now when I hear some of our own men say
That I began this war and am to blame
For all the hurt and hardship we've sustained,
And that the fault is mine for all their pain, 10625
I'm sorely tempted to give up all my claims,
And devil take the thought of further gain--
Save that I'm loath to change all for their sakes!
Let God give France to him whom more she craves!
I pay too dearly, who dear enough have paid!" 10630
"My lord," says Naimes, "pray do not fret this way!
If our Lord God was willing so to aid
Your cause that all these men joined our campaign,
Then their reward in Paradise awaits."

510

In Reggio town is Girart and his sons, 10635
Fulk and sir Claron, the brave and valiant;
Girart speaks out in a loud voice full-lunged
To Garin thus: "Step forward, worthy one!
For food and victuals how does it go with us?"
"In truth, my lord, well-stocked are we enough! 10640
Three thousand men shall not for four whole months
Complain thereof with cause worth to one glove!"
Then says the duke: "Garin, I charge you thus:
Thirty pack-mules load up for me at once,
And of our food lay on their backs as much 10645
As they can bear, till more so can they none!
Nephew Claron, get on your horse at once!
The Emir's head in its gold helm take up!
You and Gautier and Antelme and Morant,
Go all and say from me to King Carlun 10650
That in full worth I've kept my word and done;
I've called him lord, all other lords above,
Except Lord God, who is Omnipotent;
Whatever I do, tell him, in time to come,
Thanks be to God, this battle-field I've won; 10655
Give Charles this head of the Emir that was!"
"Well granted this, my lord!" replies Claron;
Without delay they do as he instructs:
By thirty troops those sumpters are packed up,

Who then with whips lay on them many a touch, 10660
While Girart's men, behind, spur stallions;
Across a slope in convoy thus they come
And find the King as he sits down to sup.

511

Into his tent come now those four companions;
Upon a plate, made once by worthy Salemon, 10665
In its round helm they've placed the head of Agolant;
White is his beard and white are his moustaches,
And white the hair which flows behind the back of him,
Which reached right down to the bows of his saddle,
And whiter is than ermine fur-lined mantle; 10670
They ride inside the tent of Charlemagne;
Claron dismounts as do his three companions;
Our King knows not as yet, nor do his barons,
If Agolant has or has not been vanquished;
He leans across to Naimes, at his right hand there: 10675
"These four young men are high of state and handsome;
They do not seem like stripling squires or lackeys."
"My lord," says Naimes, "it is the young Duke Claron,
Nephew of Girart, who came from Beuvon's family."
"With the blessing of God!" says Charlemagne. 10680

512

Claron rides in the tent of Charlemayn;
Before the King upon his feet he stays;
Upon a plate of finest gold e'er shaped,
Which Salemon in his young years once made,
In its jewelled helm the Emir's head they've placed; 10685
His beard is white as is the summer spray;
When Agolant bestrode his destrier,
Down to the knot of his sword-belt it came;
And his moustaches so carefully are trained
That they are plaited and tied with two gold braids 10690
Which lift them up and draw them back again;
And down his back his hair flows in a mane,
With lock on lock combed carefully and laid;
The plate of gold is covered with the same;
All listen well when Claron speaks and says: 10695
"Girart the duke greets you, Carlon, and hails
As the best man to be born in these days;
He has called you his lord throughout this fray,
And after God has honored most your name;
All we his troops have won a booty great; 10700
Nor would he hide what he himself has gained;
I have brought you your portion, on this plate,
Of that man's corpse who caused you so much pain,

Destroyed your lands and laid waste your domains,
And your men's lives such agony has made; 10705
Girart the duke has made him dearly pay;
Behold his head in jewelled helm still laced!"
Now Claron lifts that helmet and displays
The many stones with which it is inlaid;
The stones and gold cast off so bright a ray 10710
That Carlon's tent in brilliance is bathed;
There's not one man who on them sets his gaze,
Whose eyes straightway do not adazzle blaze;
And color floods to faces erstwhile pale;
Our King beholds the dead Agolant's face 10715
And offers God right tenderly his praise;
To Duke Girart his gratitude is great:
"Inform the duke my will now to obey;
For two whole weeks our men shall here remain
Till I have gathered the bodies of our slain, 10720
The noble-born from low to separate,
The kings, the dukes and counties' counts to claim;
Should these men go with no pomp to their graves,
All of my life I'd bear the blame and shame."
"My lord," says Claron, "there's truth in what you
    say." 10725

513

"My lords," says Charles, "so please you, give good
    ear!
Girart the duke we should indeed hold dear;
In all the lands which God has in His keep,
You could not find a better man than he;
You could not name a territory or fief, 10730
So far away by land or overseas,
I would not help this noble duke defeat,
If in his need he should but call on me;
If he wants to be king, he needs but speak
And I myself shall crown him willingly." 10735
"My lord," says Claron, "much thanks for such a
    speech;
Your trust in him is rightly placed indeed,
And these your words I'll take back and repeat."

514

"Rich King, my lord," adds Garnier in this wise;
"In Reggio town to rest the duke did ride, 10740
In the high palace built long ago in time;
We took the same without a blow required
And there we found a cellar full of wine
And granary filled up with wheat entire,

And a great larder stocked up with meat inside; 10745
Therewith the duke piled thirty sumpters high,
Which he has sent to you with us four knights."
"Much thanks for this indeed!" the King replies;
Claron says on: "Do not be angry, Sire,
But we no more may tarry or abide; 10750
Most of our men can scarcely stand upright;
Days without food and long and sleepless nights
Spent in the field have made us all so tired
That healthy men have yet no joy in life;
As for our hurt, whose sum none can surmise, 10755
There are full many of whom no one can dry
The flow of bleeding wounds and vomit's bile."
"My friend," says Charles, "I willingly comply;
To anger your great duke would not be wise."
"My lord," says Claron, "I have this well in mind." 10760
Thus from the King those envoys four retire
And hurry off in Reggio to arrive;
Its mighty tower stands by the church's side,
Where still the Queen in desperation hides
With those twelve maids who are much to be prized; 10765
See, now she leans against her window high!
Whoever seeks the limits far and wide
Of Christendom could not find twelve their like,
If beauty were and comeliness his guide;
Outside the palace walls Claron alights 10770
And squires run out to lead his mount inside;
The Emir's Queen would waste no further time:
"Young noble sir, next to your steed gray-iron,
Take off that sword of steel about you tied!
Climb up to us! It is quite safe, sir knight! 10775
We are all women and know not how to fight;
We cannot set the arrow's shaft to flight
Nor are we able to offer blows or strike;
A demon did us in this tower confine
And cut to shreds my men before my eyes; 10780
Had we been found we would ourselves have died;
But if you now will save and spare our lives
And raise us to the font to be baptized,
Each of us knows how well to serve a knight,
How to wash clothes and sew and cut alike 10785
And make a bed where both may lie at night;
We are unversed in skills of other kinds;
For your God's sake, who all your prayers inspires,
Give us some food, good sir, or we shall die!
Four days we've fasted which this day turns to five." 10790
Claron hears this and marvels in his mind;
With his right hand he makes the cross's sign.

515

"My body is, sir knight, so weak and worn;
These maids and I, we die of hunger all;
It won't be long ere our own hands we'll gnaw! 10795
Five days we've fasted which shall be six come morn,
Since we drank wine or meat or bread last saw;
I knew a time, in my young days of yore,
When I had all my heart desired and more;
So help and hear me God, I never thought, 10800
For any wealth or profit large or small,
I'd feel the pangs felt by the lowly poor."

516

Claron says this: "Lady, do not dismay!
I must go first my message to relate,
Then I'll come back to speak with you again." 10805
"My lord," she says, "then you must make all haste;
A starving mouth consents hard to delay!
With your lord's help you may well ease our pain."
See Claron then climb up that palace great!
Before the duke he hurries off and waits, 10810
Whom he finds there sitting before his plate;
Right tenderly he starts to speak and says:
"The Emperor Carlon greets you and hails,
And I myself shall speak his very phrase;
I'll not hide this, to you through me he states 10815
That there's no land on earth that you could name,
By land or sea be it so far away,
He would not help you win with his steel blade,
If in your need you should but seek his aid;
Would you be king, then doubt not his good faith, 10820
For he himself will crown you straightaway."
"God," says the duke, "how should Your name be praised,
Who let me thus in honor live my days!"
Then, turning to one of his squires, he says:
"Bring water now, so this young lord may bathe." 10825
"My lord," says Claron, "you need not make such haste;
In this your tower the mightiest and main,
At a high window I saw twelve Paynim maids,
Who at the font would be baptized and raised;
For food to eat great plea to me they make; 10830
Who at his ease upon these twelve could gaze
Might well forget all matters else I'd say."
The duke replies: "I do well grant the same;
Of such a task I'll not stand in the way."

517

Claron departs and down the steps he hurries; 10835
Behold him lords, straight to that window running!
He asks the Queen in tender tones and touching:
"My lady Queen, what service can be done you?"
She says: "Sir knight, right dreadful is our
    suffering,
And we seek naught except Baptism's comfort; 10840
Locked in this tower was I by the Almanzor;
As I looked on he killed my men unjustly,
And me myself he would have killed cold-blooded;
We fled to here, a wretched, piteous company
Of womenfolk, for whom my heart is troubled; 10845
A poor supply we had of any sustenance:
Two loaves alone of bread and wine two jugfuls,
Which we in equal part shared out among us;
On that first day full thirty queens we numbered,
The poorest one endowed with a rich country; 10850
And twenty maids there were whom we had nourished,
Who all their lives had not had a man touch them;
And eighty Christian girls, indeed one hundred
Caught by the Paynims when they the land had plundered,
The well-bred best of gentle birth each one of them; 10855
The soldiers took their pick of these poor young ones;
In torment harsh these maidens all succumbed then
And died straightway, know this in truth, of hunger;
What would you think to see this go unpunished?
As for myself, my heart nigh breaks because of it, 10860
And I await from fate a similar judgement;
There's silver here and red gold in abundance;
This tower is full from its foundations upwards;
This side alone where I bide here above you,
Contains the treasure of the Emir my husband; 10865
For one wheat loaf you can have all you'd covet!
I can no more stay locked inside this turret."
Towards the duke and down the steps she comes now,
And after her, most willing, come the others;
With timid hand the locked door she undoes then 10870
And says: "Brave lord, hear how I have been humbled!
When not long since I was crowned by Agolant,
Full thirty kings to witness it he summoned;
Yet now I see my pride has turned to nothing,
And I am one who can expect no succor; 10875
What can I say? In that God shall I trust now,
To Mary born in the town of Bethlehem;
And in His name I urge you and instruct you
To treat us not in a base way or ruffian."
At this Duke Claron takes both her hands and clutches: 10880
"Step forth, my lady, and be no further worried,

For we shall do whatever you would have us do!"
Claron's men each lead forth one of those lovelies
As up the palace steps in joy he rushes:
"Hey, Girart, lord, know this truly and justly, 10885
There never was a man so rich or lucky,
Who ever gained a gift that was this lovely!
Let us to church, for the agreement such is
That all these ladies shall have Baptism's comfort!"

518

Before the duke the Queen now stands and waits, 10890
While Girart much upon her face does gaze;
He sees how wan her visage is and pale,
Whence with her fast the color has all drained:
"My lord, if you would hear me now," she says,
"Then I shall tell a short and sorry tale; 10895
We are twelve ladies from foreign parts and strange,
Wherein we all have worn a crown of state,
And twenty maidens, the eldest still a babe,
Who crossed the sea and came here for my sake;
When I the wife of Agolant was made, 10900
I was much honored according to our ways;
Yet now I see my pride has proven vain;
Take pity, lord, upon us wretched waifs,
Till we have had the little food we crave,
And at the font have been baptized and raised; 10905
Give me not over to your varlets or knaves."
The duke hears this, then shakes his head and says:
"By this my beard that turns to white with age,
On this account you need not be afraid;
For there is none, so high he sets his blade, 10910
Who should he jostle or push one of these maids
Or even open his mouth to say "good day",
Who would not stand more chance of tempting fate
If he had pulled the beard upon my face;
I wish these maids to be such honor paid 10915
As if my father had fathered them the same."
This said, all Girart's men without delay
Vacate the room where the Queen is to stay;
Each of those maids goes with her and remains;
They ask for water without one moment's waste; 10920
See now, my lords, so many towels ornate,
So many basins each with its water-chain!
The Queen, when she is treated in this way
And has with food her strength somewhat regained,
So that the blood comes to her cheeks again, 10925
To look upon is colored now as gay
As is the rose upon a morn in May,
Whose dewy head is struck by the sun's rays.

When now the Queen sits down to eat and dine,
To serve her plate no prompting they require;   10930
Girart acts now like a fine courtly knight,
Who was ere this so fierce, so proud and wild;
Lords, see him now! He stands to his full height,
An olive branch within his hand entwined!
He calls Garnier, his seneschal, aside: 10935
"See that the Queen has all that she desires!"
Then he instructs his chief butler alike:
"Make ready for me now my choicest wines,
The best of them that you can fetch and find;
See that the Queen is sumptuously supplied!"   10940
"Well granted this, my lord," the man replies,
And does the same, wasting no further time:
"My lady Queen, you should regain your pride
And love Lord God and cherish Him likewise,
If by Baptism you may His love acquire."   10945
She says: "I owe great thanks for this much, sire,
And if my prayers proved worthy in His sight
I would not cling to one more day of life."
The Pope decides to visit there meanwhile;
He sends a message by means of a young squire   10950
And asks to lodge in Reggio town that night;
The duke strides down before the Pope arrives,
And when he does, runs up and clasps him tight;
Of his great tower two thirds he gives Pope Miles;
He says: "Good Pope, I will not try to hide   10955
That I've rushed here to tell you of my prize;
I have here both the Emir and his wife!
Within the hall of this great palace high
I've had his corpse placed in a coffin wide;
The severed head I sent to Charles betimes;   10960
He has the head in its steel helmet bright;
I've thirteen queens whom you must now baptize,
And twenty maids whom you with cross must sign!"
"Well granted this, my lord," the Pope replies,
"But let it be tomorrow at first light;   10965
I scarcely can stand up, I am so tired."

At break of day, when dawn's first light appears,
The Pope makes haste the Holy Mass to hear,
Which is intoned by Archbishop Guimer;
Duke Girart summons the Queen of the Emir   10970
And asks those girls and maidens all to meet;

He sets large tubs next to the font and near,
Then has fresh water brought to fill them deep;
They ask for oil, for holy salts and cream
And then remove the clothes from all those queens; 10975
Their mantles swapped for simple shirts and sheets,
Downcast and dumb, not one word dare they speak;
In their great fear they scarcely move their feet
To where they see so many folk convened;
They are quite sure that their fate has been sealed; 10980
Yet each can see that there is no retreat;
Will they or not all of those maids proceed;
As they come up the Pope surveys them each
And shows Girart what he himself perceives:
"These creatures, sire, whom I see standing here, 10985
Were made by God to serve a lord and keep."
"Indeed," says Girart, "I cannot but agree;
For in no land so far across the sea
Could girls be found as beautiful as these;
If Charlemayn my counsel were to heed, 10990
He'd marry them to men of high degree."

PART 12

521

Milon the Pope would now proceed at once;
Among the clergy are seven archbishops,
Who will this day the baptism conduct;
With sign of cross they firstly bless each one 10995
And then of each the mantle is undone;
In simple shirts and nothing else dressed up,
That day they plunge and bathe them in those tubs
And raise their souls to Christian favor thus;
This done they change the fair Queen's name at once: 11000
She's called Clarence--what honor hence she won;
In her own time no better wife there was--
In clothes and shoes they dress them afterwards;
Henceforth, my lords, I'll tell of great Carlun;
In Calabray he's been nigh one full month; 11005
Around a church pits thirty-one he's dug,
Wherein he lays his dead and honors much;
And high-born men whom Carlon much has loved
Inside the church are given burial;
Three hundred priests to pray there he instructs. 11010

522

Hear what Carlon the Emperor does now!

Through all the ranks his will is cried aloud:
High-born nor low shall yet be homeward bound,
Nor vavasors, nor barons, kings or counts,
Neither shall princes or dukes of wealth and power; 11015
For with their help fresh fiefs he would hand down.

523

The Emperor to linger more is loath;
Through Naimes the Duke and Otoer the old
He sends off word to Girart and the Pope;
He summons both to speak with him and both 11020
Of them arrive, for they dare not say no;
The Pope commends to God those dead men's souls,
Blessing the church where Charles has laid their bones;
Then he himself a Mass for them intones;
Rich gifts are made so their renown may grow; 11025
Six hundred marks would value these too low;
Then is an Order of sixty monks enrolled,
Endowed by Charles with wealth enough in gold
To cater for their needs and richly so;
Girart the duke sets out, his booty stowed; 11030
Three dozen he-mules and she-mules full he loads;
And then those maids new-born in Christian hope,
And those twelve queens, he dresses in new clothes;
No man who saw it done could ever hold
That on the Queen Girart did not bestow 11035
All that there was to be found there or known,
With which to honor a lady of such note;
Upon a mule they sit her now to go;
You could not find more lovely maids than those!
The duke indeed loses his self-control 11040
And courts the Queen as to her mule he holds;
He offers her his love and friendship both
And in return he sues her for her own;
All this he does to cast aside his woe;
Beside each maid one of his captains goes 11045
And in this way they ride along the road;
Carlon is standing before his tent when lo!
He turns his head and on the left beholds
Girart draw nigh, who has the Queen in tow!
His beard is white, his face both bright and bold, 11050
And his complexion like any young knight's glows;
He meets our King and greets him in this tone:
"May that High Liege called God the Lord of Hosts,
Who came to Earth to save us here below,
Who in the Virgin's womb did deign repose, 11055
May He let you on Earth in grace so grow
That to His mercy you may come ever close
And thus may find in Paradise a home!

None of my gains from you shall I withhold;
I've won all this amidst the battle's blows; 11060
The Emir's wife this is, your foreign foe;
In all the lands which God has in His hold
You'll find none lovelier, search high or low;
Show me a man who would not guard her close!"

524

As now the duke to Carlon's tent comes in, 11065
Young Duke Claron by the right hand he grips;
Upon a quilt made out of Cyprus silk,
Girart, son of Beuvon, beside him sits;
Naimon the Duke moves to the Queen at this
And from her saddle he helps her down and lifts; 11070
Counts come, and barons, to hold her stirrups still,
As do King Droon and Salemon the king;
But then the Queen, of face so fair and fit,
Looks long at Naimes, his countenance and chin,
And asks at once: "Your name, lord, tell me it!" 11075
"Lady," says Naimes, "why should it now be hid?
At Aspremont you have seen me ere this;
You gave to me your own ring as a gift."
At this the Queen sighs deeply and bows to him:
"With the blessing of God, my lord, I did! 11080
Remember this and do not treat me ill!"

525

In Carlon's tent all sit and are assembled;
Three kings are there and seven dukes attending,
And counts and barons I do not know how many;
So all may hear Girart calls on the Emperor: 11085
"Rich King, my lord, know for a fact unquestioned
There never was a man, be he so wealthy,
Who ever gained a gift more fine or precious;
For thirteen queens there are in truth, here present,
The poorest one endowed with a rich territory, 11090
And twenty maids of young years all and tender,
Who in their lives have had men touch them never;
I've won them all and in what way I'll tell you:
When from the fight the fell Almanzor went off
And in low wise quit Agolant the Emir, 11095
He came to Reggio and slaughtered all the men there;
These ladies' lives alike he would have ended,
But they escaped within the tower and fled there
With four score Christian girls, nay five time twenty,
Caught by the Paynims when they the land molested, 11100
Each one of them of well-bred birth and gentle;
The soldiers took their pick of those poor wretches;

A poor supply of sustenance they held there:
Two jugs of wine alone and just two bread-loaves,
Which they shared out to all in equal measure; 11105
They could not live like this for long, however;
Ten of them died, for whom my heart is heavy;
In mighty fear to us they then surrendered;
But my lord Pope much grace to me extended,
Who yestermorn baptized them with great pleasure; 11110
Behold them, Charles, all sitting here together!
I give them to you all, Charles, as a present,
Except the Queen, for whom I do request you."
The King replies: "Curse him who would prevent it!
Your will in this you should do and you shall do!" 11115
Immediately Girart bows low and lengthy
And then says this, in tender tones and friendly:
"He is no king whom my words will offend now;
When in my youth erstwhile a wife I wedded,
The daughter she of Hungary's Protector, 11120
Her wit and wisdom surpassed my own intelligence;
If I have ruled so long despite my enemies
It is all due to her words and directions;
The king her father died in our first melee,
But leaves behind a most worthy successor, 11125
Who is a son most handsome and high-mettled;
Equip him, Charles, and fit him out with weapons
And let him rule the land his father tended;
His father much deserved and earned this guerdon;
Yet if his son takes not this Queen as well, Sire, 11130
Then he, indeed, will lose all my affection;
From here unto the East no queen excels her;
He could not choose a mate of higher merit;
Whoso with her could spend much time together,
If to her heart she gave him a good welcome, 11135
So that he might pay her his close attention,
That man, I'd say, would live longer and better."

526

As Duke Girart commends this match be made,
The King agrees and grants it straightaway;
Between both parties the matter is arranged 11140
And fealty sworn with no delay or change;
As Florent now to Carlon swears his faith
And Charles girds him with his new kingdom's blade,
The Queen stands up and in attendance waits;
By her right hand Carlon gives her away; 11145
Young Florent kisses her in fond embrace;
Then each man's look goes to that group of maids;
Each damsel there is so radiant of face
And so well-dressed in robes of noble grace,

I could not, lords, describe their beauty great;   11150
No Frenchman there without a wife or mate
Does not now seek to get one from Charlemayn.

527

"Girart," says Charles, "I'll not conceal this
    thought--
I have no need to flatter men with talk--
You must love God and by Him set great store   11155
Above all others and praise Him and adore,
For few men's deeds are worthier than yours;
Pray give to me one of your sons and boys
To rule Apulia and Sicily by law!
And he shall wed one of these maids withal,   11160
Since at our backs the rumor runs abroad
That all these maids are not worth the least coin
In terms of faith, to keep it and exalt;
Yet this maid's sire in such dire straits I saw
To keep me safe from harm and hurt in war   11165
That from his body he let his soul be shorn;
Shall his heir now in marriage be sold short?
She could, herself, not make a better choice;
I'd have her marry one of your sons therefore,
And then your son shall join me at my court;   11170
He and Duke Naimes and Ogier, Denmark's lord,
These three alone shall be my counsellors;
Your son, indeed, shall straightway be employed
To oversee the meat before me brought,
Till I may raise his status in due course."   11175
Girart replies: "Much thanks for this reward;
To such a man should one look for support;
Now would I speak to that lad noble-born
Whom you with wife and kingdom have installed;
Florent, fine sir, pray do not be annoyed!   11180
Heed not the counsel of any man who's false;
Never harm churches or monasteries destroy,
Nor take rewards for doing what you ought;
Nor make a habit of promising men aught;
But always give, for this behooves a royal;   11185
And if you come across a knight who's poor,
In vestments mean and with an ill-fed horse,
Despise him not nor vex him more with taunts,
But sit him down to eat at your own board
And honor him with wealth from your own vault;   11190
Be merciful poor womenfolk towards
And do not force poor sons to leave your shores,
But care for them with all you can afford;
When they are grown and can defend your cause
And see you threatened by anyone at all,   11195

They'll fight for you and yours until they fall;
I do not know what else to say or more;
Thus should a prince his government perform.

528

"Florent, fine brother, to Charles be very thankful;
For he this day has recompensed the valor 11200
With which your sire served him so well in battle;
He died thereby, for my eyes saw it happen:
I held him in my arms when his soul vanished;
Heed not the words of liars or of flatterers,
For by their talk are good men often damaged; 11205
But those fine men whom your own father championed,
Heed these men not and your worth will go backwards;
You will soon learn who serves you best or badly;
What any man has lost, help him recapture,
And he'll become your closest, truest ally." 11210
"Indeed," says Charles, "your words are nothing
   lacking."

529

"Florent, fine sir, to your sister I'm wedded,
So do not mock the words that I have said here;
Make not a bishop of the son of your shepherd;
Take a king's son, or duke's or count's, I tell you, 11215
Or vavasor's, though his family be penniless;
Take such men's sons and you shall not do better;
If there be two, then take the younger fellow
And leave the elder to take up his inheritance;
Teach this one well until the time is ready, 11220
Then in God's name as your bishop invest him,
And he'll show faith and wisdom and affection;
Make not your lord he who was once your lesser,
But leave the peasant to do the work he's best at;
For honor's path is not that of the peasant, 11225
Who in the end reveals his true complexion.

530

"Florent, fine brother, pray do not be disturbed!
Tomorrow morning you must give solemn word
To break bad laws and to cast out their curse,
And champion good ones, and try to make them work; 11230
And swear to honor and serve the holy Church
And succor orphans and feed them from your purse
And maintain widows and their safety preserve;
The wicked man you should try to convert,
But none the less destroy if he grows worse; 11235

You should keep by your side men of good birth;
From their good counsel you may find out and learn
The way to govern your own soul and self first;
To promise little and give much in return
Will move the heart of everyone you serve; 11240
The wicked man who seeks his fellow's hurt,
Who would, indeed, his neighbor's fief usurp,
So that his own may grow in size and worth,
Who would rob churches and violate and burn,
Oppress the poor and tread them in the dirt, 11245
If with strong proof his guilt you can confirm
Then banish him for a full seven years;
Layman or clerk dare not say then you shirked;
In seven years, should he your mercy earn,
Then to your land allow him to return; 11250
Hence treat him so that he'll not dare be heard
Within your court nor wish to be observed;
Through him the rest may each their lesson learn
And never dare in future thus to err;
You wed your Queen tomorrow and marry her 11255
And then the Pope his blessing will confer;
Then you'll be crowned by Charles the Emperor;
When you once more to Hungary return,
Both of my sons to go with you I'll urge;
They are your nephews and you should love them, sir; 11260
And they will help you to hold your kingdom firm;
Ernault, tomorrow, will lead the Queen to church
And bring alike all of those maids and girls
To wedding high, as each of them deserves."
"Well-granted this, indeed!" Carlon confirms; 11265
"You shall not ask for any due on earth
That I'll not give, whatever the cost incurred."

531

At break of dawn when daylight starts to spread,
Milon the Pope does not his task forget;
They bring the Queen to Florent's side and then 11270
By Pope Milon to that young prince she's wed;
He blesses Florent and blesses his wife next
And then he sings the mass for both of them;
The crown of gold he sets on Florent's head,
Which Agolant had brought to France himself; 11275
Then Charlemayn invests him with his realm;
Full seven dukes that morning Charles invests
And gives new wives to counts one score and ten;
To Lord our God his army he commends;
The Christian ranks he showers then with wealth, 11280
For the world's riches about them all are spread;
Each man can take whatever makes him content.

The Emperor crowns Florent in this wise:
Before them all he's blessed with cross's sign
And his new queen is seated by his side; 11285
It was agreed by those there at the time
That Christendom had no couple so fine;
Girart speaks up, forgetting not a mite:
"Florent, fine brother, the truth I would not hide,
But give you rather some thoughts and some advice 11290
On how a king should rule his realm aright;
When our Lord God so loved His own Mankind
That He came down to Earth out of the skies
And took on flesh the Virgin's womb inside,
Three years and thirty with us He did abide; 11295
Then He Himself to new life was baptized
And ordered us and bade us do alike;
And when He then from death itself revived
And did ascend once more to Heaven high,
This other self for us He left behind, 11300
At rest and risen appearing in our sight;
He who partakes thereof, even as he dies,
And swallowing can take the smallest bite,
He shall straightway be taken to that clime
Whence for his pride the Devil was denied; 11305
I do not think, nor ever have desired,
That peasants' sons should serve this sacred rite;
Its mighty power should not with them reside
And may it never, please God the Lord on High!
Archbishops seven bear office in my shires 11310
And there's not one, so strict I've scrutinized,
Whom either king or high duke has not sired;
And bishops fifty-four I have alike,
The hand-picked best of noble birth and type;
No archbishop of mine, unless he's lied, 11315
Has ever ordained a priest for task divine
Without discussing the man with me betimes,
So we may learn of his descent and line;
He comes before me when three days have expired
And loyal men for him must testify 11320
And solemn pledge on his behalf provide,
That he is born of noble man and wife,
Whom loyal love and legal does unite;
When he forsakes the flesh and its desires,
Then may he hold the blest body of Christ, 11325
Through Whom we all are born into new life;
And I would then for all his needs provide
So he needs not in poverty decline;
If then he sins, then he deserves our ire;

267

And if he sins and is caught in the crime, 11330
Within my sight I'd punish him as vile
As if he'd robbed my fortune's stock entire;
All of my clerks are so well-versed and wise
That they need not the Pope neither require
To guide their faith or acts to authorize 11335
For baptism or any task divine;
Whatever's mine, my wealth, my land, my might,
I'll hold from no one except Lord God on High;
Ah, Charlemayn, the truth I will not hide;
In this campaign we have both won this time; 11340
Your leadership therein I've recognized
And my own lips have called you lord and Sire;
My name, at court, should never be reviled;
But all I've done I did for love of Christ;
I'm not your man nor faith to you do plight 11345
Or ever shall all the days of my life."
When this is said the gathering divides;
Girart asks for his horse--it's brought by squires,
Who hold the stirrups as Girart swings astride;
The French stare at each other as he rides by; 11350
The Emperor is lost in thought a while;
He shakes his head then gives a little smile,
And then, between his teeth, softly replies:
"If I may live a long life ere I die,
The pride of one of us shall not survive." 11355

533

Of Agolant I've sung and of Aumon,
Of Charlemayn who fierce of visage was,
And of Girart the son of Duke Beuvon,
And of the battle that was on Aspremont;
The lives of men from many ranks were lost; 11360
The vanguard troops had little choice thereof;
Their company was forty thousand strong
And with two kings and fifteen dukes was stocked;
Five thousand men with Carlon's standard stopped,
While out in front and round his gonfalon 11365
Were sixty thousand in their battalions,
And fifteen thousand in worthy Girart's squad;
From both these hosts, as you have heard in song,
Full half the men ne'er saw their homes anon;
For their reward upon the field they got; 11370
Happy their going, for they are with Lord God!
Now may that God, Who died upon the Cross,
And Who from death raised Lazarus aloft,
His mercy show both them and us upon;
Now and henceforth, my lords, the chanson stops; 11375
It ends herewith, for more I'll tell you not!

GLOSSARY

This glossary is selective only, but may prove useful for general comprehension purposes.

ABILANT:	A Pagan king from Persia; fights alongside Moadas.
ACARS OF FLORS:	A Pagan king of the Almanzor's clan.
AGOLANT:	Emir of all the Pagans; father of Aumon.
ALMANZOR (the):	A powerful Pagan emir and rival of Agolant; uncle of Amargon and Esperrant.
AMARGON:	A Pagan king and nephew of the Almanzor; companion of Esperrant.
ANCHETIN:	A Norman duke much loved by Charlemagne.
ANTELME:	Count of Tours; uncle of Richer.
APOLLO:	One of the three Saracen gods.
ASPREMONT:	lit. bitter mount; Aspromonte in Calabria.
AUMON:	Agolant's son and Champion; regent of Africa.
BALAN:	A Pagan king and Agolant's chief envoy; father of Gorhan.
BERENGER:	One of young Roland's companions.
BEUVON:	1. Girart d'Eufrate's nephew; son of Milon and brother of Claron.
	2. The father of Girart d'Eufrate.
BOIDANT:	lit. deceiving (?); a Pagan king and favorite of Aumon; fights alongside Moadas.
BRUNO:	The king of Hungary.
CAHOER:	The king of England.
CALIDES:	A Pagan king from Orcany.
CARLON, CHARLEMAYN, CHARLES:	Charlemagne, Emperor of all the Christians.
CLARON:	Girart d'Eufrate's nephew; the son of Milon and brother of Beuvon.
CORTAIN:	lit. short one; Ogier the Dane's sword.
DAVID:	The king of Cornwall.
DIDIER:	The king of the Lombards.
DRIU, DROON THE POITEVIN:	A French duke; fights alongside King Salemon.
DURENDAL:	lit. enduring blade (?); first Aumon's then Roland's sword.
EMMELINE:	The wife of Girart d'Eufrate.
ERNAULT:	One of Girart's sons; fights alongside Renier.
ESPERRANT:	lit. hoping; A Pagan king and nephew of the Almanzor; companion of Amargon.
ESTOUS (DE LENGRES):	One of young Roland's companions.
FAGON:	Duke of Touraine; Charlemagne's kinsman, seneschal and chief standard-bearer.
FLORENT:	Girart d'Eufrate's brother-in-law.

Glossary

FROMER: An abbot.

GALINDRES: A Pagan king of Batre; the Emir's closest advisor; serves as envoy alongside King Uliens.
GEOFFREY THE ANGEVIN: Geoffrey of Angers; fights alongside Hugh of Mans.
GIRART D'EUFRATE: Duke of Burgundy, Auvergne, Gascony, Cosence and Gevaudan; the son of Beuvon; rebellious to the rule of France.
GONDELBUEF: The king of Frisia.
GORHAN: A Pagan king of Garilant; Agolant's seneschal and lover of the Queen; the son of Balan.
GRAELENT: One of young Roland's companions; Charlemagne's jongleur.
GUI: One of young Roland's companions.

HATON: One of young Roland's companions; fights alongside Gui.
HECTOR: A Pagan king and standard-bearer for Aumon; one of the Almanzor's clan.
HUGH, HUON OF MANS: A count who fights alongside Geoffrey the Angevin.

JOYEUSE: lit. joyful; Charlemagne's sword.
JUPITER: One of the three Pagan gods.

MAHOM: Mohammed; the principal Pagan god.
MALADIENT: lit. evil-speaking(?); A Pagan king.
MANDAQUIN: A Pagan king; Agolant's nephew.
MATEFELON: 1. lit. killvillain; Girart d'Eufrate's horse.
2. A Pagan warrior; Aumon's seneschal.
MILON: 1. Count of Poitiers; father of Beuvon and Claron.
2. One of Girart d'Eufrate's sons.
3. The Pope.
MOADAS: A Pagan king of Jerusalem; nephew of Agolant; fights alongside Abilant and Boidant.
MOUNTJOY: Charlemagne's war-cry.
MOREL: lit. black; Duke Naimes' horse.
MOYSANT: A Pagan king; uncle of Aumon.

NAIMES: Duke of Bavaria; Charlemagne's wisest knight and closest friend.

OGIER THE DANE: Charlemagne's bravest knight.

PEPIN: Pepin the Short; father of Charlemagne.

RENIER: One of Girart d'Eufrate's sons.
RICHER: A brave knight brought up by Duke Naimes.
ROLAND: The beloved nephew of Charlemagne.

SALATIEL: A Pagan king of Valorie; belongs to the Almanzor's clan.
SALEMON: The king of Brittany.
SANSON: A French duke; fights alongside Richer.

Glossary

SYNAGON: An old Pagan king of Halape and Antioch; loved by
                 Aumon whom he brought up.

TERVAGANT: One of the Pagan gods.
THIORIN: The nephew of King Salemon.
TURPIN: The Archbishop of Reims; well-loved by Charlemagne;
                 a fighting priest.
TRIAMODES: A Pagan king of Valorie; uncle of Aumon.

ULIENS: A Pagan king; nephew of Agolant; serves as envoy
                 alongside Galindres.

VIELLANTIF: lit. wideawake; Aumon's then Roland's horse.

The Garland Library of Medieval Literature

Series A (Texts and Translations); Series B (Translations Only)

1. Chrétien de Troyes: *Lancelot, or The Knight of the Cart*. Edited and translated by William W. Kibler. Series A.
2. Brunetto Latini: *Il Tesoretto (The Little Treasure)*. Edited and translated by Julia Bolton Holloway. Series A.
3. *The Poetry of Arnaut Daniel*. Edited and translated by James J. Wilhelm. Series A.
4. *The Poetry of William VII, Count of Poitiers, IX Duke of Aquitaine*. Edited and translated by Gerald A. Bond; music edited by Hendrik van der Werf. Series A.
5. *The Poetry of Cercamon and Jaufre Rudel*. Edited and translated by George Wolf and Roy Rosenstein; music edited by Hendrik van der Werf. Series A.
6. *The Vidas of the Troubadours*. Translated by Margarita Egan. Series B.
7. *Medieval Latin Poems of Male Love and Friendship*. Translated by Thomas Stehling. Series A.
8. *Barthar Saga*. Edited and translated by Jon Skaptason and Phillip Pulsiano. Series A.
9. Guillaume de Machaut: *Judgment of the King of Bohemia (Le Jugement dou Roy de Behaingne)*. Edited and translated by R. Barton Palmer. Series A.
10. *Three Lives of the Last Englishmen*. Translated by Michael Swanton. Series B.
11. Giovanni Boccaccio: *Eclogues*. Edited and translated by Janet Smarr. Series A.
12. Hartmann von Aue: *Erec*. Translated by Thomas L. Keller. Series B.
13. *Waltharius* and *Ruodlieb*. Edited and translated by Dennis M. Kratz. Series A.
14. *The Writings of Medieval Women*. Translated by Marcelle Thiébaux. Series B.
15. *The Rise of Gawain, Nephew of Arthur (De ortu Waluuanii Nepotis Arturi)*. Edited and translated by Mildred Leake Day. Series A.
16, 17. *The French Fabliau: B.N. 837*. Edited and translated by Raymond Eichmann and John DuVal. Series A.
18. *The Poetry of Guido Cavalcanti*. Edited and translated by Lowry Nelson, Jr. Series A.
19. Hartmann von Aue: *Iwein*. Edited and translated by Patrick M. McConeghy. Series A.
20. *Seven Medieval Latin Comedies*. Translated by Alison Goddard Elliott. Series B.
21. Christine de Pizan: *The Epistle of the Prison of Human Life*. Edited and translated by Josette A. Wisman. Series A.
22. *The Poetry of the Sicilian School*. Edited and translated by Frede Jensen. Series A.
23. *The Poetry of Cino da Pistoia*. Edited and translated by Christopher Kleinhenz. Series A.

24. *The Lyrics and Melodies of Adam de la Halle*. Lyrics edited and translated by Deborah Hubbard Nelson; music edited by Hendrik van der Werf. Series A.
25. Chrétien de Troyes: *Erec and Enide*. Edited and translated by Carleton W. Carroll. Series A.
26. *Three Ovidian Tales of Love*. Edited and translated by Raymond J. Cormier. Series A.
27. *The Poetry of Guido Guinizelli*. Edited and translated by Robert Edwards. Series A.
28. Wernher der Gartenaere: *Helmbrecht*. Edited by Ulrich Seelbach; introduced and translated by Linda B. Parshall. Series A.
29. *Pathelin and Other Farces*. Edited and translated by Richard Switzer and Mireille Guillet-Rydell. Series A.
30. *Les Cent Nouvelles Nouvelles*. Translated by Judith Bruskin Diner. Series B.
31. Gerald of Wales (Giraldus Cambrensis): *The Life of St. Hugh of Avalon*. Edited and translated by Richard M. Loomis. Series A.
32. *L'Art d'Amours*. Translated by Lawrence Blonquist. Series B.
33. Giovanni Boccaccio: *L'Ameto*. Translated by Judith Serafini-Sauli. Series B.
34, 35. *The Medieval Pastourelle*. Selected, translated, and edited in part by William D. Paden, Jr. Series A.
36. Béroul: *The Romance of Tristran*. Edited and translated by Norris J. Lacy. Series A.
37. *Graelent* and *Guingamor:* Two Breton Lays. Edited and translated by Russell Weingartner. Series A.
38. Heinrich von Veldeke: *Eneit*. Translated by J. Welsey Thomas. Series B.
39. *The Lyrics and Melodies of Grace Brulé*. Edited and translated by Samuel Rosenberg and Samuel Danon; music edited by Hendrik van der Werf. Series A.
40. Giovanni Boccaccio: *Life of Dante*. Edited and translated by Vincenzo Bollettino. Series A.
41. *The Poetry of Thibaut de Champagne*. Edited and translated by Kathleen Brahney. Series A.
42. *The Poetry of Sordello*. Edited and translated by James J. Wilhelm. Series A.
43. Giovanni Boccaccio: *Il Filocolo*. Translated by Donald S. Cheney with the collaboration of Thomas G. Bergin. Series B.
44. *Le Roman de Thèbes (The Story of Thebes)*. Translated by John Smartt Coley. Series B.
45. Guillaume de Machaut: *The Judgment of the King of Navarre (Le Jugement dou Roy de Navarre)*. Translated and edited by R. Barton Palmer. Series A.
46. *The French Chansons of Charles D'Orléans*. With the Corresponding Middle English Chansons. Edited and translated by Sarah Spence. Series A.
47. *The Pilgrimage of Charlemagne* and *Aucassin and Nicolette*. Edited and translated by Glyn S. Burgess and Anne Elizabeth Cobby. Series A.
48. Chrétien de Troyes: *The Knight with the Lion,* or *Yvain*. Edited and translated by William W. Kibler. Series A.
49. *Carmina Burana*. Translated by Edward Blodgett and Roy Arthur Swanson. Series B.
50. *The Story of Meriadoc, King of Cambria (Historia Meriadoci, Regis Cambriae)*. Edited and translated by Mildred Leade Day. Series A.
51. Hrostvit: *Plays*. Translated by Katharina Wilson. Series B.

52. *Medieval Debate Poetry: Vernacular Works*. Edited and translated by Michel-André Bossy. Series A.
53. Giovanni Boccaccio: *Il Filostrato*. Translated by Robert P. apRoberts and Anna Bruni Seldis; Italian text by Vincenzo Pernicone. Series A.
54. Guillaume de Machaut: *La Fonteinne amoureuse*. Edited and translated by Brenda Hosington. Series A.
55. *The Knight of the Parrot (Le Chevalier du Papegau)*. Translated by Thomas E. Vesce. Series B.
56. *The Saga of Thidrek of Bern (Thidrekssaga af Bern)*. Translated by Edward R. Haymes. Series. B.
57. Wolfram von Eschenbach: *Titurel*. Edited and translated by Sidney M. Johnson and Marion Gibbs. Series A.
58. Der Stricker: *Daniel of the Blossoming Valley*. Translated by Michael Resler. Series B.
59. *The Byelorussian Tristan*. Translated by Zora Kipel. Series B.
60. *The Marvels of Rigomer*. Translated by Thomas E. Vesce. Series B.
61. *The Song of Aspremont (La Chanson d'Aspremont)*. Translated by Michael A. Newth. Series B.